AN EXTRAORDINARY YEAR OF ORDINARY DAYS

SOUTHWESTERN WRITERS COLLECTION SERIES

*The Wittliff Collections at Texas State University–San Marcos*

*Steven L. Davis, Editor*

# An EXTRAORDINARY YEAR of ORDINARY DAYS

*Susan Wittig Albert*

University of Texas Press

AUSTIN

*The publication of this book was supported in part by the Louann Atkins Temple Women & Culture Series, which was funded by contributions from Allison, Doug, Taylor, and Andy Bacon; Margaret, Lawrence, Will, John, and Annie Temple; Larry Temple; the Temple-Inland Foundation; and the National Endowment for the Humanities.*

The Southwestern Writers Collection Series originates from the Wittliff Collections, a repository of literature, film, music, and southwestern and Mexican photography established at Texas State University–San Marcos.

The poem on page vi is copyright © 1999 by Wendell Berry from *A Timbered Choir: The Sabbath Poems 1979–1997*. Reprinted by permission of Counterpoint.

Requests for permission to reproduce material from this work should be sent to:
Permissions
University of Texas Press
P.O. Box 7819
Austin, TX 78713-7819
www.utexas.edu/utpress/about/bpermission.html

♾ The paper used in this book meets the minimum requirements of ANSI/NISO Z39.48-1992 (R1997) (Permanence of Paper).

LIBRARY OF CONGRESS CATALOGING-IN-PUBLICATION DATA
Albert, Susan Wittig.
An extraordinary year of ordinary days / Susan Wittig Albert.
   p.    cm. — (Southwestern writers collection series)
   Includes bibliographical references and index.
   ISBN 978-0-292-72306-1 (cloth : alk. paper)
   1. Albert, Susan Wittig.  2. Authors, American—20th century—Biography.
3. Blogs—United States.  I. Title.
PS3551.L2637Z46 2010
813'.54—dc22
   [B]                                                                    2010018641

FOR THERESA MAY,
*with thanks for friendship and encouragement*

No, no, there is no going back.
Less and less you are
That possibility you were.
More and more you have become
Those lives and deaths
That have belonged to you.
You have become a sort of grave
Containing much that was
And is no more in time, beloved
Then, now, and always.
And so you have become a sort of tree
Standing over a grave.
Now more than ever you can be
Generous toward each day
That comes, young, to disappear
Forever, and yet remain
Unaging in the mind.
Every day you have less reason
Not to give yourself away.

WENDELL BERRY

## A NOTE TO THE READER

For decades, it has been my habit to keep a journal, opening each new yearly record on January 2, my birthday. In these journals, I make notes about what's happening in my life, my work, the weather, the national news. The writing is not intentionally graceful, and I don't spend time making it pretty or lyrical. It's what I'm thinking, how I'm feeling, what's on my mind on any given day. I write for myself, as a witness to my life and to the world at large, a journalist who reports events, a recorder of words, thoughts, feelings, impressions.

When I began the journal for 2008, I was looking forward to recording another ordinary year of ordinary days in the life of a working writer. I expected to meet contractual obligations for two novels; do some personal and professional traveling; attend a high school reunion (momentous: my fiftieth!); connect daily with family and friends over the Internet; enjoy the company of my husband, Bill Albert; and spend quiet evenings reading, knitting, watching television and films. Although I didn't think about this in any conscious way, I expected to end the year with pretty much the same intellectual baggage that I carried into it. New ideas, yes. New ideas would be nice, and perhaps some new creative energy—but certainly not a paradigm shift. Not in the last third of my life, at sixty-nine.

But that's not what happened.

For one thing, the presidential race turned out to be not just interesting, but electrifying. From my perspective (I'm on the liberal side of the political spectrum), it was the best and brightest thing that had happened in a long, long time. Other good things were *very* good, of course, and welcome. The writing went well; my health stayed pretty much the same; the travel went as planned; and there were no family emergencies.

The worst . . . well, let's just say it was a challenging year. Midway through January, I began to discover (via the Internet, then books) the potential seriousness of the energy depletion situation, something that shouldn't have surprised me, I suppose, but did. I spent the rest of the year educating myself to its consequences. Climate change was not news to me, but new scientific evidence of its acceleration (suppressed during the eight years of the Republican administration) heightened my concerns. Under the influence of several popular authors writing for a general audience, and others less widely known and more technical, I began to think more about the impact of both energy depletion and climate change on our system of industrialized agriculture, and I woke up with a start to the realization that our food system is simply not sustainable. It was time for me to refocus my gardening energies from ornamentals and herbs and begin gardening seriously, with the intention of producing more of our food. I started that project in late spring, although the extraordinary, record-breaking heat and drought of 2008 here in Texas (perhaps itself evidence of climate change) certainly made gardening difficult.

And there was more startling news, more unwelcome realizations. In February and March, the economic threat—home foreclosures, job losses, failures in the financial sector, tightening bank credit—began to impose itself on the country's awareness. As the summer wore on, the bleak national economic situation took on global dimensions and an intensely personal shape. By late fall, Bill's and my 401Ks had dwindled by 50 percent, and local real estate values were sinking rapidly.

We were in better shape than many. Friends and acquaintances lost jobs, homes, businesses, investments. People began trying to live off their paychecks again, instead of their credit cards, and for retailers, the change was calamitous. By December, pundits had taken to calling 2008 "The Great Disruption," "The Colossal Collapse," and "The Year of the Apocalypse." Harvard economics professor Kenneth Rogoff called it "a once-in-a-hundred-years meltdown." Whatever name you give to it—personally, nationally, globally—2008 was an extraordinary year.

And yet, as my journal records them, my days are very ordinary, filled with family obligations, work, play, and life in general. Like everyone else, I lived each day as it came, met the day's requirements, and then moved on.

Both the journal and the year are set in the context of my life, and since you and I haven't met (most likely), an introduction might be in order. I was born on January 2, 1940, on the cusp of the Second World War. I spent my childhood on a farm and in small towns in Illinois, very much a 1950s rural Midwestern girlhood. I married at eighteen and embarked on a new life as a wife, then a mother (of three, born close together, in 1959, 1961, 1962), then a college student. In 1968, I moved with my husband and young children from Urbana, Illinois, to Berkeley and began graduate study. I took my first academic position at the University of Texas in 1973 and worked as a teacher and administrator (at UT, Tulane/Newcomb, and Southwest Texas State [now Texas State University]) through 1985, when I left my academic career and began to work as a full-time writer.

Twice-divorced, I married Bill Albert the next year, and we moved to what is now a thirty-one-acre homestead we call Meadow Knoll, in the Texas Hill Country, some sixty miles northwest of Austin. For more than two decades, Bill and I have shared our lives with varying numbers and breeds of dogs, cats, chickens, ducks, geese, peacocks, cows, and sheep at the end of a rutted caliche lane, surrounded by hundreds of wild acres populated by deer, coyotes, mountain lions, armadillos, possums, raccoons, squirrels, skunks, and lovely, lovely birds. I've come to think of myself *as* that place, as Meadow Knoll, through all its changes of context and climate. And I am still that place, and still evolving, no matter where I am, no matter what other places I may become and in which I may evolve, before and since.

Living in the country has enabled me to craft a quiet, inward-turning life in a fully wired, hyperactive, entertainment-obsessed society where, as psychologist James Hillman once remarked, anything short of manic behavior is considered depression. And it has opened a daily window on the natural world, schooling me in the habit of observing our domestic animals and the wild animals that share the fields and woodlands with us. *Together, Alone: A Memoir of Marriage and Place* (University of Texas Press, 2009) is my celebration of that life and the learning it has brought, and many of its themes are threaded through this journal.

In the past few years, there has been less solitude. My books (I have been writing mystery fiction since 1992, juvenile fiction before then) reach more readers than they did in earlier years, which means that I must do more of the things that authors are expected to do: travel on book tours, visit libraries and bookstores, give talks, participate in social media on the Internet. I am also an active volunteer in the Story Circle Network, an organization for women writers and readers that I founded in 1997. The 2008 journal chronicles these various outreaches.

The books have also permitted Bill and me to enjoy the wonderful privilege (truly a luxury) of having a second home—we call it Coyote Lodge—in a tiny mountain community in New Mexico. Being at

*The beauty of thinking of ourselves as evolving places is that even from the very beginning we have been in and experienced an environment that no one but us has shared, and yet that environment is someone else who also experienced us.*

—LESLIE VAN GELDER

home in two places means that we can each have time alone, which is welcome in a marriage in which we live and work together, twenty-four-seven. The 2008 journal records my weeks at Coyote in January, August, and December.

I use my journal to record things other than my immediate life events. Like you, like all of us, I am shaped (often in more ways than I'm willing to recognize) by what happens in the world beyond me, and I'm in the habit of recording short news summaries of events that have some significance to me at the time they occur—although I can't always say exactly what that significance is until I can see a developing pattern. Years ago, I had the naïve idea that I was relatively untouched by things that happened outside my personal sphere. That probably wasn't true then; it certainly isn't true now. The world is very small: what happens in Washington or London or Baghdad or Shanghai touches me—sooner and more deeply than I expect. The news summaries track some of these events—and in 2008, there were a great many.

I'm also in the habit of making notes on my reading, and I am an incorrigible collector of quotations, with the long-standing practice of adding other people's words to my journal pages. I almost always know the name of the author, but haven't always preserved the title of the book or article. If I am currently reading the writer's work, I list the title in the month's readings—you'll find it there.

We always knew this [2008] was going to be an historic year, but we had no idea just how immense that historical change was going to be.

—SIMON SCHAMA

Readings. I am a text person. I write every day, read every evening, and keep an annotated reading diary. I soak myself in words, sentences, paragraphs the way some people soak in hot baths. For years, I read nothing but fiction; now, I read mostly nonfiction—not by intention, but by interest. If I care about what I'm reading, I am an energetic, recreative reader: I make notes in margins, rewrite sentences, argue with the writer's opinions, insert quotations from related texts, annotate the bibliography. Like a bloodhound, nose to the ground, I follow developing interests, and if something catches my attention, I'm likely to follow that trail as far as it takes me, searching bibliographies and using the Internet to actively seek out related works. Looking at my 2008 readings, however, I have to say that they are much more focused than usual. Many of the issues I encountered proved to be extraordinarily compelling, and I read more deeply and more energetically and with greater attentiveness than I have in many years.

A year in which Americans discovered the possibility of a new beginning, 2008 was a time of political change, of a new and optimistic hope, of expectations raised. It was also a year in which many were confronted by the stern reality of limited, diminishing resources we once thought unlimited and infinite. As I look back now over these pages and think about the tumultuous effect of these events on my life, on our lives, on *everyone's* lives, I am very glad that I have this personal record of what the year meant to me. I hope that as you read these entries, you will ask yourself, "What was I doing on this day, or that? How did I feel?" And most important, "What did it mean?"

For me, in my own life, eternal questions. What does it mean? And what ought I do about it?

SUSAN WITTIG ALBERT
*February 2009*

AN EXTRAORDINARY YEAR OF ORDINARY DAYS

| JANUARY | FEBRUARY | MARCH | APRIL |
|---|---|---|---|
| MAY | JUNE | JULY | AUGUST |
| SEPTEMBER | OCTOBER | NOVEMBER | DECEMBER |

## JANUARY 2, 2008, COYOTE LODGE, NEW MEXICO

Yesterday was the beginning of the new year. Today is the beginning of my personal new year: my birthday. The first day of my sixty-ninth year, the last year of my seventh decade. A good day to begin a journal, especially because yesterday, I finished the book I've been working on for the past three months: *Wormwood*, the seventeenth book in a series of mysteries featuring a character named China Bayles. It began in 1992 and will continue, I hope, for a good long time.

Finished for now, that is, since I still have a final chapter to write and some tidying up to do. But I'm ready to tackle something new. So I'm opening a new journal on the first day of my new year, a very ordinary day, as the poet Maxine Kumin says in *Always Beginning*, when I am grateful just to be going on with my life.

I've been spending the winter holidays here in New Mexico. Bill arrived the day after Thanksgiving (bringing the cat) and left (with the cat) the day after Christmas; I arrived in early December (bringing our three dogs) and will leave (dogs, too) in a couple of weeks. I would love to stay here longer, but there are things to be done back in Texas.

*Here* is Coyote Lodge, a small log house perched on a mountain slope seventy-five hundred feet above sea level, thirty miles northeast of Santa Fe, twenty-five miles northwest of Las Vegas, and forty miles south of Taos, on the eastern flank of the Sangre de Cristo Mountains, at the southern end of the Rockies. Through the wide front windows, I look north and west across the valley to a snow-covered ridge that rises to nearly ten thousand feet. Or down-valley, east and south, to Cerro Pelón, a bald, burly, white-caped sentinel standing guard at the valley's mouth. Distances are deceptive. This extinct volcano—once an inferno of fiery, liquid rock, now cold, solid stone, immovable—

*I am grateful for every ordinary day, knowing that these will draw to a close somewhere beyond our seeing. I hope to go on picking vegetables, pulling bindweed out of the fields, enjoying the birds, the dogs, even our elderly cat, whose last season this likely will be. . . . Going on is, after all, the ultimate pleasure of our lives.*

—MAXINE KUMIN

may look close, but it's thirty miles away and millions of years old. I feel some astonishment at this: at what seems to be an unchangeable landscape, but is constantly changing and being changed. In the life of the earth, it's fire one day, rock the next.

Nearer by, though I can't see it from here, is a famous mountain. Earlier people called it El Cerro del Tecolote, Owl Mountain; now it's called Hermit's Peak, in honor of an Italian recluse named Giovanni Maria Agostiani, who came there in 1863 to live in a shallow cave below the bristlecone pines that rim the eastern, dawn-facing cliff, incandescent in the morning sun. I often try to imagine the solitude of that cave in the cool blessedness of the summers, the frigid fury of the winters. I can't.

My view of Agostiani's mountain is blocked by the more familiar ridge behind our cabin, where snow-laden pines rise against a blue, oh so blue sky. But seen or unseen, Hermit's Peak is there, far beyond what is safe and imaginable. Who was the hermit, really, beyond the tales that are told about him? Where did he come from? Why? Whatever his story, Agostiani took it with him when he left the mountain in 1867. Two years later, his body was found beyond another mountain to the south of here, near Las Cruces. There was a dagger in his back.

But it's all lovely, all of this, no matter how you look at it: from the dizzying, dazzling solitude of Hermit's Peak, from the safety of my sheltering ridge, from my window.

Lovely.


JANUARY 3

The *Austin American-Statesman* printed a notice of my birthday in yesterday's newspaper. Nice—but they shortened my life by a year.

Funny thing. I'm not annoyed that my age is out there for the whole world to see, but rather that I didn't get full credit for all sixty-eight years of it, a mountain, a whole mountain range, of living and learning. The error prompts me to wonder which of those sixty-eight years I would omit from my calendar of learning experiences. One of the horrible high school years, maybe—gawky, pimply, picked-on. Or 1968–1969, that first awful year at Berkeley, a fledgling feminist trying to cope with graduate school, a floundering marriage, three active children. Or 1985, the year I was capsized in a relationship doomed to shipwreck from the beginning.

But each of those years, *annus horribilis* as it was, taught me something about myself I wouldn't have, couldn't have learned otherwise.

Each was part of the curriculum, an *annus mirabilis* in wolf's clothing. I wouldn't have missed it for the world.

Reading this week (to write a review): *Weaving a Way Home: A Personal Journey Exploring Place and Story* by Leslie Van Gelder. A strong book, arguing that we find our way in the wildness of the world through story, and through story we create our homes.

No TV here in the mountains, but several NPR stations.

NEWS SUMMARY: *The Iowa caucus, on the Democratic side: Obama, 38 percent; Edwards and Clinton with 30 percent each. Christopher Dodd and Joe Biden have dropped out. For the Republicans: Huckabee, 34 percent; Romney, 25 percent; Thompson and McCain, 13 percent each.*

## JANUARY 5

This is a presidential election year, and the news is all politics, all the time. A Democrat (although I part company with the party on some significant issues), I'm leaning toward Obama, who won a surprisingly hefty 38 percent of the vote in the Iowa caucus this week. I expected Clinton to do better since the national polling had her some eight–ten points ahead of Obama.

Obama? Clinton? A black? A woman? An astonishing choice—astonishing because it's the first time we're confronted by such a choice, astonishing because . . . my god, there it is! My heart goes both ways. But are either electable in the general election? Clinton is hampered by her gender; Obama by his race. She's encumbered by the political baggage carried over from her White House years; Obama by his lack of experience. But either would represent America more effectively to the world than the current administration, with its two ill-intentioned, unfinished wars and its anti-environment, anti-science, anti–civil rights policies.

## JANUARY 6

Out before dawn with the dogs. Zach and Lady, elderly black Labs, mellow and sedate, neither in the best of health. Lady suffers from chronic arthritis, Zach from a sudden-onset malady, new last week, which is making him drink and pee excessively. (Bill has already scheduled a vet appointment for us back home.) The third dog is Toro, a younger, energetic heeler. His job: round up his dogs and humans, nip heels, keep us moving. His ambition: catch the gophers that live in the snowbanks along the road.

The sky is transparent blue, the Sangres white with snow and rosy with the rising sun, the pines afire with frost. The thermometer read zero when we set out and Zach and Lady quickly complain of cold paws—Toro is too busy digging gophers out of the snow to think about cold paws. We cut our walk short and come home to the warm kitchen for breakfast. A painted slate plaque hangs on the kitchen wall, left behind by the former owner: *When you're lucky enough to live in the mountains, you're lucky enough.* Yes.

I am a lover of small houses, and this log house suits me. Downstairs, a bedroom and bath, a kitchen, an open space for eating and sitting. Up a flight of stairs, my writing loft. The log walls seem to bring the forest indoors. I feel enclosed by trees. But some of the logs along the deck were badly rotted and Bill has spent the last three summers restoring them—a laborious process involving cleaning, sanding, treating, staining. A lesser man might have let the logs rot (or hired out the job to be haphazardly done by somebody who doesn't care). But Bill, too, is a lover of trees—an expert wood-turner, an artist of wood. He's not about to let our log house rot.

The first time we came here together, we arrived as the moon was rising over the nighttime shoulder of the mountain. As we stood on the deck, dumbstruck by the crystalline brilliance of the stars, the clarity of the air, the absolute silence, the coyotes began to sing. They sang for a long time, to the moon and stars and each other. Some of the songs came from the dark forest above us, others from the moonlit rim of the valley—wild, ecstatic, polyphonic, the melodic voices rising, retreating, recalling, as J. Frank Dobie once said, "something lost before time began."

Their song gave our house its name: Coyote Lodge. Lucky enough.

## JANUARY 7

For me, part of the delight of learning a new landscape is learning the birds. Last summer's abundant crop of grasses and tall forbs—mullein, thistles, fleabane, sunflowers—have all been stripped, and the snow cover (nearly two feet outside the kitchen door) makes forage difficult. Looking out the window, I count three ravens, a quartet of crows, an assortment of juncos, and a pair of Steller's jays under the pine trees, eagerly cleaning up whatever the smaller birds have flung out of the feeders.

With a four-foot wingspan and a wedge-shaped tail, Raven is lord of the Overworld, wheeling, tumbling, plunging, ecstatic acrobat of air. In the summer, I watch him recklessly riding thermals along the sloping mountain, spiraling high, plunging down, black bobsled on an invisible, twisting sluice. Monogamous for life (according to Susan Tweit, in *Seasons in the Desert*), raven couples build scraggy bowls of twigs and sticks woven higgledy-piggledy with bark strips, wire, feathers, and fur, even bits of plastic. Raven is sociable, usually hanging out with a gang of buddies, strutting, swaggering, dickering, and debating. Oh, yes, he's a talker, too: I love his rough cough, his sarcastic croak, the ringing *tok* that spreads the news of danger or fresh food: insects, small animals, roadkill, promising kitchen trash. I'd join in, but I don't speak the language.

Late last night, I pulled on my coat and went outside. The sky was clear and dark, except for the lights of Santa Fe, a dim glow on the other side of the Sangres, and the stars, an infinity of diamond dust, hinting at depths and distances too great to comprehend. After I went to bed, a storm came over the mountain and the wind grew fierce and wild, waking the dogs and me.

This morning, it's blowing so hard that we've postponed our morning walk, dashing out just long enough for the dogs to do their business. Back inside, settling down to a book (Paul Gruchow's *Boundary Waters: The Grace of the Wild*—about the connection of person and place), I feel the strength of this log house, bracing itself like Cerro Pelón against the battering wind. But our black mailbox came unmoored and tumbled end over end like Raven down the road, I giving chase, sailing after it, scarcely able to keep to the ground. A wild morning.

## JANUARY 9

After a day that began with bright sun, glittering rain showers, a rainbow arcing over the valley, there was snow again in the night, and the fierce, wild songs of coyotes.

But not enough snow to keep me from driving to Las Vegas, the nearest market town, twenty-five miles to the southeast. The valley road bisects snowy grasslands, loops through an open piñon-juniper forest along a creek, and crosses the Sapello River at the hamlet of Sapello, where there is a one-room post office, a gas station, and not much else. For most of the drive, I can see Hermit's Peak rising to ten thousand feet, its eastern escarpment rugged and stern, home to hermit and owls.

*A nighttime raven roost sounds like a city of restless sleepers: the air is alive with mutters, soft cries, whimpers, sighs. The black shapes shift and rustle, jockeying for better positions in the roost trees. Now and then a few ravens will suddenly rise into the air on stiff black wings, then one by one, drift back to settle on the branches again.*

—SUSAN TWEIT

*If the deep night were revealed to us in all its naked grandeur, it would perhaps be more than we could bear. But half of infinity is still infinite. A hint of infinity is infinite too—if we can take the hint.*

—CHET RAYMO

*I remember my first winter . . . awakening one night to an intensely strange and moving sound, a frenzied chorus of falsetto yips and howls—the cold starlit dark on fire with coyote cries. . . . It was joy that rose in me, like some forgotten song of my own.*

—JOHN DANIEL

*Nuestra Señora de los Dolores de Las Vegas Grandes*, Our Lady of Sorrows of the Great Meadows: the name given to Las Vegas when it was established by a Spanish grant in 1835. Not long after, the Santa Fe Trail brought thousands of travelers through the sleepy village. There was another boom when the Atchison, Topeka, and Santa Fe Railroad arrived in 1879 and rumors of gold began to drift like fragrant piñon smoke from the nearby Sangres. The gold petered out, but Las Vegas is still here, with a population of around 15,000 (80 percent Latino, 14 percent Anglo) and some 900 buildings listed in the National Register of Historic Places—everything from Spanish adobe to Victorian Gothic.

In town, I stocked up on groceries and supplies, then drove to a local restaurant, where I spoke about the business of writing to the Rotary Club. My point: while books are vitally important to our culture, they're also an important part of the national economy, and if people don't buy books, books will go away. Then, doing my personal best to support the publishing sector, I drove across town to Tome on the Range, a well-stocked, well-kept bookstore, one of the few independents in this part of the country.

Books are my greatest vice, although I never manage to read them as fast as I buy them and hence have a towering to-be-read stack. Today I came home with half a dozen, including William deBuys' *Enchantment and Exploitation: The Life and Hard Times of a New Mexico Mountain Range*. In my favorite chair, wrapped in a blanket and with a cup of hot tea at my elbow, I devoured a hundred pages. In deBuys, I've found a guide who is exquisitely familiar with these mountains, these valleys. I'm not going up there, into the Sangres, where he's been—at least not this winter. I'll stay warm, read his journey.

*This is the paradox of the familiar: the more you know a place, or think you know it, the more it can take you where you do not expect.*

—WILLIAM DEBUYS

JANUARY 12

Working steadily while I've been here, revising the manuscript of *Together, Alone: A Memoir of Marriage and Place*, due in June to the University of Texas Press. These long, dark winter days are the perfect container for this meditative writing.

The Press published my first academic book back in the 1970s, when I was still on the faculty at UT Austin. More recently, I've been involved in two editing projects with the Press, anthologies of women's writings about their lives: *With Courage and Common Sense* (2003) and *What Wildness Is This: Women Write about the Southwest* (2007). I worked on both books for the Story Circle Network, a nonprofit organization for women writers that came into being in 1997 as a follow-on project after another of my books, *Writing from Life: Telling Your Soul's Story.*

Doing other things beside writing, too, since I've been here. Stenciled a border (turquoise, red, sand) on the kitchen walls, close to the ceiling. Watched all of *Foyle's War* and more of *West Wing* on DVD and read my way through a tall stack of good books. Invited the neighbors over for dinner. Tonight, a potluck supper at the community center. I'm taking bread pudding, baked with apples, raisins, and pecans from our trees back in Texas. It's easy, and it'll use up the eggs and bread that need to be eaten before I leave next week.

## JANUARY 13

Yesterday afternoon, the dogs and I drove up the little Rio Manuelitas, which flows out of the mountains above the village of Rociada, a huddle of adobes, wood-frame barns with metal roofs, haystacks covered with blue plastic tarps, a white-painted church. The village is mostly home to older people now, the younger ones gone to seek their fortunes beyond the mountains. I like Alice Bullock's description in her little book, *Mountain Villages*: the word "Rociada" sounds like a bell.

I push on up-creek. The snow that fell before Christmas is nearly gone from the valley, but it lingers in deep drifts in this ponderosa-spruce country above eight thousand feet. Miniature ranches and tiny farms are squeezed onto the flats between the creek and the mountain, with barns and corrals built close to small frame and adobe houses, the homes of people who've lived here for decades, for whole lifetimes. They may not have much, but in these mountains they've built a life that is in many ways richer and freer than a life lived in town.

The creek has created its own narrow valley, with willows and aspen and too much tamarisk, which was introduced in the 1820s as erosion control. Tamarisk: an aggressive bully, an invasive species ("the devil's own," one biologist calls it) that elbows aside milder-natured native willows and cottonwoods, sucking up available water and forming dense thickets that replace communities of native plants. Tamarisk foliage, flowers, and fruit provide little food for wildlife, so the shrub gives nothing back to the ecosystem. A few years ago, though, along the Mora River some thirty miles to the east, I watched a team of beavers gathering tamarisk branches for their dam. If they kept at it, maybe their dams flooded the tamarisk and killed it. Maybe, if I

*I celebrate this gathering of women's writing about the Southwest. I read with the greatest pleasure as women in all their wild diversity—in the cities, in the Sonoran Desert, in canyons and villages, in wild bosques—raise their voices in the warmth of the new day . . . [bringing] the whole ecosystem alive, a desert entire again, a dawn chorus of singing, stinging, lamenting, laughing voices.*

—KATHLEEN DEAN MOORE

*Say the name Rociada to yourself several times and listen to the music of the syllables. They sound like a sheep bell, far off across the ciénega in the early morning when timothy and foxtail grasses are wet with dew and the smell of piñon fires mixes with the more urgent smell of perking coffee.*

—ALICE BULLOCK

went there now, I'd see that the willows and cottonwoods had made a comeback.

Afterward, at home with a bowl of hot soup for supper, watching the sun fall behind the western mountains. The sunsets here are often fine, but this one was stunning: clouds drifting over the upthrust eastern flank of the Sangres, gold, copper, bronze, kindled into brilliant flame as the sun slipped behind the skyline ridge. To the north, gray-blue curtains of snow blowing out of a pewter sky over the snowfields above the tiny village of Gascon, across the trail that ranchers use to drive their cattle from winter grazing in the high valleys to the summer grass in the higher alpine meadows. The mountains, like a bulwark, make this place strong. And the people—especially those who have lived here their whole lives—seem to me to rise up from that strength.

## JANUARY 14

Heading home tomorrow, so I've spent the day cleaning, doing laundry, organizing the refrigerator and pantry, and packing the stuff that goes back to Texas. I don't want to leave. I love being alone here. (Is it fair to say I'm alone, with three dogs, each with his/her personality, needs, demands?) Love looking across the valley to the mountains, to the rugged foothills, dark green with piñon and ponderosa, to the white snowfields above Gascon. Love the silence, the small sounds: the clatter of birds, the soft brush-brush of pine boughs in the wind, the fierce sweep of storm down the mountain and across our roof.

The sky has been a clear, brilliant blue all day, although the temperature never rose above thirty. I took the dogs out tonight, the snow crunching under my feet, under the dogs' eager paws, the blackness of the sky shattered by stars. To the west, at the head of the valley, are the few scattered pinprick lights of Rociada, and to the north, the lights of a car skirting the far edge of the valley. Closer, the lights of neighbors, friends—L.G. and Sandy, Rosi and Mike. Behind me, Bob's house is dark—he's spending the evening with Donna and Al, where there's a light in every room.

They're here, they stay. I'm betwixt and between, both/and, a resident and a visitor, a Texan and a New Mexican. Tonight, in the cold, star-studded dark, counting the lights that spill across the mountain and down into the valley, naming the people who live in these lamp-lit houses and recalling their faces, I feel at home, as if I belong here.

But tomorrow I have to leave.

I belong somewhere else, too.

*This earth is my sister; I love her daily grace, her silent daring, and how loved I am. How we admire this strength in each other, all that we have lost, all that we have suffered, all that we know: we are stunned by this beauty, and I do not forget: what she is to me, what I am to her.*

—SUSAN GRIFFIN

*The work of belonging to a place is never finished. There will always be more to know than any mind or lifetime can hold. But that is no argument against learning all one can.*

—SCOTT RUSSELL SANDERS

*Some days I think this one place isn't enough. That's when nothing is enough, when I want to live multiple lives and have the know-how and guts to love without limits.*

—GRETEL EHRLICH

## JANUARY 15

*Travel Notes*

Las Vegas, New Mexico. Brilliant blue sky, low drifts of fragrant smoke over the town from piñon fires on this cold morning. Hermit's Peak, its rock face striated with bands of snow.

U.S. 84, south from Las Vegas to I-40. Juniper-studded grasslands, rugged ridges rimming the eastern horizon. The western edge of the High Plains, lapping up the eastern shores of the Sangres. Frosted grass, nuggets of small houses and trailers, smoke rising from chimneys, ruins of red rock dwellings and barns, here and there a new log A-frame tucked into the elbow of a pine-covered foothill. A relic snowdrift; a pair of chilly red-tailed hawks, breasts silver in the pale sun, hunched close together on a wire, feathers fluffed. Crossing the Pecos River, no houses, juniper thins and disappears as the road dips down into an arid landscape of yucca, ocotillo.

I-40, east to Santa Rosa. Big trucks moving fast, my minivan small and insignificant in the whipsaw of traffic on this cross-country route. The highway cuts through ancient Permian limestones, red Triassic sandstones, shales. Seas here once, unimaginably long ago.

U.S. 84, south to Fort Sumner, nearly deserted highway. The Pecos River again, the western boundary of the Llano Estacado, winding its way to the Rio Grande. Llano: "plain." Estacado: "palisaded," "enclosed," "staked." Wide arid plateau bounded by the Mescalero Ridge and the Pecos on the west, the Caprock Escarpment on the east. Arid, treeless, sparse desert grasses, sagebrush, cholla, yucca, creosote bush, scrubby juniper along the arroyos. Seldom more than twenty inches of rain a year.

Fort Sumner, east to Clovis. I glimpse a cholla starred with yellow blooms—still winter here, but this one must've been blessed by one of the brief, random rain showers and a warm southern breeze. Rabbit brush and last summer's yucca stalks, brown and dry, seedpods open, claw-like. Blowing dust, leafless trees in mostly vacant villages. Bleached skeletons of dry tumbleweed—an invader from the steppes of Central Asia, mixed with flaxseed brought to South Dakota in the 1870s. Here, they whirl across the road, snag in barbwire fences, lie heaped by the wind in huge piles along the railway, as if the desert were cleaning house.

*We are always somewhere, and it is through place that we are able to root our sense of story and our sense of self. . . . We are never nowhere, and for as long as we are alive we are bonded with a world where we experience movement, breath, and nourishment. We are here. To live is to be in relation to the body of our environment.*

—LESLIE VAN GELDER

*We simply need that wild country available to us, even if we never do more than drive to its edge and look in. For it can be a means of reassuring ourselves of our sanity as creatures, a part of the geography of hope.*

—WALLACE STEGNER

*[F]rom the point of view of humans, the tumbleweed's main function is poetic. They roll and bounce on the wind, they fly through the air like half-filled weather balloons, they pile up in throngs against fences and buildings.*

—IAN FRAZIER

As I drive, I'm listening (on CD) to David Quammen's wonderful biography, *The Reluctant Mr. Darwin*. I am sobered to learn that I am among only 13 percent of Americans who accept the theory of human evolution, unguided by a divine being. And more than half believe that God created humans in our present form within the last ten thousand years. Within the last ten thousand years!

I'm used to being in the minority—but this is amazing. I ponder it for miles.

Clovis, New Mexico. Just passed the sign pointing in the direction of Blackwater Draw, eight miles south, where in 1929, archaeologists uncovered a site occupied by humans perhaps as long ago as fifteen thousand years. (Well, good heavens. Here's the evidence.) The occupation was dated from spear points found with the remains of large animals extinct since the Pleistocene—the litter left behind by the "Clovis culture," thought to be the earliest widespread American culture. Named for the town I'm driving through right now. Main Street is littered with cheap motels, flag-festooned used-car lots, fast-food joints, pawnshops, gun shops, gas pumps, billboards, power lines. The current occupation.

Obvious irony here.

Clovis, east to Lubbock on U.S. 84. Stopped at the New Mexico tourist center at the state's border to let the dogs—contented travelers, all three—stretch their legs, do their business, slurp water, gulp treats, after which I do pretty much the same thing. A mile farther, we're in Texas, and I'm setting my watch forward an hour from Mountain to Central time. Sky no longer brilliant blue but gray, lens-shaped clouds suggesting rain.

The "sea of grass" that Francisco Coronado found here some five hundred years ago has been destroyed by overgrazing. I'm reminded of the West Texas cattlemen who, in the 1890s, declared their intention to use up the grass. Now, these flat, treeless plains are industrially farmed with oil-fueled machines, the soil enriched with fertilizers made from natural gas, the plants sprayed with petroleum-based pesticides. The crops are irrigated with paleowater (water that dates back to the last Ice Age) from the Ogallala Aquifer, which will be gone in another twenty or thirty years, pumped into irrigators that crawl like long-legged spiders around the fields, moored to a center pivot and pump. This ancient water is used to grow corn (largely for biofuels), sorghum, cotton, but mostly cotton—picked before Christmas, stuffed now into huge bales the size of semi-truck trailers scattered like loaves of white bread across the fields, wrapped in plastic tarps, blue, orange, silver.

U.S. 84, Lubbock southeast to Post. The sky has clouded over. I phone Bill, who checks the radar on the computer and reports that a substantial rain system, with embedded thunderstorms, is spreading northeastward from northern Mexico. We'll get wet before we get home.

This is the eastern edge of the Llano Estacado, and I'm looking forward to a pretty stretch of road just north of the town of Post. The plateau drops off sharply at the Caprock Escarpment, a north-south cliff line three hundred feet high, deeply cut by canyons, stretching two hundred miles south from the Canadian River in the Texas Panhandle. Rugged, scenic, beautiful.

Post. Little town, big history. Founded in 1907 by C. W. Post, the cereal millionaire creator of Post Toasties and Grape-Nuts. Fired by a dream of a Utopian community, seeking a dry, healthful climate, Post bought up a quarter of a million acres here and established a model town, complete with courthouse, the Algerita Hotel, a school, a sanitarium, a cotton gin, and a cotton mill—as well as churches, a baseball field, a bank, even a lake. He died in 1914 (a suicide—why?), but the town has carried on through the Depression, the decline of cotton, the terrible drought of the fifties, the rise of oil. The population is now about thirty-eight hundred, and the parking lot at McDonald's is full. Wouldn't have pleased Mr. Post. He preached a vegetarian diet.

South on U.S. 84 to Snyder, the far northeastern corner of the Permian Basin oil field, largest onshore oil and gas field in the United States. Near Post, industrious pump jacks line the road like rusty grasshoppers, bowing up and down, patient, persistent. When crude was around fifteen dollars a barrel, the pumps sat frozen; now it's pushing a hundred dollars a barrel, so they're at it again, up down up down.

A couple of days ago, I stumbled onto a startling *New York Times* online article, published in 2006, about something called "peak oil." The idea was first raised by Shell Oil researcher-cum-Cassandra Marion Hubbert, who in the late 1950s predicted that U.S. oil production would peak in a couple of decades—that is, it would reach the high point of its production in the seventies, level off, then decline.

At the time, "Hubbert's Peak" was an industry joke. But Hubbert turned out to be a prophet. The production of oil in the United States actually did peak in 1970—although not, of course, the demand. Now,

*The historian Donald Worster once wrote, in contemplating irrigation, that he would hate to see one more drop of water applied to his arid West, because one more drop of water would make it less free. Aridity is the soul of the place and water is the beginning of its enslavement. Irrigation is compromising its freedom by . . . making it safe and livable.*

—RICHARD MANNING

*Tackle the work just in front of you. Strive in an honest way to do the best you can.*

—CHARLES WILLIAM POST

pumps like these produce only a fraction of what this country demands, and we import the rest—nearly 70 percent. But according to the article, global oil is finite, too. Globally, production will peak. But not demand. Demand just keeps rising. Then what? Seeing the pumps, I'm reminded of the question and wonder again: then what?

I'm still pondering this as I listen to *The Reluctant Mr. Darwin*. Quammen quotes Thomas Malthus, who had a significant influence on Darwin: "Every species has a tendency to expand beyond its available resources."

Clovis man, Clovis Main Street, Main Streets across the country. And gas pumps everywhere.

Expanding beyond our available resources. Fossil water, fossil fuel.

Then what?

But here, along U.S. 84 near Snyder, a hopeful sign of species resourcefulness: wind farms, sprouting miles of stalwart wind turbines. Unlike paleowater and Permian oil and gas, wind is a renewable resource, and there's plenty of it on these flat plains. Two hundred feet high, the turbines and their contiguous electrical transmission lines aren't pretty—but certainly no uglier than rusty pump jacks and irrigation equipment.

Wind and solar. This is the future. This is where we need to be going. Will we? Or will we simply continue on as we are, exploiting what we have, until it's too late?

This is in my mind as I stop to buy gas ($3.10 a gallon) and wonder what Bill and I are doing with houses in two different states, almost seven hundred miles apart. Mentally, I change the subject. Not something I want to think about.

I-20, east of Sweetwater, nearing Abilene. The light is an expressive presence here, like the wind, constantly changing, golden, gray, bright, shadowy. Clouds building to the southeast, the rain system Bill told me about. The dogs are tired, occasionally growly and snappish, but overall, they're fine travelers (quieter than children, less quarrelsome and whiny), comfortable companions.

U.S. 183, southeast of Cisco, on the last leg of the trip, only one hundred and fifty miles to go. Twilight now. A stealthy owl, large, heavy, glides low across the road in front of me. Gray sunset clouds brushed with fuchsia and gold, darker clouds and rain to the east. Lights coming on in farmhouses, ranch houses, little houses, like the ones I grew up in back in the Midwest. I've always loved little houses, modest, tidy, unimposing, settling into the landscape, like the little house where Bill and I live in the Hill Country.

Home, and shortly.

Home. Full dark, cold, raining hard. The dogs are ecstatic. The cat (here with Bill all this time), wary of the dogs, takes to the kitchen bar where she sits, flicking her tail in irritation. I'm weary but happy and hungry, ready for a bowl of Bill's chili in front of the fireplace and the embracing comfort of our familiar bed.

*It would be nice to travel if you knew where you were going and where you would live at the end—or do we ever know, do we ever live where we live? Or are we always in other places, lost, like sheep?*

—JANET FRAME

## JANUARY 17, MEADOW KNOLL, TEXAS

The Hill Country: home since Bill and I married, more than twenty years ago. We're some sixty miles northwest of Austin, right on the ninety-eighth meridian, that "institutional fault line" described by Walter Prescott Webb as the great divide between the eastern woodlands and the grassland west, arid and harsh. I believe it. Our average rainfall is only about thirty inches, a little more in some years, a lot less in others.

The lives of modern settlers in this place are comforted and buttressed by electricity, gasoline-powered engines, deep water wells. But I often think how the first Europeans must have seen this land, with its wide expanse of sky and grass—mostly grass, then, for this is the southern tip of a prairie that once stretched a thousand miles, from here into Southern Canada. Mostly gone now, destroyed by overgrazing, annual cropping, urbanization. John Madson once wrote that the people were changed by the land—I'm sure that's true. But in these latter days, the land has been changed by the people—although Nature has a persistence we lack. Perhaps she will turn us out and the native prairies will make a comeback.

Chilly this morning, in the low forties, blustery wind whipping bare branches, but balmy after below-zero mornings in New Mexico. The sharp green spears of early daffodils push through the leaves along the edge of the woods, and there's a cardinal celebrating in the tree outside my window: *cheer-cheer-what-cheer.*

What cheer. The dogs are celebrating, too. No snowy paws.

*As one contrasts the civilization of the Great Plains with that of the eastern timberland, one sees what may be called an institutional fault (comparable to a geological fault) running from middle Texas to Illinois or Dakota, roughly following the ninety-eighth meridian. . . . When people first crossed this line they did not immediately realize the imperceptible change that had taken place in their environment, nor, more is the tragedy, did they foresee the full consequences which that change was to bring in their own characters and in their modes of life.*

—WALTER PRESCOTT WEBB

## JANUARY 18

Unpacking, opening mail, sorting e-mails. Just saw the cover for the next book in the China Bayles series, *Nightshade.* Nice colors, but the plant is wrong. I query the art department at Berkley (my mysteries are published by Berkley Prime Crime, a Penguin imprint) and am told that it's too late to make changes and that nobody but me is likely to notice. Not true. A couple of years ago, a newspaper reviewer—a garden writer—took me to task for using the "wrong" variety of bleeding hearts on a book cover. If I were a "real" gardener, she wrote, I wouldn't have made such a mistake. (My opinion: If she were a "real" reviewer, she'd know that in most cases writers see their book covers after the fact.)

*Writing prejudicial, off-putting reviews is a precise exercise in applied black magic.*

—WILLIAM S. BURROUGHS

**NEWS SUMMARY:** *The nation's mayors launched a new appeal for federal aid to deal with the home foreclosure crisis. More than two hundred and fifty mayors met in Washington, D.C., with the United States Conference of Mayors. The conference president called the rise in foreclosures an "economic tsunami" in need of immediate attention.*

## JANUARY 19

Reading: A good book called *Bad Money* by Kevin Phillips, about the ballooning U.S. debt—national, corporate, personal.

Scary, but not news to me. Over the past five years, I've been shaking my head at the huge escalation in home prices, to the staccato beat of TV shows like *Flip This House* ("tips on the art of flipping for profit") and *My House Is Worth What?* There's something wrong with this picture, when home is converted from home-place to a hunk of real estate profit, "flipped" as fast as possible for as much as possible. The idea of home—the need to find affordable, sustaining shelter; the deep human need to be at home in a place—has been repackaged as a gilt-edged, low-risk investment opportunity, sending the home-building and home finance industries into turbo-drive but impoverishing our spirits. And now we hear about thousands, perhaps hundreds of thousands of people enticed by subprime mortgages into buying homes they couldn't afford and losing them in a tidal wave of debt: "an economic tsunami."

Homeless, dispossessed, unrooted. We are truly entering, as Terry Tempest Williams says, a place of desolation.

*I truly believe that [we need] to stay home, to learn the names of things, to realize who we live among. . . . If we are not rooted deeply in place, making that commitment to dig in and stay put . . . then I think we are living a life without specificity, and then our lives become abstractions. Then we enter a place of true desolation.*

—TERRY TEMPEST WILLIAMS

Eighteen degrees this morning, the frost a bright, brittle crust of diamonds on grass, weeds. At dawn, the dogs and I walk the east meadow loop. We're still getting reacquainted with our territory: the dogs with the trace scents of the deer, coons, possums, mice, and coyotes that travel this same path every night (their territory, too, their homeland, their place); I with the sights and sounds of home—the cardinals flashing scarlet through the dark green junipers, the grasses of our remnant scrap of native prairie, the lamentations of mourning doves.

Back in the kitchen for pancakes, golden, crunchy with Bill's pecans. We gathered an astonishing two hundred pounds last fall from the trees he's grafted, cultivated. Won't run out of pecans for a while.

After breakfast, Bill and I drove up to the barn to break the ice on the tank that supplies water for Texas and Blossom, our longhorn cows, and Mutton, the lone survivor of a flock of six Barbado sheep slaughtered by dogs a few years ago—no leash law in our rural county, and some irresponsible dog owners think it's fine to let them roam at night. I fed the animals their wintertime ration of cow cake, chopped corn, and sorghum and molasses and scattered corn for the ducks and the pair of large white ganders we call Mutt and Jeff. The seven white and four black ducks were released on our little lake last summer by a neighbor and were adopted by Mutt and Jeff, who clearly needed something to do besides swimming and eating. They take their parenting duties seriously, herding their unruly charges with a nip here, a tuck there, an occasional wing-swat. Little things, as Henry Beston says. Small events in a tiny world. Fun to watch.

Meadow Knoll—the name we gave to this Hill Country property when we came here in 1986—is a thirty-one-acre stretch of meadows and woods on the east side of a variable-level lake, scooped out in the early 1970s by a small-time developer with overblown ideas and an oversized bulldozer. When it's full, the lake, fed by a spring, a creek, and rainwater runoff from nearby fields, covers about twenty acres. During droughts (like the one we're living through now), it shrinks to the size of a wading pool. Before white settlers arrived, the area was the site of a Tonkawa Indian campground—perhaps a trade camp, where Tonkawa, Caddo, and Jumano came together to swap goods and food and news. The modern road to the lake is called Indian Wells, reflecting the old-timers' knowledge of the campsite.

If there were any archaeological remains at the Indian Wells spring, that fool with the bulldozer chewed them up. That's a great pity, for

*We need another and wiser and perhaps a more mystical concept of animals. . . . In a world older and more complete than ours they move finished and complete, gifted with extensions of the senses we have lost or never attained, living by voices we shall never hear. They are not brethren, they are not underlings; they are other nations, caught with ourselves in the net of life and time, fellow prisoners of the splendour and travail of the earth.*

—HENRY BESTON

*Who would live happily in the country must be wisely prepared to take great pleasure in little things.*

—HENRY BESTON

*Where I grew up . . . people had home-places. . . . The home-place was the settling place, the one your forebears had come to from the old country; the place where, for better or worse, they had concluded to try their fortunes; or it was the final stop in the family's wanderings, the place where luck, or money, or resolve had run out, where one made a last stand.*

—PAUL GRUCHOW

researchers in nearby Williamson and Bell counties have uncovered human-occupied campsites dating back some twelve thousand years. This might have been one of these. The Hill Country was home to a network of hunter-gatherer families, clans, and tribes, moving north and south, east and west, in the regular pursuit of deer and bison and seasonal harvests: pecans, mesquite beans, prickly pear cactus.

All this changed in the mid-1800s when the fierce Comanches attacked from the north and the land-hungry Anglos pushed in from the east. Together, they squeezed out the friendly, transient Tonkawas. But I think of them often, especially on nights when the moon is full. Imagine them camped at the spring, on the sloping hill, relaxing beside their fires or asleep in tipis and brush huts. Sometimes I think: if I look hard enough, maybe I'll see them, see their spirits or the drifting smoke from their campfires, hear the barking of camp dogs, the singing of the children. But they're gone, removed to an Oklahoma reservation in 1884, their homeland carved into ranches and farms and subdivisions. And in place of their camp, a developer's lake, home to herons, kingfishers, migrating cormorants, a flock of resident ducks, and Mutt and Jeff.

Home. Home.

NEWS SUMMARY: *Responding to fears that the United States is headed for an imminent recession, stocks fell dramatically in all major markets of Europe, Asia, and America. In response to the global plunge, the Federal Reserve Bank cut interest rates by three-quarters of a percent, the largest single-day reduction in the bank's history.*

## JANUARY 22

The global bad news, really bad, is eclipsed by bad news here at home. Zach, our senior black Lab, is staying overnight at the vet's for a second round of tests. The preliminary diagnosis: Cushing's disease, a problem in either the pituitary or the adrenal gland—hard to tell which. This accounts for the constant drinking and peeing of the last several weeks.

Zach came to us from the Round Rock pound eleven years ago, via Dick and Luann Lindsey, who started the Austin-area Lab Rescue. This tail-wagging, tongue-lolling, goofy guy won our hearts, and there's never been a minute since that we didn't love him, even when he ate the (expensive) wooden blinds at the living room window

*No matter how much one may love the world as a whole, one can live fully in it only by living responsibly in some small part of it. Where we live and who we live there with define the terms of our relationship to the world and to humanity.*

— WENDELL BERRY

*You ask of my companions. Hills, sir, and the sundown, and a dog as large as myself that my father bought me. They are better than human beings, because they know but do not tell.*

—EMILY DICKINSON

and my great-grandmother's velvet-and-satin crazy-quilt pillow. Four years later, we adopted Lady, another black Lab, another rescue. Three years after that, Toro—a heeler, a cow dog with the temperament of a Texas trail boss—bounced into our lives and announced that he was adopting us.

Ours is a small house and full, especially when I'm trying to cook dinner with three dogs underfoot. But they've worked out their territorial agreements and are surprisingly congenial: Zach is mellow and old-dog tolerant; Lady, decorous, lady-like; Toro, in-your-face but eager to please. The dogs teach me something new every day. New about them, new about myself.

I slept hard last night: no Zach to get us out of bed at one a.m., and three, and five. I hadn't realized I was so tired. But I missed him, dreamed that I was tossing sticks for him, which he loved to fetch when he was young and lively. Woke up worrying, the way you worry about a child in the hospital, or a dear friend. Zach is thirteen, close to the time we'll have to say goodbye. I'm not ready—but will I ever be ready for this? I don't think so.

*Dogs' lives are too short. Their only fault, really.*

—AGNES SLIGH TURNBULL

*A dog is one of the remaining reasons why some people can be persuaded to go for a walk.*

—O. A. BATTISTA

JANUARY 23

Ordinary days.

The best days, ordinary days, begin about 6:30 a.m.—waking from a warm dream to a kiss from my husband and an ecstatic canine greeting. (The cat is not particularly affectionate, except with Bill.) Make the bed, brew fresh coffee, start a load of laundry. Coffee in hand, turn on the computer, check the e-mail for urgencies (happily, none on this ordinary day), glance at the weather radar and the front page of the online *New York Times*.

Twenty minutes with e-mail, and it's time for the dogs to take me for our morning walk, through the pale wintry sunshine and across the east meadow to the Ramsey Ranch fence; along a path under live oaks, cedars, and mesquite; up the old lane behind the abandoned workshop to the pasture where our cows and sheep stand broadside to the winter sun, warming their brown flanks. Down the gravel lane and home to fix the dogs' breakfasts and mine—Bill takes care of himself.

A pot of tea brewing, a casserole out of the freezer for supper, laundry into the dryer, another load into the washer, a quick sweep of the kitchen floor (oh, the dog fur!) and I'm on my way to my computer to finish the e-mail, post to the blog, make an entry in this journal, and open the file on the current writing project (*Wormwood*, nearly finished).

I start the day with work that I did the previous afternoon, editing, expanding, cutting, revising—usually adding five hundred words in the process. Some of the revisions are stylistic, local, a few words adjusted, a paragraph recast, detail layered in, an irrelevancy deleted. Other revisions are non-local: I go back to earlier parts of the work, making changes in situation, characterization, timing, and so on—easier on the computer than it used to be on a typewriter. When I began writing short stories in the late 1950s, I worked on an antique (even then) Royal that required a jackhammer wrist action. Making revisions and tinkering with text on the computer is an indescribable pleasure likely felt most keenly by writers who remember those old days, those old ways—without a shred of nostalgic pleasure.

In the afternoon, new work: pushing ahead through the chapter or scene, producing another thousand words to add to the morning's count. That's my goal, anyway. Some days I make it, or better; other days, not. Interruptions are part of the process (I don't write in an ivory tower), although sometimes I have to shut the door or put my fingers in my ears. But I'm fairly focused, and by 4:30 on an ordinary day, the book is fifteen hundred new words to the good, and I'm moderately happy with the work.

## JANUARY 24

Bill is back from the vet with the news: Cushing's, definitely. Not good. Zach is going on a twice-a-day medication, but it's not a cure, only a temporary mitigation of the symptoms. We won't see any change for at least a month. (Translation: we'll continue taking turns getting up at night to take him outdoors.) Lady isn't doing well, either: her arthritis is making it harder for her to negotiate the back steps. I sympathize with Lady. Sometimes I have trouble with those steps, too. We're both feeling older.

NEWS SUMMARY: *The Bush administration and the House are working out the terms of a $146-billion stimulus package that gives rebates of $300–$600 to individuals earning up to $75,000 and to couples with incomes up to $150,000. Families will be eligible for up to $300 in rebates for each child.*

Rebates? I'm sure the money will be welcome to many, but it's not going to change the basic situation. It'll go to the banks because people will use it to pay this month's credit card bill. But maybe that's the idea. Maybe this is a way of getting money to the banks. Indirectly.

Still thinking about that "peak oil" business I happened on in the *Times* piece a couple of weeks ago and doing some focused reading. *The Geography of Nowhere: The Rise and Decline of America's Man-Made Landscape* by James Howard Kunstler, which has been on my shelf for a while. More sobering, mind-altering, even life-altering: *The Party's Over: Oil, War and the Fate of Industrial Societies* by Richard Heinberg. Seriously scary.

I am an educated, well-read person. How is it that I have managed to remain ignorant of the cataclysmic idea that the Industrial Age, founded on nonrenewable energy sources, may come to an end in the next few decades, in my lifetime, in my children's lifetimes? I am almost as stunned by my lack of awareness of this idea as I am by the idea itself.

I'm remembering an event during the seventies' Arab oil embargo: I drove to the corner gas station to fill up my little tomato juice–red Volkswagen and encountered an "Out of Gas" sign on the pump. I remember being astonished, incredulous at the notion that a gas station could be out of gas. But why was I so surprised? Surely I didn't believe that every gas station tapped into an endless underground source of the stuff?

But I did. I grew up with cheap oil. It fueled my life, shaped my footloose, fancy-free lifeways, but I never thought of how much I depended on it. I was completely oblivious to everything but the cost per gallon of what I put into my car. I have a lot to learn about this subject. And the lessons may be painful.

Can't think about this every minute, can't write about it in every journal entry. But I'm thinking about it a lot.

*We are about to enter a new era in which each year, less net energy [from fossil fuel sources] will be available to humankind, regardless of our efforts or choices. The only significant choice we will have will be how to adjust to this new regime. But we will not be in a position to navigate wisely through these rapids of cultural change if we are still living with the mistaken belief that we are somehow entitled to endless energy.*

—RICHARD HEINBERG

*We must face the prospect of changing our basic ways of living. This change will either be made on our own initiative in a planned way, or forced on us with chaos and suffering by the inexorable laws of nature.*

—JIMMY CARTER (1976)

JANUARY 26

It's not true—at least for me—that writing is a lonely business.

On an ordinary day, I depend on essential people. Bill reads most of what I write and points out the dangling story lines, plot snarls, and repetitions (the characters' multiple sighs, shrugs, eye-rollings). As our literary agent, he manages our writing business.

He also pays the household bills and does the taxes, collaborates on household chores, and keeps our thirty-one acres functioning. From 1994 to 2006, we wrote together as Robin Paige, producing a dozen Victorian-Edwardian mysteries. Before that, we worked together in young-adult mass-market fiction, writing nearly seventy books in six years. Hard to imagine my work—and my life—without him.

Essential Webmistress and assistant since 1997, Peggy Moody (She-Who-Makes-Things-Happen) manages our Web sites and e-mail newsletters. Incredibly fast, astonishingly cheerful, even when the world is going to hell in a handbasket. One of those irreplaceable people without whom the right things just don't get done in the right way. Every time.

Essential editors. Natalee Rosenstein at Prime Crime/Berkley Books/Penguin U.S.A. has been my editor since 1994, and I fervently hope we go on together for many more years. Over at the University of Texas Press, it's Theresa May who is indispensable, an enthusiastic and helpful editor, a friend.

Essential networks, women, mostly. The Story Circle Network keeps me focused on lifewriting. Sisters in Crime, connecting me with other mystery authors. Women Writing the West, a network of women who share a subject and a passion.

It takes a village to live any kind of life, especially a writing life. Can't be done alone.

## JANUARY 27

A friend sent me a copy of Lillian Rubin's *60 on Up: The Truth About Aging in America*. The first line: "Getting old sucks!" Even now, Rubin says, when aging isn't quite the steep slide into the long, dark night that it used to be, getting old "is a time of decline and loss."

Mmm . . . well, yes. Declines. My back hurts and my bones are brittle enough that I take a medication to slow bone loss. In the mirror, I see that my post-menopausal face is showing a fair number of wrinkles and crinkles and that my hair (muddy, ashy brown-blonde) is shot through with silver. Definitely on the downside of sixty.

But whether these losses outnumber the gains, I'm not sure. When I think about the things I can do now that I couldn't do then, seems like a pretty fair trade. There's the profoundly satisfying relationship with Bill and with my three grown children. I have good work to do. There's the Internet for research and information and e-mail for keeping in touch. Oh, and the computer itself, making me more productive—far more productive—than I was when I was half my age.

I don't plan to jump out of an airplane to celebrate my next birthday, or run the Boston Marathon, or climb the Himalayas. But I didn't do those things when I was thirty years younger. I taught then and read books and wrote books and enjoyed myself, and I'm still doing all these things, except that I'm doing more of them, especially reading and writing. And if I had to gauge my "contentment" level (whatever that is), I'd have to say it's been a damn sight higher in my sixties than in any other decade of my life. I can certainly lay claim to more hard-won self-knowledge and self-acceptance, maybe even a little more wisdom. A fair trade, if you ask me.

Take that, Lillian Rubin!

## JANUARY 28

Speaking of reading.

I've been seriously addicted since *The Tale of Peter Rabbit*, the first book I can remember reading (rather than being read to). I love the weight of a book in my hand, the smell of ink, the feel of the paper as I turn the pages, the enveloping, enlivening sense of belonging to a reading-and-writing culture. I confess to reading in restaurants, in the bathtub, at stoplights. I agree with whoever said that the closest we will ever come to an orderly universe is a good library.

Until recently I have not been interested in reading electronic books. I like to see print on paper pages, between covers. But for my birthday, I got an e-book reader. This electronic gizmo has the heft of a skinny paperback book, a screen the size of a Hallmark card, and a mini-keyboard, for people with mini-fingers. Looks like a toy.

But, oh my goodness. I turned it on: "Hello, Susan," it said, right there on the screen. I haven't yet met a book that could do that. I ordered Sue Grafton's Kinsey Millhone mystery, *Trespass*, published a few weeks ago. Seventy seconds later, via cell phone hocus-pocus, *Trespass* is on the screen in front of me. The *screen*? No paper pages to turn? No matter. Pulled into the message, I forget all about the medium.

And best of all, this skinny little gadget can hold two hundred books—more, if I buy a stick-in whatzit to increase the storage. This means that I can save my precious shelf space (space that has to shrink when Bill and I start to downsize in a few years) for print books I can't bear to part with or that don't exist in this electronic for-

*First you are young; then you are middle-aged; then you are old; then you are wonderful.*

—LADY DIANA COOPER

*I cannot remember a time when I was not in love with them—with the books themselves, cover and binding and the paper they were printed on, with their smell and their weight and with their possession in my arms, captured and carried off to myself.*

—EUDORA WELTY

*A book reads the better which is our own, and has been so long known to us, that we know the topography of its blots, and dog's ears, and can trace the dirt in it to having read it at tea with buttered muffins.*

—CHARLES LAMB

*Change can be scary. When papyrus replaced clay tablets, and the Gutenberg press calligraphy, did a bit of panic set in? Are we in the midst of a revolution of similar proportion? Very probably.*

—SUSAN MCLESTER

mat. (Although checking online, I see that Dickens, Thackeray, Austen, and god-only-knows-who-else are all available in downloadable format, free.)

And paper, and trees? Think of all the trees being saved, and the oil now used to truck printed books from warehouse to bookstore!

I love it. Absolutely love it. It's like having an entire library, a university, a universe of knowledge in my hands.

But I can't help wondering how this is going to change the publishing industry. Bookstores. How will bookstores deal with this?

## JANUARY 29

Bill is organizing the taxes and updating the year's budget. Hard to overstate the challenge of managing money when income is intermittent and you don't use credit, a decision we made in the early months of our marriage. One or the other of us had a second job the first year or two, but since then, we've supported ourselves with the writing. Some years it was (in my mother's Depression-era phrase) "slim pickin's," but we never treated the writing as a hobby, or even as supplementary income, always as the family business. In recent years, the income has become more predictable, because the books are written on contract, but when you get paid only a couple of times a year . . . well, that requires planning. Bill says it doesn't take rocket science to manage this intermittent flow, just a lot of adding and subtracting.

## JANUARY 30

Another of Bill's responsibilities: dealing with our computers. This morning, he's doing a periodic backup on mine, made easier by a slick doohickey called a "flash drive," which is about the size of my thumb and (amazingly) contains all my data files.

In an earlier incarnation (before we were married), Bill was a systems analyst and a mainframe manager for the state's birth control records: this computer stuff isn't rocket science, either, as far as he's concerned. So he says. I'm awed. Everything depends on these machines—writing, promoting books, communicating with editors and readers around the globe. I'm always impressed when I see him solving the problems in our systems caused by poor documentation, forced obsolescence, and speed-of-thought changes on the Internet.

A "volatile environment," he says. No kidding.

Foggy morning, in the forties, damp and chilly, the bare, black trees receding into the misty woods outside my window. Next month's daffodils, a few hardy daylily spears poking up through the soggy brown blanket of leaf mulch in the flower bed. *Wormwood* is just about wrapped up, so I am occupying myself with the necessary business of book promotion. Today is going to be a different kind of ordinary day. I have to put on my marketing hat.

These days, I can't just drop a manuscript in the mail and forget about it. An author is expected to be a full partner with the publisher's publicity department: touring and talking to libraries, book clubs, garden groups, hockey teams, riot squads, whoever is patient enough to sit and listen. She has to host a Web site and send out e-letters; blog and arrange blog tours; and show up at mystery conferences and conventions, scrubbed and smiling. Whether she wants to or not.

*Publicity is like poison. It doesn't hurt unless you swallow it.*

—JOE PATERNO

I'm lucky. In my fifteen-year incarnation as a university professor, I learned to like standing up in front of an audience to talk about books. And I don't dislike managing Web sites (with Peggy's help) or blogging or going to conferences. I've learned to accept this stuff as a necessary part of the writing business—and yes, yes, oh, yes, and yes again, it is a business.

But it all takes time. This morning, it took a couple of hours to e-mail the groups that have invited me to talk to their libraries, garden clubs, bookstores, and so forth, during April, when *Nightshade* comes out. Next, I had to list these tour events and e-mail them to Peggy (She-Without-Whom-Nothing-Gets-Done) for posting on the Web site. After that, I set up the March blog tour, which involved finding suitable online blog hosts, selecting dates, choosing topics, writing posts. An all-day job.

*Publicity in women is detestable. Anonymity runs in their blood. The desire to be veiled still possesses them. They are not even now as concerned about the health of their fame as men are, and, speaking generally, will pass a tombstone or a signpost without feeling an irresistible desire to cut their names on it.*

—VIRGINIA WOOLF

I can't complain. Writing books is only part of the job. Selling them is another. A day like this one, dedicated to getting the word out, is just another ordinary day.

But I have to admit, sometimes, to wanting to be back in New Mexico, just writing and reading and walking the dogs in the snow.

## January Reading and Listening

(Print, e-books, audiobooks, significant online publications)

*Bad Money: Reckless Finance, Failed Politics, and the Global Crisis of American Capitalism*, by Kevin Phillips

*Behind the Mountains*, by Oliver La Farge

*Boundary Waters: The Grace of the Wild*, by Paul Gruchow

*Enchantment and Exploitation: The Life and Hard Times of a New Mexico Mountain Range*, by William deBuys

*The Geography of Nowhere: The Rise and Decline of America's Man-Made Landscape*, by James Howard Kunstler

*Grassland: The History, Biology, Politics, and Promise of the American Prairie*, by Richard Manning

*If Mountains Die: A New Mexico Memoir*, by John Nichols

*Landscapes of the Sacred: Geography and Narrative in American Spirituality*, by Belden C. Lane

*One Writer's Beginnings*, by Eudora Welty

*The Party's Over: Oil, War and the Fate of Industrial Societies*, by Richard Heinberg

*The Reluctant Mr. Darwin: An Intimate Portrait of Charles Darwin and the Making of His Theory of Evolution*, by David Quammen

*Seasons in the Desert: A Naturalist's Notebook*, by Susan Tweit

*T Is for Trespass*, by Sue Grafton

*An Unspoken Hunger: Stories from the Field*, by Terry Tempest Williams

*Weaving a Way Home: A Personal Journey Exploring Place and Story*, by Leslie Van Gelder

| JANUARY | **FEBRUARY** | MARCH | APRIL |
|---|---|---|---|
| MAY | JUNE | JULY | AUGUST |
| SEPTEMBER | OCTOBER | NOVEMBER | DECEMBER |

## FEBRUARY 3

Home again, after a nourishing, enriching weekend at the Story Circle conference in Austin. The Story Circle Network (which I founded in 1997, with the help of a dozen Austin women) is now an international organization with members in almost every state and a half-dozen foreign countries. I led a couple of workshops at the conference: one on personal mapping, the other ("Here Be Dragons") on writing about difficult life situations. Also chaired a five-member panel on blogging.

Daughter Robin came from Colorado and we roomed together, talked until wee hours. Robin is a strong woman, focused, serious but playful, generous with her energies. I'm proud of her. Proud of all the Story Circle women, too. Women who aren't afraid of their stories, aren't afraid to share them.

Back home: answering e-mails, checking on the responses to the blog tour proposal Peggy posted online for me (several promising ones), sweeping, dusting, doing laundry. Funny how filthy the house can get in just a couple of days, with husband, three dogs, and a cat left to their own devices.

Outdoors, a blustery southeast wind blowing in from the Gulf. Today's temperature topped out at eighty-two, tying a record. But a Pacific front is due in from the northwest tonight, bringing cooler temperatures, maybe even some rain. An evening for reading: Paul Gruchow's *Grass Roots: The Landscape of Home*. Also on the stack: *Long Life* by Mary Oliver, a book of essays for dipping into, too rich, too heart-filling to be read all at once.

And James Howard Kunstler's *The Long Emergency*, on life after oil. Dark topic, bleak outlook. Not a book I'm looking forward to reading, but feel I must.

*Stories are a way of explaining the inexplicable, of giving shape to that which has no shape, meaning to that which eludes meaning.*

—MARY CLEARMAN BLEW

*The literature of women's lives is a tradition of escapees, women who have lived to tell the tale. . . . They resist captivity. They get up and go. They seek better worlds.*

—PHYLLIS ROSE

Rain. Rain would be good. Last week, sixteen hundred acres went up in flames a few miles south of here (downwind, luckily). Some idiot thought it was a good day for a "controlled burn." Never mind that the county had issued a burn ban or that the Forest Service had posted a "red flag day." Barns, outbuildings, and miles of fence were destroyed. The fire burned all afternoon, took five volunteer fire departments to contain it just short of a cluster of houses.

There's a huge irony here. We actually *need* fire. We probably need fire as much as we need rain. When settlers moved into Burnet County in the 1850s, this area was part of the Southern Plains, a vast, open prairie with widely scattered clumps of live oak and cedar, shaped and maintained by the buffalo that made it their home and the lightning-caused fires that periodically swept across it. The U.S. Army slaughtered the buffalo, and the farmers and ranchers suppressed the fires. And now that sprawling subdivisions have replaced the farms and ranches, the populated prairie has morphed into a vast cedar brake that produces more fuel every year. Dangerously flammable.

The land needs fire. Fire has been part of the story of the land for longer than people. But fire is no longer welcome. When it happens, it's catastrophic.

*When we're finished grazing in the garden, I want there to be some garden left. This is more than an aesthetic desire—though surely it is the beautiful complexity of nature that woos me. It is a moral desire. To use nature beyond its capacity to restore itself is to destroy the force and power that have given us our lives.*

—ALISON HAWTHORNE DEMING

*There is a way that nature speaks, that land speaks. Most of the time we are simply not patient enough, quiet enough, to pay attention to the story.*

—LINDA HOGAN

NEWS SUMMARY: *The U.S. economy lost jobs for the first time in more than four years. The Bureau of Labor Statistics reported that seventeen thousand jobs were eliminated in January. The data increased fears of an imminent recession.*

FEBRUARY 5

Scary stuff in the news these days, job losses, foreclosures. No immediate effect on Bill and me and our quiet life here at Meadow Knoll, but I worry about the children—about my kids, always pushing their lives (and budgets) to the limit. About other people's kids, trying to get along in a difficult world.

Also worried about Zach. The medicine he's taking for Cushing's suppresses his appetite. He's already pretty scrawny—can't afford to lose any more weight. This morning, I cooked chicken with rice and carrots and was happy to watch him eat enthusiastically. He's still getting us up at 2 and 4 a.m., and I'm learning to live with puddles of pee on the floor, just as I've learned to live with shoals of dog fur under the furniture and Lady needing a boost up the steps. No big deal: I can wipe up the pee, sweep up the fur, give Lady a boost. There's more to my life than dogs, of course. But they're a huge part of it. Obviously.

Watched *A Crude Awakening: The Oil Crash* on DVD last night: a documentary (won six major film prizes) about the world's dependency on oil and what is likely to happen as it becomes less available and is finally depleted. Sobering, very. I've been putting off reading Kunstler's book—afraid it's time to dig into it.

But today is Super Tuesday. Big political news. Huge.

*Dogs are not our whole life, but they make our lives whole.*

—ROGER CARAS

NEWS SUMMARY: *Super Tuesday, February 5. Primaries and caucuses were held in twenty-four states, with Senator John McCain emerging as the clear Republican frontrunner. Hillary Clinton won big states such as California and Massachusetts and garnered 46 percent of the popular vote to Barack Obama's 45 percent. Obama took more states, winning 847 delegates to Clinton's 834.*

FEBRUARY 6

Super Tuesday, always interesting, this year a commanding event. A black man, a strong woman, a senior senator. Something for everyone, especially for those who like to talk about how racism, sexism, and ageism might affect the electorate. Still no clear Democratic favorite.

A windstorm (no rain, sadly) blasted through the Hill Country this morning, dropping the temperature forty degrees in three hours. The first brave daffodil, unruffled, survived the wind. I won't have many garden flowers this year because of the flood damage last July, when it rained for nearly the full month without letup. Not many wildflowers, either: too much rain last summer, none at all since September— nothing measurable, anyway. Five months, dry as old bones. The April bluebonnets will be sparse.

But there's a blessing in inhabiting a place for a long time. I am consoled with the knowledge that although there may be only a few flowers this spring, those few will be beautiful, and that when the rains come—next autumn or the autumn after—we'll have bluebonnets again. I know that the hummingbirds will arrive around the fifteenth of March, give or take a week, and that the monarchs will be sailing through our woods not long after, on their way north from Mexico. Scarlet paintbrush and blackfoot daisy and purple monarda, all in their time. And eventually it will rain again.

Someday.

*To inhabit a place means literally to have made it a habit, to have made it the custom and ordinary practice of our lives, to have learned how to wear a place like a familiar garment, like the garments of sanctity that nuns once wore. The word habit, in its now-dim original form, meant "to own." We own places not because we possess the deeds to them, but because they have entered the continuum of our lives.*

—PAUL GRUCHOW

*A journal as an experiment in consciousness. An attempt to record not just the external world, and not just the vagrant, fugitive, ephemeral "thoughts" that brush against us like gnats, but the refractory and inviolable authenticity of daily life: daily-ness, day-ness, day-lightness, the day's eye of experience.*

—JOYCE CAROL OATES

*The Internet is the first thing that humanity has built that humanity doesn't understand, the largest experiment in anarchy that we have ever had.*

—ERIC SCHMIDT

*The Internet is the world's largest library. It's just that all the books are on the floor.*

—JOHN ALLEN PAULOS

*All the necessities, comforts, luxuries, and miracles of our time—central heating, air conditioning, cars, airplanes, electric lighting, cheap clothing, recorded music, movies, supermarkets, power tools, hip replacement surgery, the national defense, you name it—owe their origins or continued existence in one way or another to cheap fossil fuel.*

—JAMES HOWARD KUNSTLER

Between writing projects at the moment, sort of. I'm working on this journal most days. I still have the final chapter to write and some cleanup work to do on *Wormwood*, due on the editor's desk at the end of March. But I don't want to go back to *Wormwood* unless I have a clear space of about three weeks. I need the long, steady flow of uninterrupted work, when I can follow the story lines from beginning to end. And any day now, I'm expecting the page proofs for the next book in the Cottage Tales series, *The Tale of Briar Bank*. Correcting the proofs is a three-day job.

In the meantime, I'm working ahead on the weekly e-letters that are a spin-off of the calendar book I wrote a couple of years ago, *China Bayles' Book of Days*. The book has a piece about plants (gardening, crafting, cooking, healing, and so on) for every day of the year: lends itself well to transformation into a weekly e-letter with Web links, added information, photos, graphics.

I can handle the content, but the rest of it is a job for an expert. So I e-mail the file to Peggy, who codes it and sends it out into cyberspace every Monday morning, and thence into computers across the country and—amazingly—around the world. I don't pretend to know how this sort of thing works, but Peggy does, and that's what counts.

Being between writing projects means more time for reading: Kunstler, slowly—a difficult, uncomfortable read. Listening to Robert Reich's *Supercapitalism* (an audiobook) and thinking about American over-consumption of globally produced goods, about social responsibility. Thinking about my own recent trip to Walmart: I value the low prices and—living in the country—the one-stop shopping. But the goods are mostly foreign-made (jobs and trade dollars flowing out of the country) and Walmart's wages and employee benefits are low. About this, Reich says accurately, "The awkward truth is that most of us are of two minds." Both of my minds go with me to Walmart, and I come home with about half of what I intended to buy. Which is good, probably.

In lighter moments, dipping into a couple of favorites from earlier, easier days: Deborah Tall, *From Where We Stand: Recovering a Sense of Place* and Annie Dillard's *Pilgrim at Tinker Creek*. Wishing I could stay with just these lovely books and ignore the darker stuff, the awkward truths, just shove it away.

But I can't. The world feels different to me now, more fragile, somehow. Odd, because it looks the same. Almost.

Walking the dogs in the crisp morning chill of a February Sunday. Absent the usual weekday traffic noise from the highway two miles to the south, all I can hear is the nimble polyphonic conversation of the mockingbird in the willow by the creek, the perky chirping of a pair of gossipy wrens, the excited honking of geese at the lake.

These open fields on a chilly winter morning remind me of the fields I walked when I was a girl in eastern Illinois, only a few prairie miles from the Indiana border. We were tenant farmers on a small farm that was home to a herd of four or five dozen young beef steers fattening for market—which, back in those days, meant grass feeding, supplemented with a little corn. The owner of the farm was an optometrist who lived in nearby Danville. We lived rent-free in the old frame farmhouse, at the end of a lane lined with hickory trees and maples and birch. Well, not exactly rent-free, because my father tended the livestock in return for the rent.

And it wasn't my father who did the tending. He had a factory job in town, so my brother John and I did the farm chores, some of which I positively hated. Tumbling hay bales out of the loft, for instance, clipping the baling wire, breaking up the bales, and pushing hay into the mangers—all this in the pre-dawn dark before we caught the school bus. Nose running, face frozen, fingers like sticks, sheer misery on mornings when the temperature trembled at twenty below.

But I didn't mind feeding chickens or working in the garden or raking leaves on a fine autumn Saturday under the flaming maples and the gloriously golden birch. And I loved walking fence (making sure that none of the steers had broken through and hightailed it off somewhere) on hot evenings in summer when green seemed to swallow every other color and the warm air clung like damp silk to my skin. And the early winter twilight when I was alone with the curious cattle and the birds and the fields, the grasses frost-bleached, the color of old bones, and the bare-limbed trees and the low, gray, all-embracing sky.

It was those years on the farm that fed my love for country, for the everyday world of overworked fields and sagging fences, untidy woods, winter pastures. Nothing special, nothing extraordinary, not even (to most people, anyway) very beautiful.

"Home is where we have a history," Terry Tempest Williams says. Unkempt fields, tangled woods: my history. Home.

*The mockingbird that nests each year in the front-yard spruce strikes up his chant in high places. . . . He sings a phrase and repeats it exactly; then he sings another and repeats that, then another. The mockingbird's invention is limitless; he strews newness about as casually as a god.*

—ANNIE DILLARD

*I've learned to watch for character in the lived landscape, to look to the ground for information. . . . My project is to find what's legible here.*

—DEBORAH TALL

*We humans have a strong desire for groundedness in place. We want to be rooted; we want to be somewhere real. The saying, "Wherever you go, there you are," seems also to be an acknowledgment that wherever you go, of course, you take places and people from the past with you.*

—GRETCHEN LEGLER

Saw an American kestrel perched on the power line beside the lane just at dawn this morning, and then later, hovering on a strong north wind above the meadow, waiting for an unwary mouse. This one is a female, rufous wings barred with black and a streaked breast. The most colorful raptor in the world, says the bird book. I believe it.

Still reading *The Long Emergency*, thinking that everything in our house is in one way or another oil-based. Every single thing.

But not the kestrel.

## FEBRUARY 11

My firstborn's birthday today: Bob is forty-nine. We still relate as mother and son, but as the years have slipped by, we've begun to connect more like contemporaries—another of those aspects of growing older that you don't think about until you find yourself doing it.

Bob is the successful owner of his own home repair business in Reno, Nevada. He knows tools, knows how to use them, and manages jobs and clients with aplomb. More, he's the only parent his three kids (all in college now) have been able to count on for more than a decade: a responsibility that he's carried out with amazing grace, weathering the tempests of on-the-job parent training with equanimity.

Where did he learn these skills? Not from his mother, certainly. We grew up together, my children and I, in a time when kids were considerably less "parented" than they are now. I was in my late twenties and they were in elementary school when I took the family to California, enrolled as a graduate student at uc-Berkeley, divorced their father, and rewrote my future—and theirs. It's to their credit, certainly not mine, that they have grown into the productive adults and attentive parents they are. (I sometimes think that the best thing I did for my children was to let them read past their bedtimes.)

But I might have had something to do with their self-reliance. They still remember the Saturday mornings when I gave them pillowcases into which they were required to stuff their own dirty clothes, doled out quarters for the washer and dimes for the dryer, and sent them off to the self-serve laundry across the street from our apartment in the graduate student village. They didn't think it was funny then, although they're able to chuckle about it now. I tell them that's because they have children of their own.

But how in heaven's name did Bob get to be forty-nine?

I'm barely forty-nine myself.

*We're lucky to find places that become the unalterable on the daily borders of our lives, places we can entrust with the loyalty of our gaze, imaginative territory into which the mind may safely stray and return to tell its tale. . . . Devoting ourselves to a place, we gain the boldness to name, project, reconstitute, see it in our own light. . . . On my best days, I feel as if this place is family now.*

—DEBORAH TALL

*I would be most content if my children grew up to be the kind of people who think decorating consists mostly of building enough bookshelves.*

—ANNA QUINDLEN

NEWS SUMMARY: *Each person in the United States is responsible for around twenty-one tons of $CO_2$ emissions per year, according to the United Nations Human Development Reports (UNHDR).*

FEBRUARY 12

Twenty-one tons.

I was thinking about climate change and carbon footprints this morning, when UPS showed up with a box of twenty advance reading copies (ARCS, in the trade) of *Nightshade*. I'll mail these to the people who have invited me to post to their blogs on my "blog tour" next month. The invitations have been coming in steadily; I've chosen most of the hosts and settled on dates and topics. It's not really a tour, of course. I'll do it from my computer, in my jammies (if I choose), at an enormous savings of time, dollars, personal energy, $CO_2$, and gasoline.

Which is a good thing. I'm measuring our personal carbon footprint and trying to think of ways to reduce it—although as Bill points out, nothing the two of us do will be significant enough to change the outcome of this situation.

But twenty-one TONS? *Somebody* has to do *something*, I argue.

Bill points to the box of ARCS I'm holding in my hand. "Probably twenty-one tons right there," he says. "And how many books have you written?"

Good grief.

*Each book's footprint is different, depending on factors such as whether the paper came from sustainably managed forests, whether the paper is glossy or matte, and whether any copies are flown or shipped to foreign countries. But to give a rough idea, a 500-page paperback . . . will typically account for around 2.5 kg [5.5 pounds] of dioxide emissions per copy.*

—PENGUIN PUBLISHING COMPANY WEBSITE, HTTP://WWW.PENGUIN.CO.UK

FEBRUARY 13

Well, I can't change what I do for a living. I write. I'm sorry, but writing is a given. For now, for the foreseeable future. Period. Paragraph. End of story.

Still. I don't commute to work, and even counting the New Mexico trips, we drive fewer miles annually than most families. We're thrifty and frugal. We repair, repurpose, reuse, recycle. We drive fuel-efficient vehicles and don't think about replacing them until they pass the 200,000-mile mark. We've already shortened our showers and replaced the lightbulbs with compact fluorescents. (If everybody replaced just three, I've read, we could keep a trillion pounds of $CO_2$ out of the atmosphere.) In winter, we burn downed trees from our woodlot to heat the house. In summer, we turn up the thermostat to spare the AC. We consume about 60 percent less electricity than the average American household.

But we can do more. We can reduce the number of trips we make for groceries and mail. I've put up a clothesline in the backyard to reduce my use of the electric dryer. Bill is wrapping the water heater in a blanket of insulation. We've decided to get a new roof, which will help reduce AC costs even more. We'll look at everything we do with new eyes.

Some things I can't change.

Some I can.

Ways to conserve energy, reduce $CO_2$:

Move your heater thermostat down two degrees in winter and up two degrees in the summer. Save 2,000 pounds of carbon dioxide and $98 per year.

Keep your water heater thermostat no higher than 120°F. Save 550 pounds of carbon dioxide and $30 per year.

Buy minimally packaged goods. Less packaging could reduce your garbage by about 10 percent. Save 1,200 pounds of carbon dioxide and $1,000 per year.

—stopglobalwarming.org

## FEBRUARY 14

Bill and I are celebrating Valentine's Day, the twenty-third time we've done this together since we met in 1986. I had just left the university and was writing young adult fiction; he was working as a statistician and computer systems analyst with the Texas Health Department.

He had done a great deal of technical and analytical writing (software documentation, government reports), and as the relationship got more romantic and more serious, we began to talk about the possibility of writing together—especially after he untangled a plot problem I had created for myself in *Heart of Danger*, the Nancy Drew mystery I was working on. That bit of happy teamwork settled it for us, and we took on the adventure of marriage.

A lifelong adventurer—pilot, skin diver, spelunker, photographer, world traveler—Bill was ready for something new. He had bought Meadow Knoll a dozen years before we met, with the dream of living in the country, working from home. My dream, too. A dream we could share.

To the dream, he brought not just the skills that allowed us to write together, but also the practical skills that made it possible to live in the country, where nothing gets done unless you do it yourself. He owns every tool ever devised, I swear. He collects and restores antique tools and knows how to use them. Knows how to build a fence, too, install a septic tank and sewage system, wire an electrical box, construct a building, repair or rewire or rebuild or reorganize almost anything.

We've lost count of the books we've written during these years, more than a hundred now, many written together. Even the books I've written alone have happened, in large part, because he encourages, urges, supports, sustains.

I can't imagine life without him. My valentine.

## FEBRUARY 15

Drat. My editor just e-mailed that the copy editor won't be finished with *Briar Bank* until February 25, which turns my calendar upside down. I was expecting the copy edit this week and intended to finish it, then wrap up the *Wormwood* manuscript.

Anyway, *Wormwood* is substantially finished, except for the last chapter and the resource notes. But to make sure that I've tied up all the story threads (and there are quite a few), I need to go through the whole book again. I usually manage about twenty-five pages a day on a final pass, and since the text will finish out at some 275 pages, I'm looking at ten or twelve writing days.

So I'd better stop fiddling around. Go straight to *Wormwood* and spend the next two weeks cleaning it up. When that's done, *Briar Bank* will be here. And both projects will be finished by the time I have to focus on the promotion of *Nightshade*.

And when I'm not doing that, I can work on this journal.

Writing can be a very full life.

## FEBRUARY 16

I'm an inveterate list-maker, a scheduler. Today's list:

revise pp. 66–100 in *Wormwood*
wash Zach's bedding (he peed on it again last night)
wash sheets and towels, hang out on the new clothesline
finish knitting Paula's sock
prune some of the roses
patch Bill's jeans
take dogs to the vet for shots

This week's list, some of it (admittedly) wishful thinking:

revise the rest of *Wormwood*
prune *all* the roses
find out who to call about getting satellite broadband installed
call them
rake leaves from the iris bed
come up with questions for e-mail interview with Heather Cariou
    for the Story Circle book review Web site
start Paula's second sock
help Bill fix the fence so we can move the cows
move the cows

A word or two of explanation. I'm knitting socks for Paula Yost because she's my co-editor on the Story Circle book review Web site, and she's done more than her share of the work. The socks are a thank-you present. But I pitch in by editing reviews and occasionally doing an interview—like the one with Heather Cariou, author of *Sixtyfive Roses: A Sister's Memoir* (also on the list). Fixing the fence is a fairly big job, requiring barbwire, wire cutters, staples, a hammer, two people, and muttered curses. Moving the cows and sheep is not a big job. They've been lusting after the grass on the other side of the fence (it's greener and there's more of it). The minute we open the gate, they make a break for it.

List-making isn't so much a matter of organizing what I have to do as organizing my understanding of who I am. We are what we eat, people say. We know who we are by the way we spend our money. I know who I am by the way I spend my time, divide my attention, focus my energies.

It's true that there's something artificial about lists (things tend to get done whether I write them down or not), and a little chaos and whim can be a good thing in life.

But sometimes a scaffold is necessary. I wouldn't try to paint a two-story house without it.

FEBRUARY 17

A dull day brightened by a flock of daffodils, supremely sunny King Alfreds, blooming along the edge of the woods like buckets of spilled sunshine. I sat down on the ground beside them and drank in that luscious yellow, all, all yellow. Later daffs will have orange centers the color of Cheez-Its, or will be pure white, or display white petals with tiny orange cups in the center, or will offer triplets or quartets of miniature blossoms on a single stem, or an indescribably sweet scent. But these King Alfreds are the loveliest of all.

Unlike the bluebonnets, there'll be a wealth of daffodils this spring because there was an abundance of rain last July and August, and the bulbs prospered mightily and multiplied. That doesn't always happen. In years when there's little rain, the daffodil population shrinks, and I treasure the few that struggle to bloom.

But the daffodils don't care how many they are, or how few. Each one just goes on being entirely, exclusively, serenely beautiful. That's comforting, somehow. Just as comforting: once they're in the ground, daffodils are entirely self-sufficient. They don't need pruning, fertilizing, coaching, or debugging. They don't have a carbon footprint.

No, wait. That's not right. They must have a *negative* carbon footprint because they absorb $CO_2$ and turn it into flowers. Isn't that what I learned in science class?

Come to think of it, all the trees in our woodlot and the grass and shrubs and native plants on our thirty-one acres absorb $CO_2$.

I need to look into this.

*What does it mean . . . that the earth is so beautiful? And what shall I do about it? What is the gift that I should bring to the world? What is the life that I should live?*

*—MARY OLIVER*

## FEBRUARY 19

Ah. From the Colorado Tree Coalition, I learn that a single mature tree can absorb carbon dioxide at a rate of forty-eight pounds a year. And we have at least two hundred mature trees in our woodlot and fencerows, probably more, plus lots of grass. . . .

Grass! From the National Farmers Union, I learn that an acre of unmowed, untilled grassland can absorb about three-quarters of a ton of carbon dioxide each year. And we have about twenty-seven acres of grass.

Trees plus grass. . . . The calculator tells me that we're talking some twenty-four tons of carbon dioxide a year absorbed—the technical term for this is "sequestered"—right here at Meadow Knoll every year.

I'm feeling better already.

But I'm not giving up my clothesline. We're still getting the new roof. And I'm sure there is more we can do.

*When I bought my farm, I did not know what a bargain I had in the bluebirds, daffodils and thrushes; as little did I know what sublime mornings and sunsets I was buying.*

*—RALPH WALDO EMERSON*

Yesterday was not an ordinary day.

For the dozen years that we've been on the Internet, we've been on "dial-up." I could grow old, very old, waiting for the monitor screen to fill.

But that's changing. Yesterday, we had a satellite dish installed on the house and I am now plugged in to the wide, wide world. Now, the signal whizzes twenty-three thousand miles up to the satellite and back down to my desktop in less time than it takes to type a sentence. Fully wired, always on.

So? Does any of this make me a better writer? Without a doubt. The facts I might be tempted to guess at if it meant a trip to the library (or even a trip to a bookshelf in the other room) are now as handy as a Google search. The writing is more richly detailed, more comprehensive and accurate, more up-to-date.

And having e-mail makes it easy to reply to readers, a task that many writers have found difficult. In her journals, May Sarton complains bitterly about having to write (by hand) replies to "friends of the work." In *Life Work*, poet Donald Hall says that he solves the problem by spending a couple of hours every evening dictating, then turning the dictation over to a typist. I spend an hour a day—sometimes morning, sometimes evening—cleaning up the e-mail. Yes, it takes time. No, it's not a burden. I'm just glad that there are people out there in the world, reading what I've written and caring enough about it to tell me what they liked—or didn't. (Which they do.)

But now I wonder: am I too dependent on the Internet? What would I do if it went away? How would I do the research, read newspapers, pursue information? Would I have to go back to using what we contemptuously call "snail mail"?

Hope it never comes to that. I wouldn't care to be responsible for what might happen.

> *Entire new continents can emerge from the ocean in the time it takes for a Web page to show up on your screen. Contrary to what you may have heard, the Internet does not operate at the speed of light; it operates at the speed of the Department of Motor Vehicles.*
>
> —DAVE BARRY

> *When I took office, only high energy physicists had ever heard of what is called the World Wide Web. . . . Now even my cat has its own page.*
>
> —BILL CLINTON

NEWS SUMMARY: *There have been two recent suicide bombings in Iraq and Afghanistan. Nearly a hundred people died when two women suicide bombers attacked a crowded market in eastern Baghdad. Eighty people were killed and nearly a hundred injured in a suicide bombing near Kandahar, the worst such attack since 2001. In Pakistan, President Pervez Musharraf's party lost the election. The defeat is considered a protest against Musharraf's attempts to suppress dissent and his alliance with the United States.*

I treasure my physical isolation here, but there's no disconnecting from the world's events or shielding myself from the world's anger at U.S. policies. I sometimes feel like a spectator forced to sit in the stands and watch a horrific exhibition of mass slaughter—people, animals, the earth—which I am required to subsidize and which is being carried out in my name, on principles I cannot support, for reasons I cannot accept, by an administration I didn't vote for.

*We have two choices. Either we change the way we live, or we must change the way they live. We choose the latter.*

*—DONALD RUMSFELD*

In the past two weeks, two more suicide bombings related to U.S. occupations of Iraq and Afghanistan. What might be a bright spot—Musharraf's defeat—is dimmed by the fact that without his strong-man rule, there'll be political chaos. And Pakistan is a nuclear power.

Feeling helpless. Going out to the garden.

## FEBRUARY 22

Another out-of-the-ordinary day.

The crew is here today, putting the new roof on our house. It's a roof-over job: that is, the old roof stays put and the new roof, panels of blue sheet metal, is laid down on top of it, with a three-inch layer of insulation sandwiched in between. More insulation, more energy savings, we hope.

When we moved to Meadow Knoll in 1986, we installed a single-wide trailer twelve feet wide and fifty-six feet long. We bought it for forty-five hundred dollars cash, less than you'd pay for a used car. Not a spiffy place to live, but we wanted to write and we couldn't be sure of a reliable income. Staying small, paying cash, we'd have no rent, no mortgage. It was a serious choice, carefully considered.

We expected to live in the trailer for two or three years, four, at the most. But there was just so much to do: the vegetable garden, the chickens and geese and ducks, the writing that paid the bills. We kept putting the house off. Every year, as stuff piled up around us—knee-high, hip-high, waist-high—we'd say, "Next year. We'll deal with it next year."

*As much as we live in a place, we live in place; we inhabit a condition of the soul. We live where we have made defini-tions, and in the process of making definitions, we create a place in which to live.*

*—SALLIE TISDALE*

But by 1995, we knew there was no next year. We *had* to have more room. In fact, we either had to get a larger house or a divorce.

But building would take too much time, and as writers, it's difficult (it was then, anyway) to get a mortgage. We weren't inclined to get a divorce, either. So we went shopping for a house. We found a double-wide on a lot outside of Dallas, and two weeks later, it was delivered.

We had just finished another book; we added the acceptance check to some savings and handed the broker a check. We named the house Serenity. And why not? Like the land it sits on, Serenity was paid for, which—especially in the current climate of foreclosures—remains a great comfort.

As we could afford it, Serenity got a new back deck and a patio door, a front porch, a corner fireplace that heats the house in the winter, wood floors, a brick patio and walks, and now this spiffy blue roof. I love living here, love looking out windows into the woods and meadows and wide, bright skies; love living in a small house that's easy to clean (well, relatively); love the financial freedom of owning a house with no mortgage—low taxes, too.

And every time I hear someone say scornfully, "*I'd* never live in a trailer," I just shrug and smile.

*Worm or beetle—
drought or tempest—
on a farmer's land
may fall,
Each is loaded full o'
ruin, but a mortgage
beats 'em all.*

—WILL CARLETON

FEBRUARY 23

Pruning roses.

Actually, Valentine's Day is the appointed day for pruning roses in this part of Texas. But on Valentine's Day I was writing, and the roses didn't get done. Didn't even get started.

I can't put the job off any longer because the roses are already unfurling their glossy new leaves. The bushes—which enjoyed a glorious season last year, energized by July's heavy rains—are exuberant and unruly. I need to remove the dead wood, clip and reshape the old growth, thin the new growth. Of course, all this is all a matter of judgment, and my rose-pruning judgment seems not very sound. Every year, I either overdo it or underdo it. I never quite get it right.

But these roses—not patented hybrids, but "antiques," heirlooms from (mostly) antebellum gardens in the South—are forgiving. In a culture that values novelty, transformation, and genetic transmutation, these stubborn survivors from forgotten gardens have staying power. Ducher, Cecile Brunner, Queen of Bourbons, Souvenir de la Malmaison, Zepherine Drouhin, Céline Forestier, Duchesse de Brabant, Old Blush, Lady Banks—lovely, romantic names for shapely plants with muted pastel blooms and remarkable perfumes. Unlike fragile hybrids, they're cold-hardy and drought-resistant. I'm grateful for that now; we've had no significant rain for five months. But they do appreciate being restrained: they profit from an assertive pruning in February, and another, milder pruning in August, before the autumn rains (we can only hope) and the chilly winter.

There's a lesson here somewhere.

*One day, the gardener realizes that what she is doing out there is actually teaching herself to garden by performing a series of experiments. This is a pivotal moment.*

—MARGARET ROACH

*The more one gardens, the more one learns; and the more one learns, the more one realizes how little one knows. I suppose the whole of life is like that.*

—VITA SACKVILLE-WEST

Just finished reading Barbara Kingsolver's *Animal, Vegetable, Miracle*, a wonderful memoir about her family's year-long adventure in becoming food self-sufficient: growing as much food as they could and buying the rest locally—a locavore adventure. She points out that if every American ate one meal a week of locally, organically raised food, we could cut weekly U.S. oil consumption by more than 1.1 million barrels of oil. And cutting oil consumption means cutting $CO_2$ production.

One meal a week. Yes. I can do that.

I'm "cluster-reading" this week, and learning. Michael Pollan's *In Defense of Food: An Eater's Manifesto*, intelligent, informed, compelling, passionate. *Eating Fossil Fuels: Oil, Food and the Coming Crisis in Agriculture* by Dale Allen Pfeiffer. This book, about our fatal dependence on industrial, fossil-fueled farming, ought to be on everyone's reading list. "If global food shipments were to stop tomorrow," Pfeiffer says, "we would no longer be able to feed ourselves."

Okay. I get it. Things are about to change around here. I'm getting serious about gardening. Not herbs or flowers: I have plenty of those. I'm talking about a full-scale vegetable garden that will replace the much-traveled green beans, peas, carrots, cabbages, and other veggies that have been flown and trucked nearly fifteen hundred miles to our table.

For a number of years, Bill and I had a large garden here. We also had chickens for eggs and meat, and for the freezer, pigs raised by a neighbor and a calf purchased from a local rancher. In the 1990s, when book promotion began requiring more travel, I stopped growing vegetables and we gave up our chickens. But in the meantime, I learned a great deal.

Gardening in Central Texas is tricky business. For a spring vegetable garden, I should have started weeks ago, with broccoli and cabbage transplants (wearing little paper collars to deter cabbage worms), tomato and pepper and squash seedlings under fluorescent lights. Seed potatoes should have been in by Valentine's Day.

So this will be a fall garden, going into the ground in August and September. Chore list: rehab the old garden, construct new raised beds, cook up a batch of compost, build a deer-proof fence, purchase seeds—open-pollinated, non-hybrid vegetables and varieties that do well in this climate. There's no point in planting a ninety-six-day beefsteak tomato, because tomatoes don't set fruit once the nighttime temperature goes above 70 degrees. Here (in the spring garden), that can happen in mid-May, so I need an early tomato. Early Wonder,

*Small changes in buying habits can make big differences. Becoming a less energy-dependent nation may just need to start with a good breakfast.*

—BARBARA KINGSOLVER

*Eat food. Not too much. Mostly plants.*

—MICHAEL POLLAN

*[I]t takes only 20 minutes of labor to provide most Americans with their daily diet—as long as that labor is fossil fueled. Unfortunately, if you remove fossil fuels from the equation . . . the current U.S. daily diet would demand nearly three weeks of work from each American to produce the amount of food they eat each day.*

—DALE ALLEN PFEIFFER

*Of the tomato or love apple, I know very little. . . . No one, it is believed, regards it as very nutritious; and it belongs, like the mushroom and the potato, to a family of plants, some of the individuals of which are extremely poisonous. Some persons are even injured, more or less, by the acid of the tomato.*

—WILLIAM ANDRUS ALCOTT (1846)

maybe, which matures in fifty-five days. Or Early Girl. Used to be, I had to sift through dozens of seed catalogs to find what I wanted. Now, I can seed-shop online.

I feel better. There's nothing like having a list.

## FEBRUARY 25

On Saturday I drove down to San Marcos for the launch of *Lone Star Sleuths: An Anthology of Texas Crime Fiction*, which included an excerpt from *Rosemary Remembered*, one of my early China Bayles mysteries. A strong turnout: some one hundred and fifty mystery lovers showed up to snack, schmooze, buy books.

It is not always thus. Book signings can be a desert experience. I've been in bookstores where I was displayed inside the front door like a cardboard cut-out. In mall bookstores, I've been stationed outside the front door, where my most significant encounters were coy requests for directions to the little girls' room. (Only rarely am I asked about the little boys' room.) Once, I drove two hundred miles to a bookstore, to discover that the manager had failed to advertise the event or order a single book. Another time, I reached a store that was full of eager fans and friends, but the new book was still in the warehouse, a hundred miles away.

"The signing from hell," as writer Joan Hess has called it.

What else can you do but laugh?

NEWS SUMMARY: *Ralph Nader announced that he will run for president as a third-party candidate.*

## FEBRUARY 26

Oh, please. Not Nader again.

I agree: there are problems with our two-party political system. But it will hang around our necks like an albatross until some compelling third-party candidate comes along who is charismatic enough to rip it off and stomp on it. Even then, this person had better have a heckuva lot more money than the other guys.

It won't be Ralph Nader, not after what he did to Gore in 2000.

I voted today, early, in the Texas primary. There was a spirit of community and camaraderie among the folks lined up at the courthouse. I had the same feeling I always have when I'm voting: a feeling of privilege, empowerment. Except that I feel more empowered when I vote in the primary, where my vote actually counts for something. In the general election, my vote for the Democrat counts for nothing. The Electoral College swallows it.

## FEBRUARY 27

*Wormwood* is ready for printing. Each time I do this—pull up the file, set the printer to run the pages back to front so I don't have to restack them, load the paper, and push the button—I think back to the typewriter era, when preparing a manuscript for submission was no task for the faint of heart. Now, the process is so easy that a third grader can write and print her stories and have them bound into a book, although I'm not sure that this ease of production has improved the quality of the books out there.

The printed manuscript goes to my Berkley Prime Crime editor, who reads the old-fashioned way, with the manuscript on the desk and a pen in her hand. The electronic file goes, via e-mail, to her assistant. I'll see it again when the copyedited pages come back to me in October, and in December, when I get the page proofs. By this time next year, the advance reading copy will be out for review, and I'll be making plans for an April book tour.

In the book business, we think ahead.

NEWS SUMMARY: *A major new study warns that the continued rise of global average temperatures from emissions of man-made greenhouse gases is likely to result in sudden, dramatic, out-of-control changes in oceans and land masses. The report, in the Proceedings of the National Academy of Sciences, identifies nine "tipping points" that may result in abrupt, nonlinear ecosystem change. The report calls upon all governments to note the potential for small changes to be amplified into massive, abrupt, and potentially irreversible ecosystem failures.*

## FEBRUARY 28

I've been looking around online to see how other people—ordinary people—are feeling about the prospect of climate change and energy depletion in the next couple of decades. The idea is beginning to dawn on Web sites, in blogs, and many who have lived their whole

*The flood of print has turned reading into a process of gulping rather than savoring.*

—RAYMOND CHANDLER

*Some books are to be tasted, others to be swallowed, and some few to be chewed and digested: that is, some books are to be read only in parts, others to be read, but not curiously, and some few to be read wholly, and with diligence and attention.*

—FRANCIS BACON

*Energy will be one of the defining issues of this century, and one thing is clear: the era of easy oil is over. We need your help. At Chevron, we believe that innovation, collaboration, and conservation are the cornerstones on which to build this new world. But we can't do it alone. Corporations, governments, and every citizen of this planet must be part of the solution as surely as they are part of the problem. And so, we ask you to join us.*

—CHEVRON OIL COMPANY COMMERCIAL

*We can't conserve our way to energy independence, nor can we conserve our way to having enough energy available. So we've got to do both.*

—GEORGE W. BUSH
(2001)

lives with all the energy they wanted are wondering how they'll get along without cheap energy in an era of global warming. Many seem to hold on to the hope that we'll muddle through without having to give up too much. Natural gas, "clean" coal, electric cars, hydrogen fuel, nuclear: alternative energies that will allow us to keep on living the way we've always lived.

Happily, I also found something else, a clearer-headed, more heartening point of view. For example, Pat Meadows, on her blog, "Entire of Itself," writes about what she calls the "Theory of Anyway." She points out that using less, living more lightly, being more frugal— these efforts allow us to leave more for others, relate more directly to our food and shelter needs, strengthen our connections to community, and give us the opportunity to take personal action. These are all things we should be doing now, rather than waiting until we're forced to do them. Things we should be doing *anyway*, simply because they are the right things to do.

The Theory of Anyway. Yes.

## February Reading, Viewing, and Listening

*Animal, Vegetable, Miracle: A Year of Food Life*, by Barbara Kingsolver, Camille Kingsolver, and Steven L. Hopp

Colorado Tree Coalition, www.coloradotrees.org

*A Crude Awakening: The Oil Crash* (documentary film), www.oilcrashmovie .com/film.html

*Eating Fossil Fuels: Oil, Food and the Coming Crisis in Agriculture*, by Dale Allen Pfeiffer

*From Where We Stand: Recovering a Sense of Place*, by Deborah Tall

*Grass Roots: The Landscape of Home*, by Paul Gruchow

*In Defense of Food: An Eater's Manifesto*, by Michael Pollan

*The Long Emergency: Surviving the Converging Catastrophes of the Twenty-First Century*, by James Howard Kunstler

*Long Life: Essays and Other Writings*, by Mary Oliver

National Farmers Union, www.nfu.org

*The Omnivore's Dilemma: A Natural History of Four Meals*, by Michael Pollan

*Pilgrim at Tinker Creek*, by Annie Dillard

*Sixtyfive Roses: A Sister's Memoir*, by Heather Summerhayes Cariou

*Supercapitalism: The Transformation of Business, Democracy, and Everyday Life*, by Robert Reich

"The Theory of Anyway," by Pat Meadows: http://entire-of-itself.blogspot .com/2007/01/theory-of-anyway.htm

| JANUARY | FEBRUARY | **MARCH** | APRIL |
|---------|----------|-----------|-------|
| MAY | JUNE | JULY | AUGUST |
| SEPTEMBER | OCTOBER | NOVEMBER | DECEMBER |

## MARCH 1

Segued from winter to summer without missing a beat. Eighty-two degrees a couple of days ago, eighty-eight yesterday, ninety-four this afternoon. Time for shorts, a tee shirt, no shoes.

The flowers don't mind. The daffodils are still lush and golden along the edge of the woods, the redbuds are frosted in purple, and the blue-eyed grass (a miniature wild cousin of the iris) is blooming in the fields. Yesterday, I spotted our first Indian paintbrush. The brightly colored bracts—red, orange, yellow, lavender—are an attractive come-hither lure for hummingbirds and bees.

When I see this bright beauty blooming in the grass, I know the hummingbirds will be here soon. Better go out to the garden shed and look for the hummingbird feeders.

*Joys come from simple and natural things, mists over meadows, sunlight on leaves, the path of the moon over water. Even rain and wind and stormy clouds bring joy, just as knowing animals and flowers and where they live. Such things are where you find them, and belong to the aware and alive.*

—SIGURD OLSON

*Every spring is the only spring: a perpetual astonishment.*

—ELLIS PETERS

*It was one of those March days when the sun shines hot and the wind blows cold: when it is summer in the light, and winter in the shade.*

—CHARLES DICKENS

## MARCH 2

I can postpone the hunt for the feeder. A cold front just barreled down from the Panhandle, bringing sleet and snow to Dallas and Waco and gusty winds, gray skies, and a morning temperature of twenty-four to Meadow Knoll.

The dogs and I took a quick walk around the east meadow, double-timing. My face was freezing and the wind was like ice water down my neck. By the time I got back, chilled to the bone, Bill had built a fire of cedar and oak logs in the fireplace. Pancakes and hot chocolate and the fire warmed me up considerably.

The UPS delivery truck arrived at eleven with the promised copy-edited manuscript of *The Tale of Briar Bank*. This book is the fifth in a series of eight mysteries centering on eight years in the life (1905–1913) of Beatrix Potter. A perfect day to settle down in front of the fire with a shawl, a cup of steaming Earl Grey tea, and a good book.

*Briar Bank*, like the four previous books in the Cottage Tales series, is set in the English Lake District, where Beatrix bought a farm. In addition to the people who live in the village of Near Sawrey, the story includes animals, domestic and wild. And the animals talk.

Talking animals go back to Aesop and his fables—certainly not a new thing. I love Kenneth Grahame's *The Wind in the Willows* and Richard Adams' *Watership Down*. And I was captivated by the idea of inviting Beatrix's storybook creatures—Mrs. Tiggy-Winkle, Jemima Puddle-duck, Tom Thumb the mouse, Tabitha Twitchit, and others—to join a flock of animals of my own invention. Took some doing to negotiate the licensing requirements with Potter's publisher (owner of her copyrights), but once that was settled, the project moved forward. Judging from the mail I receive on the series, readers are enjoying it—even the talking animals. Some people even like the talking animals more than the humans.

I'm finding dozens of things to change. Mostly small, happily—a word, a couple of sentences, a detail or two, superficial stuff. The copy editor has done a good job of catching the real errors.

> *A novel can educate to some extent. But first, a novel has to entertain—that's the contract with the reader: you give me ten hours and I'll give you a reason to turn the page.*
>
> —BARBARA KINGSOLVER

> *In writing, you can make a silk purse out of a sow's ear, but first you have to create the sow's ear.*
>
> —CHARLES PARNELL

NEWS SUMMARY: *In the March 4 Texas primary, Hillary Clinton took 51 percent of the vote to Barack Obama's 47 percent. Primary wins in Texas, Ohio, Rhode Island, and Vermont brought John McCain enough delegates to secure the Republican presidential nomination. Mike Huckabee dropped out of the race.*

## MARCH 5

Warmer today, plenty of sun, mild breeze.

McCain's sewn it up, but the Dems are still at it, with Clinton and Obama neck-and-neck, Edwards a distant third. I voted for Obama in the primary, but I'd be happy with either Obama or Clinton—although I wish they'd both pay more attention to energy depletion. They dance around the subject but never address it directly—maybe because it's easier to talk about climate change (which they can conceivably do something about) than the end of oil (which they can't).

Nobody wants to talk about energy depletion. "Don't worry," one woman says, patting me on the shoulder in a comforting way. "Scientists will come up with an alternative. They always have."

> *The energy IQ of our Congress is 55. If you think there's a problem in getting oil company CEOs to address the [oil depletion] problem, try convincing a politician to address it.*
>
> —TOM PETRIE, ENERGY CONSULTANT

Another: "Oh, come on—don't be such a Cassandra. There's enough oil for everybody, if the environmentalists will just shut up and let the oil companies drill offshore and in the Arctic."

A third: "Nothing to fret about. Oil shale, that's the answer. Or maybe natural gas."

The trouble is that energy is still readily available, its sources and real costs invisible to its users. As long as this is true, we can pretend we'll always have as much as we have today, if not more.

## MARCH 7

The corrected pages of *Briar Bank* went back to New York, and Bill and I celebrated by driving to Marble Falls for dinner.

I read somewhere that the American family eats out three or four times a week (surely this contributes to the obesity epidemic). For us, it's more likely to be a couple of times a month. We prefer to eat at home because we like knowing what's in what's on our plates, and because we'd rather not drive sixty miles just for the privilege of paying for a meal cooked and served by someone else. When we do go out, we combine the trip with shopping—and in this case, dropping the manuscript into a FedEx pickup box.

"Are we having a date?" Bill jokes as we get into the car. He follows that up with the crucial question: "Did you remember the grocery list?"

A week of ordinary days, happily topped off with the return of a manuscript, dinner with my favorite date, a trip to the grocery store, and an evening's reading. Tonight, *House of Happy Endings* by Leslie Garis. I chose the book because Garis' grandfather was one of the writers in the Edward Stratemeyer syndicate, the producer of the Hardy Boys and Nancy Drew books. Light years ago, when Bill and I first started out as writers, we worked in both series. We have the distinction of being both Carolyn Keene and Franklin W. Dixon.

## MARCH 8

*Wormwood* was the final book in a three-book China Bayles contract—Books Fifteen, Sixteen, and Seventeen—which means that it's time to negotiate a new contract. Thereupon hangs a dilemma. A happy one, but still a dilemma.

Nonfiction and mainstream fiction are written "one-off," a book at a time. Genre fiction (mystery, romance, science fiction, western) is

*What does it take [to make our world work]? It takes 85 million barrels of oil per day globally, as well as millions of tons of coal and billions of cubic feet of natural gas. The supply network for these fuels is globe-spanning and awesome. Yet, from the standpoint of the end user, this network is practically invisible and easily taken for granted. We flip the switch, pump the gas, or turn up the thermostat with hardly a thought to the processes of extraction we draw upon, or the environmental horrors they entail.*

—RICHARD HEINBERG

usually written in a series format with contract agreements for two or three books. A multi-book contract makes it easier for the editors (who work two to four years ahead) to plan production. Makes it nice for the writer, too, who is happily aware that she can count on several years of good work.

My input into the contract is usually confined to the proposal itself: title and a brief synopsis for each book. The rest of it—payments, payment schedule, due dates, rights—is between Bill (who has served as our literary agent since 1999) and the editor. But coming up with the titles and synopses also involves thinking about the direction of the series. How are the characters likely to develop in these two or three books? What might happen to them? How might they change? Do I want to try any storytelling experiments?

Readers say they enjoy the comfortable familiarity of Pecan Springs and China's circle of friends. I have the feeling that most would love it if I kept on writing the same book over and over again. But I can't bring myself to do that, so I've been experimenting with point of view, setting, narrative construction.

With a new contract in the offing, I'm thinking ahead. What comes first to my mind is how amazingly fortunate I am to be able to choose my projects and define my work—especially in this last year of my seventh decade when, according to conventional wisdom, I should be planning to pack it in.

So I'm thinking about the next three books. Feels like a blessing.

MARCH 9

Still thinking about the next China Bayles books. And talking to Bill. He's made several suggestions, good ones. He's also reminded me that I have three more Cottage Tales to write, with an annual deadline of August 31. Whatever I propose has to be in synch with that existing obligation.

MARCH 10

While I'm thinking, I'm also writing—or rather, revising, polishing, and making another pass through *Together, Alone*. At the same time, I'm making sketches for the mapmaker, Molly O'Halloran. I'm lucky to have her. She provided illustrations for the ambitious book *Home Ground* (edited by Barry Lopez) and for one of Wendell Berry's novels.

*Inevitably, you repeat yourself. The only thing you can do is avoid looking at your previous books so you don't become sad about it. That way, you never fall into, "I should be writing this well now," or, "This isn't very good."*

—JOHN MADSON

*In nearly all good fiction, the basic—all but inescapable—plot form is: A central character wants something, goes after it despite opposition (perhaps including his own doubts), and so arrives at a win, lose, or draw.*

—JOHN GARDNER

*I would like [my epitaph] to read . . . : Here lies a teller of tales.*

—RAY BRADBURY

And there's a bonus: she's worked with the editors at the University of Texas Press and knows what they need from the get-go. No learning curve.

Today: Story Circle Reading Circle in Austin. The book: *Garlic and Sapphires* by Ruth Reichl. Pert, lively memoir, an interesting look at the food business by a critic who knows it inside out.

## MARCH 11

Zach is back at the vet's for another overnight, with tests tomorrow and (we hope) a medication he can tolerate. In spite of our efforts to tempt him to eat, he's lost six pounds, about 10 percent of his body weight. But tonight—ah, tonight we can sleep. It hasn't been all bad, though: Zach is remarkably cooperative, and the 3 a.m. stars are remarkably beautiful.

## MARCH 12

*A day of rain, another bright week, and all earth will be filled with the tremor and the thrust of the year's new energies.*

—HENRY BESTON

*Oil has literally made foreign and security policy for decades. Just since the turn of this century, it has provoked the division of the Middle East after World War I; aroused Germany and Japan to extend their tentacles beyond their borders; the Arab Oil Embargo; Iran versus Iraq; the Gulf War. This is all clear.*

—BILL RICHARDSON, SECRETARY OF ENERGY (1999)

A little rain this morning, sunshine this afternoon. I came up with a three-book idea and e-mailed a brief description to Natalee, my editor. An hour later, back comes an encouraging e-mail: "Make a proposal." I'd already roughed it out, so with a little spit and polish, it was ready to go.

An interesting thought, as I clicked "send" and the proposal flew off to New York, where (thanks to the magic of e-mail) it will arrive in Natalee's inbox before I finish my coffee. This project represents three years of my future. Three years of research and writing, of livelihood—right livelihood, to my mind. When this contract is completed, in 2011, I'll be in my seventy-second year. It will feel like an entirely new life-territory.

## MARCH 13

Who knows? With so many things changing in the world, it may be an entirely different *country* out there in another three years—or six, or nine.

I'm reading Michael Klare on resource wars, *Rising Powers, Shrinking Planet: The New Geopolitics of Energy*. The book is an education for me, and I'm seeing our military presence in the Persian Gulf, the current disputes in the Caspian, and the wars in Afghanistan and Iraq in a whole new light. It's been all about oil for a very long time, and most of us just haven't understood it.

I'm thinking that I'm glad to find new teachers—like Klare, Kingsolver, Pollan, others—in my sixty-ninth year. I may not like what I'm learning, but I'll know when I'm *really* old: I'll be ready to stop.


## MARCH 14

This morning, the first bluebonnet, under the ash tree outside my window—the first of few in this year of deepening drought. For me, the lack of bluebonnets is an aesthetic disappointment. I love to look out across the meadow and see it blooming blue. For the towns in the Hill Country, it's a different matter. A healthy crop of April wildflowers ensures a healthy bottom line for local businesses. When wildflowers are sparse, business is sparser. Nature as commodity.

This afternoon, good news. Natalee e-mails that she's planning to make an offer on the proposal. She'll call on Monday to discuss it. Nice of her not to keep us in suspense—there'll be an offer. But that doesn't necessarily mean she'll want what I proposed. Maybe she'll have a different idea.

Rereading: Barry Lopez, *About This Life*, one of my favorite books about landscape, imagination, memory. Lopez reminds me of the tremendous soul-price we are paying for our oil-fueled affluence, our footloose ways, our broken connections to place. We are a society, he says, "in which it is no longer necessary for human beings to know where they live."

*We abuse land because we regard it as a commodity belonging to us. When we see land as a community to which we belong, we may begin to use it with love and respect.*

—ALDO LEOPOLD

*In the forty thousand years of human history, it has only been in the last few hundred years or so that a people could afford to ignore their local geographies as completely as we do and still survive.*

—BARRY LOPEZ


## MARCH 15

March? More like May, June.

It was sixty-five when we got up, heading for mid-nineties this afternoon. The Chickasaw plum is blooming in the woods, and the cypress trees along the creek are showing a fresh, up-to-the-minute chartreuse.

Spent a couple of hours in the warm morning sunshine pruning the last of the roses—the climbers, so formidably, fatally thorny that I always put off pruning them as long as I can. My arms are bloody. The roses are unbowed, and only slightly diminished—I'm not brave enough to do much damage.

Cowardly with the climbers, I am more courageous with the crape myrtles, the mustang grape on the fence, and a Mexican oregano

*Pruning hurts. Pruning helps you grow.*

—EMILIE BARNES

with the musical name of *Poliomentha longiflora*. I always think of this oregano—now lush and beautiful, especially during its lush June bloom—as the "rooster bush." We used to have chickens, laying hens, in the charge of a black-and-white rooster named Chaunticleer, after the lusty rooster in Chaucer's *The Nun's Priest's Tale*. Our rooster always took his hens to have their daily dust baths under the Mexican oregano, and to me, it's still his bush. Pruning the crape myrtles and the grapevine and the rooster bush are pure pleasure, compared to those roses. No thorns.

All the while, of course, I am thinking about that phone call and wondering how it's going to turn out. It's nice to know there'll be an offer—that's relieved some of the tension. But times are tough right now. Book sales are down across the board. Maybe Natalee won't want three books. Maybe she won't be able to offer as much as she's offered in the past. Maybe . . . o.

### MARCH 17

Natalee says yes to the three-book package I proposed, beginning with *Holly Blues*, which will be delivered next March (2009) and published in April 2010. I'm delighted.

### MARCH 18

Thinking about the new contract and remembering my first sale as a writer. I was eighteen, and I sold a short story called "Her First Violin" to a Sunday school take-home newspaper. I was paid a penny a word: fifteen dollars for fifteen hundred words. I danced around the room, yipping like a puppy. It wasn't just the money, although in those days, fifteen dollars came near to buying a week's groceries; today, with inflation, it would come to about $110. It was the idea that somebody valued my writing enough to print it—and pay for it. It was a pivotal moment in my life.

I once read a story about Norman Mailer, whose agent was negotiating payment for a *Playboy* piece. The magazine wanted to pay the going rate of twenty-five cents a word. Mailer wanted a dollar. The agent kept pushing, pushing, until finally the editor agreed. "Okay," he said, "we'll pay a buck for words like 'usufruct' and 'eleemosynary,' but not for every 'and,' 'but,' or 'the.'"

Excuse me. I'm going to look up "eleemosynary."

AN EXTRAORDINARY YEAR OF ORDINARY DAYS

**NEWS SUMMARY:** *The Bush administration has intervened in an attempt to avert a nationwide financial crisis. The Federal Reserve proposes a $200-billion loan package for banks. It also plans to loan $30 billion to JPMorgan Chase so Chase can buy out the now-bankrupt Bear Stearns. It is hoped that the emergency acquisition will avert a financial panic.*

## MARCH 19

Television, radio, the Internet—every channel, all the media, boiling over with financial disaster. Not much immediate impact on us, at least at the moment: Bill is a deficit hawk who has always insisted on pay-as-you-go, and since we're writers and our income is irregular, cash-only has been a practical necessity. But this debt/credit situation is looking like those horizon-to-horizon dust storms of the 1930s: it is so massive that it will envelop everyone, even people who don't have monthly auto payments or a house that's mortgaged for more than it's worth.

*We're a what's-my-monthly-payment nation. The idea is to have my monthly payments as big as I can take. If you cut interest rates, I'll get a bigger car.*

—PAUL KASRIEL,
ECONOMIST

## MARCH 20

Speaking of storms.

Yesterday, the wind yanked the metal roof off the barn. Last night, it wrenched the roof panels off our front porch and sent them sailing like a pack of cards over the house into the backyard. Luckily, we were indoors, and nobody got hurt by flying metal. Bill is out there now, collecting the twisted wreckage. The rafters were ripped loose, so we'll have to replace the entire structure.

Humidity low, wind whipping, perfect wildfire weather, and there it is: gray-white smoke like a massive thunderhead billowing up beyond the ridge to the south. Likely, it's on the other side of Route 29, some three or four miles away, and the wind is blowing out of the north, which means we're safe—from this fire, anyway. I hear on the news that this weekend alone, some 140,000 acres of Texas land have burned.

Bill has devised an emergency evacuation plan. In case of a wildfire:

Put the dogs and cat (with various leashes and carry cases) into the van, add the computers, the data backups, and the big file box from his office (which weighs a ton), plus whatever else there's time to collect.

If the fire is coming from the north, drive south across our neighbor's pasture.

If the fire is coming from the south, drive north up the lane to the county road.

This is one list I don't like looking at.

## MARCH 21

*At 5:30 the vernal equinox occurs. I go outside and stand in the middle of a hayfield with my eyes closed. The universe is restless, but I want to feel celestial equipoise: twelve hours of daylight, twelve of dark, and the earth ramrod straight on its axis. Straightening my posture to resist the magnetic tilt back into dormancy, spiritual and emotional reticence, I imagine the equatorial sash, now nose-to-nose with the sun, sizzling like a piece of bacon, and the earth slowly tilting.*

—GRETEL EHRLICH

The spring equinox, celebrated with a delicious rain. An inch and a quarter, the first significant rain in six months. Overnight, the grass has turned a bright emerald green. But the soil is still dry, and although the rain raises our spirits, there wasn't enough of it to lift the county's burn ban.

Working today on travel plans for next month's *Nightshade* events—sixteen, all in Texas. April is a pretty month, and I don't mind the travel. It's something I have to do to support the books, and I genuinely enjoy talking to readers. But I would really rather be writing.

Or reading. This week, reading Gretel Ehrlich's *Islands, the Universe, Home*, written when she lived on a ranch in Wyoming. Resilient prose, rich in metaphor, evocative. Also, *This Organic Life: Confessions of a Suburban Homesteader* by Joan Dye Gussow—"one part memoir, one part manual, one part manifesto," as Michael Pollan says about the book. Gussow may have been the first eat-locally, eat-seasonally gardener and memoirist.

## MARCH 22

Nice news today. The Mystery Guild has selected *Nightshade* as its April alternate. There's a payment for this, but it's the advertising that counts. The Guild has more than a quarter million subscribers and the alternate is featured as prominently as the main selection in multiple mailings. This isn't the first time a China Bayles book has been chosen: it's always something to celebrate.

More nice news. Zach's medication has reduced his Cushing's symptoms—drinking and peeing—and we've all been sleeping through the night. His appetite is better, too. Lady, though, is having even more trouble negotiating the back steps, and our slick wood floors make it hard for her to get around in the house. Toro is healthy, thank heavens. And the cat.

And the vet's bottom line.

Breathtakingly beautiful spring day, daffodils massed along the woods, redbuds clouded in purple, Chickasaw plum, its blossoms as frilly as the finest lace. A trio of turkey hens stalked through the yard last night, clucking and trilling, and this morning, at dawn, I heard the gobbler's wobbly, plaintive call. I'm sure the hens heard it, too. The fellow was probably mobbed.

Wild turkey hens (I've read: I don't have a close personal acquaintance with them) lay a dozen eggs, but the predation loss is high. A researcher at Texas A&M University recently set up cameras beside turkey nests and found out that more than 60 percent were destroyed by raccoons, foxes, and snakes. But there are enough survivors to keep the wild turkey population growing, and we see more of them every year. When I hear the gobblers raising their seductive voices, I know that we'll be watching the turkey chicks—poults, they're called—in just about two months.

Dipping into, here and there, an edited collection of Joyce Carol Oates' journals, 1973–1982. Fascinating account of her daily life, private thoughts, writing, and the creative process.

*The first day of spring was once the time for taking the young virgins into the fields, there in dalliance to set an example in fertility for nature to follow. Now we just set the clocks an hour ahead and change the oil in the crankcase.*

—E. B. WHITE

Easter Sunday yesterday, and the Texas mountain laurel (*Sophora secundiflora*) is in bloom. I loved the lilacs I grew up with in Illinois and can smell their delicate, distinctive scent still. But not when the mountain laurel is blooming. It smells like grape Kool-Aid, buckets and buckets of it. Soaks up every other scent, real and remembered.

This year's bloom is the best we've had from these little trees, grown from seed I collected from a laurel growing in a curbside plant container on Sixth Street in Austin twenty years ago. There's something magical about growing a tree from seed. I sometimes imagine that it's grateful to me for giving it root room and putting it where it can reach up to the sky and welcome the birds. But I'm the one who's grateful—to this tree for consenting to make its home here, for growing and blooming where I can visit it every day.

*Sophora secundiflora* apparently feels at home with its roots in our thin, dry Edwards Plateau limestone. A member of the pea family, it isn't a laurel at all. It has some interesting folk names, most of them having to do with its large red seeds: coral bean, mescal bean, bigdrunk bean. The local Indians used strands of the seeds as currency (a six-foot strand, according to Cabeza de Vaca, bought a small horse)

*Two days of extraordinary weather. Easter Sunday in the high seventies and today just as warm, though windy. . . . Forsythia blooming everywhere. Daffodils out back. Tulips slower, not yet blossoming. Hyacinth very pale, sluggish, slow. A lovely, enchanting time of year.*

—JOYCE CAROL OATES

*Nature—wild Nature—dwells in gardens just as she dwells in the tangled woods, in the deeps of the sea, and on the heights of the mountains; and the wilder the garden, the more you will see of her there.*

—HERBERT SASS

and wore them as good luck necklaces. They brewed the leaves and seeds into an intoxicating ritual drink. And back in the innocent days before video games and the mall, Texas kids entertained themselves with "burn beans." They'd rub the seed on cement and push them against another kid's arm, with a predictable result.

Reading: *Pompeii* by Robert Harris—a recommendation from my son, who is reading the novel for a class in ancient history and thought I'd like it. He's right. I love the historical detail, vivid descriptions, appreciate the meticulous research. Great story, too.

**NEWS SUMMARY:** *A roadside bomb in Baghdad killed four U.S. soldiers, bringing the deaths of American troops to four thousand, less than a week after the fifth anniversary of the war. George Bush says, "I will vow so long as I'm president to make sure that those lives were not lost in vain, that, in fact, there is an outcome that will merit the sacrifice."*

## MARCH 25

Four thousand!

What "outcome" could possibly "merit" (doesn't Bush mean *justify, rationalize?*) those deaths—as well as the other eighty-some thousand documented civilian deaths that have occurred in the five years since our invasion? The only visible outcome is a dubious, debilitated democracy, established for the purpose of giving America a place for Middle Eastern military bases, from which vantage points we can "protect" Middle Eastern oil.

And we're not even allowed to see the coffins of our dead soldiers as they come home. The implicit instruction to American citizens: Forget about the war. We'll handle it. None of your business.

Dark times. Dark times.

*In March [2003], on the eve of the Iraq war, a directive arrived from the Pentagon at U.S. military bases. "There will be no arrival ceremonies for, or media coverage of, deceased military personnel returning to or departing from Ramstein airbase or Dover, Del., base, to include interim stops," the Defense Department said.*

*—DANA MILBANK,*
*WASHINGTON POST*

## MARCH 26

Census figures published this week show that Travis County (metropolitan Austin) is the ninth fastest-growing county in the nation, with Williamson County only two places behind. Not a pretty thought on an otherwise lovely spring morning, since both Travis and Williamson counties adjoin our rural county. Checking the census figures,

I happened on a blogger who noted that many of the new residents will move to the "new sprawling suburbs strangling [Austin] like a gasoline-fueled robotic python."

Picturesque language, sadly accurate. The bright side: the suburbs haven't sprawled out as far as we are. Yet. Maybe this economic downturn—combined with the threat of high gasoline prices—will put on the brakes.

## MARCH 27

Got my hair cut this morning at the Mane Attraction in Bertram (population: 1,100—up by about 30 percent in the last ten years). The Mane Attraction is quintessential small-town Texas: a rank of hair dryers, a pair of shampoo stations, a long shelf with mirrors and barber chairs, a manicure desk, a playpen for Becky's grandbaby (Becky is the owner), notices of church pie suppers and the quilt raffle at the bank—all in one large room.

I always learn something while I'm getting my hair cut. Today I learn that Becky's cows have twenty-five new calves this spring. (She has only one bull—he had a busy year.) I also hear about an intriguing local mystery. A dozen families out on Oatmeal Road were evacuated (nobody knows why) from their homes yesterday and were put up for the night in City Hall (the old post office).

Over at Carolyn's Market, I heard that somebody opened a shed and found 125 five-gallon containers of unidentified chemicals and a bag of highly explosive benzoyl peroxide, so they evacuated everybody. Terrorists, maybe?

The truth (heard on the five o'clock TV news) was more prosaic: the stuff was stored there by a retired chemist some ten or fifteen years ago. The state Hazmat team carted it off, and the evacuees went home.

By all accounts, this adventure was almost as exciting as the annual Labor Day Oatmeal Festival. The parade takes place on Bertram's main street because Oatmeal (too small to show up on the map) doesn't have a main street, or any street at all. Several years ago, my ninety-year-old mother got to ride on the Bertram Nursing Home float. She'd never been in a parade before. I asked her how she felt about this. She said she felt like a queen.

## MARCH 28

We don't go to movies—too far to drive, and there aren't many current movies we want to see. But we do subscribe to one of those rent-movies-by-mail outfits and indulge in an amazing variety of films. This week, we watched *Blood and Oil*, a documentary about the Middle East during World War I, a couple of episodes of *West Wing* (we're viewing them in order), and *Wit*, based on Margaret Edson's Pulitzer Prize–winning play.

In *Wit*, Dr. Vivian Bearing (English professor, John Donne scholar) is dying of ovarian cancer. Bearing is played by Emma Thompson, whose dry, self-deprecating irony lightens a dark role. I loved the way Edson wove Donne's poetry into the script, loved Emma Thompson's performance, loved even the awkward young doctor, so captivated by the esoteric technical aspects of his craft that he loses sight of his own humanity. In the end, we understand that it's not intellectual brilliance that redeems us, but simple kindness and loving steadfastness—summed up by (of all things) the story of *The Runaway Bunny*, read to the dying Bearing by her mentor. "If you become a crocus in a hidden garden," said his mother, "I will become a gardener and find you." Donne's metaphysics, made real.

Watching this sophisticated, moving film, I'm grateful for the technology that allows me to see it here, so far out in the country. Grateful again when I take the dogs for their before-bed outing and hear a screech owl and the frogs along the creek. I'm not a believer in a beneficent deity, but if I were, I might imagine Her as a gardener and myself as a crocus. It would be a comforting thought.

> *"If you are a gardener and find me," said the little bunny, "I will be a bird and fly away from you."*
>
> *"If you become a bird and fly away from me," said his mother, "I will be a tree that you come home to."*
>
> —MARGARET WISE BROWN

## MARCH 29

Our friend Dolly, a local rancher, stops by with jars of ruby red prickly pear and hog plum jelly for me and a couple of Caribbean Red habanero plants for Bill. He and Dolly are pepper-loving chileheads. They talk hot stuff while I fetch a book for Dolly, my author's copy of *Nightshade*, since I don't have other copies yet.

An appropriate trade. Chiles are nightshades.

> *If you will follow my counsell, deal not with Nightshade in any case, and banish it from your gardens and the use of it also, being a plant so furious and deadly.*
>
> —JOHN GERARD (1598)

## MARCH 30

Home again, after a two-day book trip to Pearland, a suburb south of Houston, where I gave a talk at the Red Hat Literacy Luncheon—

three hundred–plus ladies wearing outrageous red hats and an abundance of purple.

Six hours drive time to Pearland (I cleverly managed to hit the Sam Houston Tollway at rush hour) and five back—eleven hours plus an overnight in a motel. When I arrived at the luncheon, I learned that the organizers had reduced my talk time to twenty minutes. I wangled five more minutes, feeling (forgivably, I hope) that it was a very long trip for such a short presentation.

Barnes & Noble brought books to the luncheon and sold plenty—all but *Nightshade.* The book isn't officially available until next week, and all pleas to the publisher for its early release for this event were met with "Sorry, it's the rule." (Irony: I arrived home yesterday evening to an e-mail from a reader in Missouri, who bought a copy of *Nightshade* at her local chain bookstore last weekend.)

"The rule" has to do with the on-sale date: the day bookstores are permitted to offer the book for sale. On-sale dates are required to be observed strictly (witness the ruckus when *Harry Potter* was let out of the bag early) with penalties for violators who break the embargo. The rationale: publishers sometimes promote a new release heavily, hoping that consumers will so lust after a book that they will stand in line at midnight (think *Harry Potter* again), thereby enhancing its shot at the best-seller lists.

But most books (including *Nightshade*) aren't heavily promoted by the publisher. Most books aren't candidates for the best-seller lists. The on-sale date is no big deal, and there's no good reason for the book to be embargoed.

Sometimes you wonder if publishers enjoy shooting themselves in the foot.

## MARCH 31

The hummingbirds are here.

Two, anyway, ruby-throats. The black-chinned will be along a little later. I've hung two feeders, a dozen feet apart, so the less aggressive birds can feed without disturbance. Hummingbirds pack an incredible ferocity into their small bodies and defend their territories with all the power and speed they can muster, zipping at the speed of thought, their wings a blur. Not much out there to feed on except for a few paintbrush, so they're focused on the feeders. Makes for some fascinating viewing.

An appropriate finale to March, a fine welcome for April.

*I hope you love birds too. It is economical. It saves going to heaven.*

—EMILY DICKINSON

*Some delight through song; others with showy plumage; the hummer, with flight.*

—JAY NEVILLE

## March Reading and Viewing

*About This Life: Journeys on the Threshold of Memory*, by Barry Lopez

*American Household Botany: A History of Useful Plants, 1620–1900*, by Judith Sumner

*Blood and Oil: The Middle East in World War I* (documentary film)

*Garlic and Sapphires: The Secret Life of a Critic in Disguise*, by Ruth Reichl

*House of Happy Endings: A Memoir*, by Leslie Garis

*Islands, the Universe, Home*, by Gretel Ehrlich

*The Journal of Joyce Carol Oates, 1973–1982*, edited by Greg Johnson

*Pompeii: A Novel*, by Robert Harris

*Rising Powers, Shrinking Planet: The New Geopolitics of Energy*, by Michael Klare

*This Organic Life: Confessions of a Suburban Homesteader*, by Joan Dye Gussow

*Wit*, a film, based on a play by Margaret Edson, directed by Mike Nichols, starring Emma Thompson

| JANUARY | FEBRUARY | MARCH | **APRIL** |
|---------|----------|-------|-----------|
| MAY | JUNE | JULY | AUGUST |
| SEPTEMBER | OCTOBER | NOVEMBER | DECEMBER |

## APRIL 1

Six cartons of *Nightshade* arrived today.

Never mind that this is not a novel event, that I've been here, done this before. Every time I pick up a new book, turn the pages and feel the stiff binding and smell the ink—every time is like the first time. I am never not amazed, never not thrilled. It's like reaching out to take your baby in your arms, not quite believing that this creature has finally made its way out into the world from some mysterious place inside you. You say: Did I do that? *How* did I do that?

Up early on this bright April Fool's morning to walk the dogs before I begin a day of signing and shipping books sold from our Web site by Story Circle. Bill hauls them to the post office for me, bless him.

I work all day, with brief breaks for laundry, lunch, dog-walking, and a sandwich-and-salad supper. It's nearly eight when I finish, sit down with a cup of hot chocolate, put up my feet, and pick up a book. Rereading Edwin Way Teale's *A Naturalist Buys an Old Farm*, a delight in any season. Teale speaks to the reason that Bill and I are here at Meadow Knoll:

> *In such a country place as ours the near-at-home also has its special attraction, its continuing charm, the hold of the familiar that is also the ever-changing . . . . Here, in every season of the year, we [live] on the edge of wildness. All these acres around us, all these fields and woods fading into the night . . . form a sanctuary farm—a sanctuary for wildlife and a sanctuary for us.*

A sanctuary for us. Seems even more important these days.

*For several days after my first book was published I carried it about in my pocket, and took surreptitious peeks at it to make sure the ink had not faded.*

—J. M. BARRIE

*You write a book and it's like putting a message in a bottle and throwing it in the ocean. You don't know if it will ever reach any shores. And there, you see, sometimes it falls in the hands of the right person.*

—ISABEL ALLENDE

**NEWS SUMMARY:** *The Iraqi Army dismissed thirteen hundred soldiers who refused to fight in the Battle of Basra, while the BBC estimated the battle's death toll at three hundred. Suicide bombings in Afghanistan and Iraq killed fourteen last week. North Korea fired warning missiles into the sea, and pirates seized a ship off Somalia. The lagging economy and increased fuel costs forced Aloha and Skybus Airlines to cease operations.*

APRIL 2

I cleaned out the metal tank where I keep potted geraniums and discovered a toadlet about the size of a baby's fist, mottled gray and black, looking remarkably like a lumpy rock covered with lichen. A Texas toad (*Bufo speciosus*), likely born in the bottom of the tank where I found him, one of a multitude. My handbook reports that his mother would have laid a clutch of some eleven thousand eggs—nature's allowance for death and destruction, Teale says. A good thing for us that all eleven thousand haven't survived to the size of this fellow, or we'd be up to our knees in toads.

But it was a pleasure to meet this one, and a reminder that there are whole worlds of creatures around us who live out their modest lives without being troubled by resource wars or missiles or energy depletions or pirates or lagging economies.

They simply are, and are simply beautiful, whole, and entire to themselves.

I need to take a lesson from the toads.

*[T]he warm shallows seemed paved with pollywogs. By taking sample countings, one year, we estimated our pond contained 10,000 tadpoles. So great is the allowance nature makes for death and destruction!*

—EDWIN WAY TEALE

APRIL 3

Today, my father's birthday: John Hamilton Webber, born in 1903. *His* father (so the story goes) was not my grandmother's husband but a family friend: the editor of the local newspaper in one version of the story; in another, an associate in the family jewelry business.

Whatever the truth of Granny's indiscretions, John was her indulged darling. Wild, unruly, he didn't go to college (unlike his sister, two brothers), didn't even finish high school. He worked in the family jewelry business, and when it collapsed in the Crash of '29, he was stranded. He went through a couple of wives before he married my mother—the two of them were still married, incredibly, when he died at 85. He was an alcoholic, and, I think now, manic-depressive.

*My father was often angry when I was most like him.*

—LILLIAN HELLMAN

60    AN EXTRAORDINARY YEAR OF ORDINARY DAYS

It's impossible to decipher how much or what part of my father's self-destructive behaviors were due to his internal conflicts or to the chaotic decades through which he lived: World War I, the rowdy twenties, the gray years of the Great Depression, World War II. An intelligent, capable man who read obsessively (Westerns, detective fiction, Dickens, Trollope, Thackeray), he passed the love of books and libraries on to me. I worked as hard as I could in school to make him proud of me and learned to love the learning itself—a good thing, for there were no rewards of pride or affection from him. I was in my forties before the swamps of the old unhappinesses drained away; even now, twenty years after his death, I still can't say I love him.

But today is a bright spring day, the birds are singing, the sky is blue, and the world is too pretty to harbor grudges. I'm sorry, Dad, that you were so unhappy. That's the best I can do.

*We bear the influences of our parents, but we are not fated to remain merely the products of our parents. There is within us as well the positive and creative aspects of the inner archetypal father, which can compensate for many of the negative influences in our actual life histories.*

*—LINDA SCHIERSE LEONARD*

NEWS SUMMARY: *In the past twenty-four months, the average world price for rice has risen by 217 percent, wheat by 136 percent, corn by 125 percent, and soybeans by 107 percent. In the past three months, food riots have broken out in Bangladesh, Egypt, Cameroon, Haiti, Latin America. "While many are worrying about filling their gas tanks," said World Bank President Robert Zoellick, "many others around the world are struggling to fill their stomachs." Among the culprits: biofuel programs, climate instability, destruction of local agricultures by cheap global imports.*

APRIL 4

I love soybeans. Last time I was at the grocery store, frozen soybeans were on my list. I checked the label. They came from China. China! Soybeans? When fields of soybeans stretch across the American Midwest? But the problem with American soybeans, it seems, is that most of the seed is now genetically modified. And people (even Americans) don't like to eat GM plants—when they know what they're eating, that is. That's why we're getting our soybeans from China.

Maybe I can raise some—it's worth a try, anyway. I can't grow all of our food, by any stretch, but I can at least raise some of our veggies. So I've been laying out the fall vegetable garden.

When we moved here in the mid-eighties, Bill double-dug a large garden in a sunny spot where the soil was best. This isn't saying much, since the existing soil on the Edwards Plateau is thin and alkaline—

*Modern agriculture has charted a course for disaster. Our soils and water resources, and our weakened food crops, will fail us just as energy depletion makes it increasingly difficult to make up for these deficiencies through artificial means. The fossil fuel–based agriculture that allowed our population to climb so far above carrying capacity in the last century will soon falter most cruelly.*

*—DALE ALLEN PFEIFFER*

caliche soil, it's called. It's what's left after years of cotton-cropping and over-grazing destroyed the rich topsoil produced by centuries of decaying native prairies.

But double-digging and soil enrichment (we've put tons of compost and chicken manure into the garden space over the years) improved the situation dramatically. I was a student of John Jeavons' bio-intensive methods (still have my first edition copy of *How to Grow More Vegetables*, which I am rereading), and we had a productive garden until the books began to require so much of my attention. Now it's time to return to gardening. Happily, the space, the improved soil, my tools—it's all still there, waiting to go back into production.

The plan: raised beds (built with recycled landscape timbers), with space for movable containers for tomatoes and lettuces. The beds are designed for interplanting and succession planting. The whole thing is fenced to keep out the deer and rabbits, who love lettuce and peas as much as we do. But the fence can be moved, the space expanded, as we see the need.

There's plenty of room on thirty-one acres.


## APRIL 5

Yesterday, book travel. Drove to Kerrville to speak at a meeting of the Kerr County Master Gardeners. I always enjoy talking to master gardeners, who know enough about plants to ask interesting questions. I talked about the nightshade family in all its fascinating ambiguity: nutritious (potato), delicious (tomato, tomatillo, chile pepper), and poisonous (tobacco, datura, deadly nightshade).

After the program, I backtracked from Kerrville up Route 16 to Berkman's Books in Fredericksburg. The owners, David and Lucy Berkman, are ardent bibliophiles, and their attractive bookstore, which spills over into the family living room, is crammed with new releases and fascinating collectables. I love being in a shop that is so clearly at the center of the owners' family life.

Bookstore signings are always unpredictable, but this one was gratifying. There was a notice in the local newspaper, the books arrived, and so did the people. We sold a stack of the new hardcovers and a goodly number of the backlist. I drove home through the darkening Texas night, indulging in a chocolate milkshake and listening to a disturbing book, *The World Without Us* by Alan Weisman, thinking that if humans were suddenly to leave the world, there'd be no one left to read books.

APRIL 6

At four thirty this morning, our emergency weather radio jerked us awake with a severe thunderstorm warning, which was interrupted by a bolt of blue lightning and a bone-rattling crash of thunder. The dogs got up to see what was going on. We got up, too, to check the radar on the computers and unplug them, before we decided that the worst of the storm was sliding south of us and went back to bed.

Falling asleep, I remembered Grandpa Franklin—my mother's father—rousing us in the middle of the night to go to "the cave," the cellar where Grandma Franklin stored the bounty of her Missouri garden. We'd take pillows and blankets and sleep there in the cool, damp dark, while Grandpa stood on the cellar steps, testing the wind, gauging the danger. When he gave the all-clear, we'd trail back to bed, half-asleep. I wonder what he would make of the storm images I can see on the radar.

At eight, Bill and our neighbor Jesse left to drive to Burnet, while the dogs and I took our morning walk. It was wet and chilly, and Lady was even slower than usual. I dawdled along the creek, running fresh with the morning's rain, while the dogs pawed and sniffed at animal scents. Overnight, the drought-dried grasses have turned green, greener, greenest. A galaxy of wild blackberry blossoms spangles the meadow, tiny blue-eyed grass and purple and white anemones bloom along the path, and redwing blackbirds trill with bright abandon in the cattail marsh, their calls warming the chilly morning like a smile.

Rereading: *Writing from the Center*, Scott Russell Sanders. A favorite book, deep, rich, memorable. "For each home ground we need new maps, living maps, stories and poems, photographs and paintings, essays and songs. We need to know where we are, so that we may dwell in our place with a full heart."

*A bookstore is one of the only pieces of evidence we have that people are still thinking.*

—JERRY SEINFELD

*Our ancestors spoke to storms with magical words, prayed to them, cursed them, and danced for them, dancing to the very edge of what is alien and powerful—the cold power of ocean currents, of chaotic winds beyond control and understanding. We may have lost the dances, but we carry with us a need to approach the power of the universe, if only to touch it and race away.*

—KATHLEEN DEAN MOORE

*I value my garden more for being full of blackbirds than of cherries, and very frankly give them fruit for their songs.*

—JOSEPH ADDISON

APRIL 7

Bill's errand ends in disappointment. The problem he and Jesse are trying to solve has to do with the road through our rural subdivision, which a few of the property owners volunteer to maintain. One of the owners (a non-volunteer) built a fence on the right-of-way where ditching needs to be done and refuses to move it back to her property line. Bill and Jesse are asking the county to tell her to move it.

But the Burnet County attorney, county commissioner, and county judge refuse. They claim that the road—poorly constructed to start with, the source of much neighborhood wrangling—belongs to the developer, who has been dead for a decade and insolvent long before that. In effect, they say, nobody has the legal authority to tell this person to move her fence.

Later in the day, I drive past the trespasser's place, indulging in the imagination of vandalism. Garbage on her front lawn. A bucket of spilled paint across her driveway. Roadkill hung on the offending fence.

Or maybe I'll put her into a book and arrange a little murder. Fictionally, of course, since I'm a law-abiding person.

Most of the time.

## APRIL 8

*The shelf life of a modern hardback writer is somewhere between the milk and the yogurt.*

—CALVIN TRILLIN

*When writers die they become books, which is, after all, not too bad an incarnation.*

—JORGE LUIS BORGES

Royalty statements arrived today. Strong sales for the Cottage Tales and the Robin Paige mysteries, even though the last mystery in that series was published in 2006. The most recent China Bayles hardcover has done well, but the backlist hasn't. All the paperbacks in that series are in multiple printings, which means that there are hundreds of thousands of available used copies out there, resold on the Internet and in garage sales and flea markets. Why would somebody pay $6.99 for a book they can buy for a quarter? Still, we're content. And feel fortunate for becoming established before used-book sales totally swamped every author's backlist.

And when I stop to think about it, I realize that there will be a tide of those books out there, ebbing and flowing, long after I'm gone. Makes me happy. Sort of.

## APRIL 10

Spent the afternoon with Molly O'Halloran, going over the information she needs for the maps she's making for *Together, Alone*. We met at a coffee shop in East Austin, not far from where she lives. Beautiful day, outdoor table on a sheltered patio, interesting company, good project. "For each home ground," as Scott Russell Sanders says, "we need new maps, living maps, stories and poems." Molly's maps will be just fine, I'm sure of it.

The evening was a waste of time: a book signing at a chain bookstore in Round Rock, an Austin suburb. No advertising, no copies of the new book. Five people bought books—by accident, I suspect.

The last day of the blog tour, and if I'm feeling stressed and too busy, it's my own damn fault. The tour is interesting and (I hope) productive; at least, there's been plenty of traffic, measured by visitors to the blogs. Pragmatic, Bill asks, "Is all this going to result in book sales?" I can only shrug. I don't know. But at least the word's getting out. That's what this is all about. Shameless promotion, as Sisters in Crime reminds us, by brazen hussies.

This morning, I'm answering e-mails, replying to comments on blog posts, and working on promotional materials for book clubs. This afternoon, a telephone interview with Windows Bookshop in Monroe, Louisiana, to be broadcast in streaming audio over the Internet tomorrow, then podcast and archived on the bookstore's Web site. Streaming audio. Podcast. Where do we learn these words?

And in the interstices of this activity, I've been helping Bill with a project that has a much more solid and satisfying result. He has replaced the siding on the storage shed he built some twenty-five years ago. The new siding, freshly painted, looks wonderfully neat and trim.

As I admire Bill's handiwork, I feel a twinge of guilt. What he does has substance, durability. Repaired, the shed will be usable for years to come. This book promotion? Feels flimsy, ephemeral. No idea whether the hours I've spent and will spend this month have any value at all.

To remedy this, I drive the ranch truck to the cow pasture, collect a twenty-gallon tub of cow pies, and bring it home for the compost heap.

There's nothing like hauling cow manure to make you feel of the earth, earthy.

Back in 2001 or so, I helped Story Circle start a book review Web site: reviewing books "by, for, about women." Paula Yost took it over for a number of years, then last year, I joined Paula for a remake and a relaunch of the site and currently volunteer as editor and reviewer.

Now, reading (for a review on the Web site) *Spring's Edge: A Ranch Wife's Chronicles*, a memoir by Laurie Wagner Buyer about her life on a Colorado ranch. When I think I have it hard, I reach for books like this one. Reminds me that women can be tough and tender at the same time, that the seasons can break your heart, the earth can make you whole. Reminds me that there is a way to live on the land, and a time to leave it.

*To get famous, be shameless.*

—ANON.

*To establish oneself in the world, one does all one can to seem established there already.*

—FRANÇOIS, DUC DE LA ROCHEFOUCAULD

*My whole life has been spent waiting for an epiphany, a manifestation of God's presence, the kind of transcendent, magical experience that lets you see your place in the big picture. And that is what I had with my first compost heap.*

—BETTE MIDLER

*More snow, some rain, lots of sun, and our world will dance a greening jig. . . . Snipe song ripples through the sky. Spring comes again fresh-faced and welcoming. . . . I sense the atmosphere hanging on life's balanced scale, ready to tip into full spring with the weight of one more robin, one more blooming pasqueflower.*

—LAURIE WAGNER BUYER

## APRIL 13

*Whether consciously or unconsciously, like the tides, we are always leaving, and always going home, leaving invisible strands of connection behind.*

—LESLIE VAN GELDER

It's spring-beautiful here, and I always hate to leave Meadow Knoll in April. But this year, the book travel is all in-state, broken into several short trips with time at home between—nothing like the marathon five-week tour I did two years ago or last year's three-week tour of the Southwest. The first trip, just three events, four days: Brownwood, Abilene, Dallas, and home.

Before I leave, Bill hands me a sheaf of tax forms and a pen—the end of an active process that's been on his desk for several months. Even with the computer tax program he uses, the taxes take days of work, and we both feel better when the forms are signed and on their way to somebody else's desk.

## APRIL 14

*Journeyer: one who whirls through Other worlds, Spinning/Spiraling on multidimensional Voyages through Realms of the Wild, which involve Quests, adventurous Travel, the Dispelling of demons, cosmic encounters, participations in Paradise.*

—MARY DALY

Nomad thoughts on a bright, breezy spring morning when everything—clouds, trees, birds, cows, even a small brisk dog trotting along the road—seems on the move.

Got here (Brownwood, Texas, 110 miles west of home) about noon. The event is in the community center, and the ladies from the garden club (the sponsor of today's event) pitched in to help me set up the book sale table. The host group set out refreshments—food made from recipes in the mysteries (always great fun, and a compliment)— and we munched and chatted until time for my talk, with questions afterward. Fifty-two people, and much, much, much more fun than a bookstore event.

Then I headed off for my motel, where I had a salad for supper, a steamy bath, and settled in for an evening's reading: James Howard Kunstler's *World Made by Hand*, a novel about a post-oil, post-apocalyptic world. Not exactly the happiest kind of reading. But the story and the characters draw me strongly into the world of the novel, which is exactly what Kunstler wants to do. The book (which I read about in a review in *Orion*) is a polemic about the end of the oil age. Environmental writer Bill McKibben, in a back cover endorsement, says that the coming of peak oil means that the story may not be "entirely fictional much longer."

The trips this month are a mix: events where I bring books for sale and events where the host or a local bookstore handles the sales. Today, here in Brownwood, I sold books for Story Circle. Tomorrow, at the Abilene library, a local bookstore will handle the sales. All I have to do is talk, field questions.

A beautiful morning for driving, a short trip this time, a hundred miles from Brownwood to Abilene. There's been plenty of rain here, obviously. Bluebonnets, paintbrush, primroses, yellow daisies decorate the roadside. The grass is lush, the tanks are full, and the animals—cows, sheep, goats—are sleek and fat, beautiful. Wanting to know more about the subprime mess, I'm listening to a reading of Charles Morris' *The Trillion Dollar Meltdown*. Sounds like things are going to get a whole lot worse before they get very much better. Interesting. This book has just been published, but it was written over the two previous years. The author could see the problems created by subprime lending and predict their effect on major financial institutions like Bear Stearns. Why was everyone else so utterly blind?

At the library, sixty-some people for a sandwich-and-cookies lunch. The library book club has read a couple of the books. Nice, because people could ask informed questions. Gave a talk, answered questions, signed books, chatted with readers, then drove across town to the hotel, arriving in time for a nap, then a phone call to Bill.

When we're apart, we try to keep in touch several times a day, since unexpected things crop up. A for-instance: the new three-book contract arrived today, but the payout schedule isn't what we agreed to. Bill is our agent, so he'll deal with it, but he wants to be sure that I understand our options. The rest of the conversation is homey, husband-wife stuff. I tell him about the library turnout and the talk and the book sale; he tells me what he did all day (mowing, cutting trees). He's having a pizza for supper. There's nothing on my schedule for this evening: dinner is another salad, my standard on-the-road food fare. I resist the temptation to indulge in big meals on the road. Too much unhealthy food, too many extra pounds.

Nice to have the time alone. Bill and I live in one another's pockets as it is, and being apart gives us both a welcome break. Long trips are a challenge (getting older, I sometimes find it hard to keep going all day without a break), but these short trips can be a mini-vacation, almost. A comfortable hotel room; a book; a knitting project (Christmas socks for son Michael, he of the big feet); and these notes, which I'm making on my AlphaSmart, a smart keyboard that stores text for uploading to my desktop computer. It's smaller and lighter than a laptop and does everything I need it to do, on four AA batteries that never seem to run out of juice, all compliments of the oil industry.

Because, yes, the AlphaSmart and its batteries are manufactured with oil products, like the furniture in the room around me, and like almost every other thing I've come in contact with today—thoughts

*Where I am going I have never been before. And since I have no destination that I know, where I am going is always where I am. When I come to good resting places, I rest. I rest whether I am tired or not because the places are good. Each one is an arrival. I am where I have been going.*

—WENDELL BERRY

inspired by Kunstler's novel and the other disquieting books I've been reading.

It's not even nine o'clock when I run out of juice myself and fall asleep with the light on.

## APRIL 16

Up early to drive to Fort Worth, a hundred miles east of Abilene. Two events today: lunch at Texas Christian University, evening talk at Barnes & Noble.

A friend, another author, is about to launch a ten-day tour of ten major cities. Goes like this: get on a plane, get picked up at the airport by an escort and driven to the bookstore and the hotel, then back to the airport. Rinse and repeat. I've done that, and it's no fun. Too rushed, not personal enough, and it doesn't take me to places where my readers like to gather: libraries, women's clubs, garden groups. Not to mention that a ten-city tour involves at least eleven airplane flights, some percentage of which are bound to be late. When (if) you get where you're going, you're scheduled so tightly that all you see is the inside of the bookstore—a lovely place, a delightful place, when you have the time to browse. On that kind of tour, you don't have time.

That's not the way I like to do it. I'd rather choose my own venues, make my own schedule, and drive myself, listening to an audiobook and enjoying the view. This morning, magnificent colors across the Texas landscape: chartreuse mesquite, dark green cedars, drifts of primroses like pillows of pink snow along the highway. This afternoon, there was time to drop in at the nearby botanical garden. This evening, the bookstore event, a good turnout.

I need to get on the road earlier tomorrow. It's four hours home, and I need to be there by mid-morning. Bill wants to drive to Marble Falls to get roofing material to repair the front porch roof. Our truck is older than our marriage. One of us doesn't set off in it unless the other one is available at the other end of the phone, in case the truck quits before it gets where it's going.

Speaking of going. I'll be home just long enough to hug my husband, pet the dogs, do the laundry, deal with the e-mail, and cook a couple of meals. Day after tomorrow, South Texas.

NEWS SUMMARY: *The nation's housing market continues to deteriorate. Foreclosure filings jumped 57 percent in March compared with the same month last year. Compared to March 2007, the number of homes repossessed by banks are up 129 percent.*

## APRIL 18

I'm sitting on a fourth-floor balcony looking north along the dunes on the beach of South Padre Island, watching a big surf foaming onto empty sands, twilight falling. I'm here to do a couple of library talks, tomorrow morning, afternoon. This evening: drinks and dinner with two librarians and the president of the local library board—interesting, energizing talk about reaching readers, creating community, involving authors. Librarians are terrific people, absolutely dedicated.

Barbara Kingsolver once wrote that she wanted to embrace "every living librarian who crosses my path, on behalf of the souls they never knew they saved." True for me, too. My soul has been saved, over and over, through books, beginning when I was young and in dire need of salvation. The only books available to me were in libraries, and librarians held the key, literally. Now, I rely less on libraries, but more than ever on books. I *am* what I read, and the reading I'm doing these days—significant stuff, tough stuff, on climate change, energy depletion, the economy—is changing me. Not into a happier person, certainly. (What's to be happy about the human role in climate change? Nobody can be glad that we've squandered so many of the earth's resources.) But into someone better informed. Which counts for something. Maybe.

The sun is coasting down a cloudless sky, dropping fast into the Laguna Madre, the narrow strip of water on the western, mainland side of this barrier island. A flotilla of antic kites rides the breeze like chips of bright confetti. A trio of brown pelicans, buoyed on the stiff inshore wind, silently, solemnly patrols the air space above the beach. The breaking surf is a constant roar, punctuated by the shrill, peremptory cries of watchful gulls. The smell of salt air, windows open to the sound of the sea. Reading: *A Voice in the Wilderness*, a collection of conversations with Terry Tempest Williams.

## APRIL 19

Bright, high clouds, brisk onshore breeze, temperature in the low sixties. I don't see beaches every day, or the ocean, or pelicans, so I'm up early and out on the sandy beach, looking as hard as I can.

When I first visited this island some thirty years ago, the sand was

*As a child, my number one best friend was the librarian in my grade school. I actually believed all those books belonged to her.*

—ERMA BOMBECK

*To me, writing is about how we see. The writers I want to read teach me how to see—see the world differently. In my writing there is no separation between how I observe the world and how I write the world. We write through our eyes. We write through our body. We write out of what we know.*

—TERRY TEMPEST WILLIAMS

a blinding white. Now, it's stained with residual oil and the high tides strand shoals of human trash along with shells, seaweed, driftwood. But the walk along the empty early morning beach is as I remember it: an orange-red sun rising out of a ceaselessly moving ocean; gangs of sandpipers and sanderlings darting along the strand line; choirs of terns and gulls, sedately meditative; the constant, beating, foaming rush of the surf.

But I'm not alone. Comes a gray-bearded man riding along the sand on a red ATV with a plastic crate lashed to the rear and a sign: TURTLE PATROL. Later, I learn from a lady at the Friends of the Library brunch that the turtle patrolman was her husband, looking for loggerhead turtles, sea turtles, green turtles, and the endangered Kemp's Ridley. These native turtles are laying their eggs now: if he finds a nest, he gathers the eggs and takes them to safe harbor. If he finds an injured or sick turtle, he takes it to turtle rescue/rehab, where it is cared for and released into the Gulf. A good Samaritan for turtles.

South Padre Island, the cut-off tip of the longer Padre Island, is three miles wide, thirty-four miles long. The northern section, empty, wild, is covered with sand dunes, some actively on the move, others moored by grass and beach shrubs. The southern part is heavily, depressingly developed—hotels, restaurants, gift shops, multi-story condos.

In the 1970s, when I first came to South Padre to fish, the development was still primitive: picturesque wood frame beach cottages, a handful of restaurants and shops, and two hotels, the tallest just three stories. The cottages are gone now. Luxurious condos have sprouted in their places, and the hotels rise to twelve stories or more, with taller construction underway. The main access road thrusts ten miles north up the middle of the island, and for-sale signs stud the wild dunes. A park affords public access to several miles of narrow beach, but this fragile, wind-sculpted wildness is fast disappearing.

The growing mortgage crisis is injuring many homeowners, and I am deeply sorry for their pain. But as I survey what's happened here—and think about what's happening all over America—I can't help feeling profoundly glad for anything that slows this frantic development. There are too many houses in places where houses don't belong. Too many huge houses that use too much of our limited resources for construction, for heating and cooling. Too many *expensive* houses—not houses to live in but to display the owner's wealth and status.

The only way I can enjoy the ocean here is to turn away from what humans have done to the land, choose not to see it, not to think about it, not to put it into words. But that doesn't work, either. I can't turn my back on the earth: if I do, there's nothing left to turn toward.

We have to look at everything, the beautiful, the ugly. We have to *see* it. We have to bear witness.


## APRIL 21

Glad to be home again, doing everyday chores, catching up on the mail and e-mail. Reading another unsettling book about energy depletion. This one is probably the most influential, the one that looks hard at actual and potential production: Matthew Simmons' *Twilight in the Desert: The Coming Saudi Oil Shock and the World Economy*. It's technical and difficult, and I'm grateful for the college courses I took for my geology minor. I know just enough to appreciate the research behind Simmons' book, which argues that Saudi oil production is likely to peak soon or has peaked already, just as U.S. oil production peaked in 1970. And Saudi oil accounts for nearly 10 percent of the global oil supply.

Simmons has credibility: he's an oil industry insider, was a member of Cheney's Energy Task Force. If he spoke his piece there, it's no wonder that the Bush administration won't allow Task Force documents to be made public. This oil-allied administration (Bush's oil wells, Cheney's Halliburton ties) has a vested interest in pushing over-consumption. But no administration—Republican or Democrat—could warn the public about diminishing oil supplies without sending the markets into a death spiral. We're not supposed to discover that cheap oil is not an infinite resource. We're supposed to use it, use as much of it as possible, use all of it, use it until it's gone, all gone—or costs so much to produce that it's out of reach of ordinary people.

And then what?


## APRIL 22

The roses are blooming, courtesy of that severe pruning a couple of months ago. The deer like them, too, unfortunately, and the population of our native whitetails is growing. I don't want to fence the rose garden because it borders the walk from the driveway to the house, and anything tall enough to deter deer would be unsightly. Guess I'll have to resort to other means. Spraying the leaves with garlic and cayenne might work.

*What will happen to our global society if (or when?) legitimate, empowered oil demand begins to exceed available supplies on a regular basis by 2 or 5 percent? Unless we carefully formulate and swiftly adopt a plan to use oil in increasingly less intensive ways . . . The world could find itself on a precarious global tipping point between peaceful prosperity and an era of sinister conflict.*

—MATTHEW SIMMONS

*Taking the living earth seriously means taking seriously our responsibility to protect her skin. Estimates for Nature to grow one inch of topsoil range from thirty to one thousand years, although any ardent earth-tender knows she can do much better than even the low figure by providing more food to the army of organisms that generate humus from waste. Which is why we help Nature along.*

—JOAN DYE GUSSOW

My major outdoor project right now: compost for the fall vegetable garden. Manure (generously contributed by Blossom, Texas, and Mutton), layered with green clippings from Bill's late spring mowing, dried grass from last fall's mowing, kitchen refuse, dog hair (contributed by Zach, Lady, and Toro), and human urine (contributed by Susan and Bill). A family enterprise. The compost should be fully cooked and ready to serve up to the garden by September. Unfinished compost will go into another pile to rot until spring.

There's not much I can do about peak oil and climate change, except cut back on our uses of energy. But I can make compost, and compost makes food. I like Joan Dye Gussow's description of herself in *This Organic Life*: "an ardent earth-tender." I like that. I'll think of myself as ardently tending the earth.

*A good compost pile should get hot enough to poach an egg, but not so hot it would cook a lobster.*

*—ANON.*

## APRIL 23

*To discover our true address, we will have to stay off the interstates, avoid the friendly franchises, climb out of our cars, hunt up guides who have lived heedfully in place, and we will have to walk around with eyes and ears open to the neighborhood.*

*—SCOTT RUSSELL SANDERS*

On the road again. Tonight, I'm speaking at the library in Columbus, halfway between San Antonio and Houston. The town was founded in 1835, just a few months before the defeat at the Alamo and the massacre at Goliad. The hapless settlers, squeezed between the victorious Mexicans and the vanquished Texans, made a break for it and didn't return home until Sam Houston's army defeated the Mexicans at San Jacinto in April 1836. The county voted for secession in 1861: this was tobacco and cotton country and most of the farmers owned slaves. In the decades after the war, cattle became the cash crop, then rice, finally oil and gas. Now the community celebrates "heritage tourism," featuring an ornate Victorian mansion, the opera house, and other buildings built by previous booms. I'm told that all you have to do is turn on your radio, drive past the historic site, and listen to a prerecorded message.

Local history is vitally important, yes. But sound bites of "heritage tourism," delivered to your car like a cheeseburger and fries from Sonic—this runs the risk of trivializing both past and place, glossing them over, turning them into entertainment for people who want to grab a quick bite of Texas history on the interstate between Houston and San Antonio. Not quite a theme park, but something like it.

NEWS SUMMARY: *The Pennsylvania Democratic primary was won by Hillary Clinton. Financial sector bad news continues, with Citigroup, other major banks facing huge losses. The Senate passed a bill designed to help homeowners faced with foreclosure.*

APRIL 24

A full house at the Columbus library last night, fifty-some people. I like to talk to a responsive audience, and last night's group was enthusiastic.

Next stop, Conroe (about sixty miles north of Houston) and the Texas Master Gardeners Conference, a two-day affair at the convention center.

APRIL 25

I was astonished at the number of people who came to the master gardeners conference—more than six hundred. I talked about Shaker herbs to a group of nearly a hundred and astrological herbalism to another, smaller group. Did a good job with the Shaker material; it has a strong story line and is easy to handle. But the second presentation (on the seventeenth-century herbalist/astrologer Nicholas Culpeper) was complex and dense, and there's almost no story line at all, just facts. I don't think I'll offer that topic again. And not right after lunch. Maybe if I had brought in a half-dozen dancing girls . . .

Astounding, the construction going on here, north of Houston. Malls, office parks, vast enclaves of expensive homes artfully snugged into master-planned communities, the entire landscape reconfigured, reconstructed, manufactured. Few signs of economic downturn here. But this is the Oil Patch, where oil is next to godliness. And the price of a barrel of oil is sharply up, which translates into new construction—at least for now.

Somebody invited me to a party this evening, but I'm spending the evening in my hotel room, rereading a collection of essays by Gary Snyder, *The Practice of the Wild*. And knitting: more socks.

It's islands of quiet that keep me going on a trip like this, with multiple events on most days. And I'm bone tired. I think that's the aspect of aging that disturbs me most. Once upon a time, I could teach all day, give a dinner talk, follow it up with a party. Looking back over those years, I think I expended too much energy in doing things that didn't count for much in the long run. Now, an evening's quiet is bliss.

*Our place is part of what we are. Yet even a "place" has a kind of fluidity: it passes through space and time. . . . A place will have been grasslands, then conifers, then beech and elm. It will have been half riverbed, it will have been scratched and plowed by ice. And then it will be cultivated, paved, sprayed, dammed, graded, built up. But each is only for a while, and that will be just another set of lines on the palimpsest. The whole earth is a great tablet holding the multiple overlaid new and ancient traces of the swirl of forces. Each place is its own place, forever (eventually) wild.*

—GARY SNYDER

To find your own way is to follow your bliss. This involves analysis, watching yourself and seeing where real deep bliss is—not the quick little excitement, but the real deep, life-filling bliss.

—JOSEPH CAMPBELL

Suppose it is not possible to be lost, and that feeling lost is simply an interpretation of how I do not know where I am. Suppose that you are right here where you are.

—DIANNE CONNELLY

Grrrr. Lost the folder that had detailed directions to today's event in Houston. But I remembered the map well enough to navigate the labyrinthine nightmare of freeways to the Garden Center at Hermann Park. To my vast surprise, I managed to arrive at the right place, at the right time for lunch with the South Texas Unit of the Herb Association of America. Lucia Bettler, an energetic, bubbly woman with a great love of travel and the arts, sold books at the lunch. Lucia owns and manages Lucia's Garden, an herb shop in Houston, and also teaches cooking classes and offers workshops, reads, and writes— one of my models for the character of China Bayles.

I took some time to admire the rose garden (would've stayed longer but the sun was blistering, the humidity wilting), then drove to Murder by the Book. I've visited this mystery bookstore at least once a year for the past sixteen years, and I always look forward to it. David Thompson and the gang make it fun, with wine and good fellowship.

One thing I don't worry about on these book trips: clothes. I learned a long time ago that I don't need—and definitely don't want—to look "glamorous." A couple of pairs of jeans, two or three colored tees, a khaki jacket for dress-up, a couple of roll-sleeve blue denim big shirts. That's it: like it or lump it. I have enough to do with driving myself to the event; delivering an interesting talk (funny, when I can manage it); selling books if necessary (involves packing, hauling, and minding the cash); and driving myself back to the hotel.

Clothes and hair are the least of my worries. What you see is what you get.

## APRIL 27

Now in Tomball, a suburb thirty-plus miles northwest of Houston, for a Sunday signing at Arbor Gate Nursery. Another hugely built-up area. This was once Texas coastal prairie—abundant rainfall, fertile soil, rich in acres of native grasses. Also rich in oil. The first gusher came in here in 1933. For a half century, Humble Oil gave the town's citizens all the free gasoline they could pump in exchange for drilling rights. The oil is depleted here (as elsewhere in this region). The grasses are gone, too. In their place: thousands of acres of tract homes.

Woke up this morning to a fifteen-degree temperature drop, wind sweeping down from the plains, moisture streaming up from the Gulf. I expected a rainout at Arbor Gate, but enjoyed a dry (if windy) afternoon with plenty of garden shopper traffic. One gal drove all the way from Richmond—a great compliment, given the ferocity of Houston traffic. Beverly (the nursery's owner) sold out of *Nightshade* and most of the other titles. As a thank-you, she gave me a basket of plants for my herb garden. Basil, a couple of varieties of thyme, sage, and pineapple mint, some catnip for our cat, and two pots of parsley, enough to get me through the summer.

An evening's unquiet reading: the latest of Richard Heinberg's books on resource depletions—*Peak Everything: Waking Up to the Century of Declines*. We are just beginning to glimpse the planet's limits and our own, Heinberg says, an awakening that "entails an emotional, cultural, and political catharsis. . . . [W]aking up implies realizing that the very fabric of modern life is woven from illusion—thousands of illusions, in fact."

Depletion, decline, limitation—these are hard sells to a nation of people who are used to an infinite abundance of everything, to the idea of limitless progress, infinite possibility. It's time to learn to live within limits.

In the midst of this unsettling reading and thinking, parsley, thyme, and sage seem extraordinarily comforting. And I have a day off tomorrow—although not really "off." Have to drive into Houston, to Murder by the Book, and pick up a box of *Nightshade*. Don't have enough left for the last two events on the schedule.

*[T]he problem of our dependence on fossil fuels is central to human survival, and so long as that dependence continues to any significant extent we must make its reduction the centerpiece of all our collective efforts—whether they are efforts to feed ourselves, resolve conflicts, or maintain a functioning economy.*

—RICHARD HEINBERG

## APRIL 29

An exhausting day today, two events, and now, after 10 p.m., I think: I am getting too old for this. I've caught a bad cold—occupational hazard on book tour, where people are constantly sneezing on you. Runny nose, very sore throat. Had a luncheon at Blinn College in Brenham; a dinner with the Friends of the Library in Angleton. Both events were large—60 at the luncheon, 160 at the dinner. Enthusiastic listeners, laughed in the right places, bought lots of books.

Tomorrow, a five-hour drive home. I'm ready, more than ready, to settle down to the next writing project. But before that, house cleaning and gardening. The prospect of both (like parsley and thyme) seems extraordinarily comforting.

*It just may be that the most radical act we can commit is to stay home. Otherwise, who will be there to chart the changes? Who will be able to tell us if the long-billed curlews have returned to the grassy vales of Promontory, Utah? Who will be there to utter the cry of loss when the salmon of the McKenzie River in Oregon are nowhere to be seen?*

—TERRY TEMPEST WILLIAMS

Home again, to Bill (bless him for his patience), three dear dogs (all of whom need a bath), and the cat (who has to relinquish her sleeping spot on my pillow). Only one more book event this spring, in mid-May. So I can lay aside these travel tales, these side trips, and get on with my own at-home story, the central story of my life, the story I inhabit and that inhabits me, that holds the key to all my paradigms and maps and imaginings of myself.

But the travel is undeniably important, too: there is no coming home without going away. And when I go elsewhere, see what is to be seen and reflect on what it means—to the people who live there, to those traveling through, to the land—I come home all the gladder.

## April Reading and Listening

*How to Grow More Vegetables (and Fruits, Nuts, Berries, Grains, and Other Crops) Than You Ever Thought Possible on Less Land Than You Can Imagine,* by John Jeavons

*A Naturalist Buys an Old Farm,* by Edwin Way Teale

*Peak Everything: Waking Up to the Century of Declines,* by Richard Heinberg

*The Practice of the Wild,* by Gary Snyder

*Spring's Edge: A Ranch Wife's Chronicles,* by Laurie Wagner Buyer

*The Trillion Dollar Meltdown: Easy Money, High Rollers, and the Great Credit Crash,* by Charles Morris

*Twilight in the Desert: The Coming Saudi Oil Shock and the World Economy,* by Matthew Simmons

*A Voice in the Wilderness: Conversations with Terry Tempest Williams,* by Michael Austin

*World Made by Hand: A Novel,* by James Howard Kunstler

*The World Without Us,* by Alan Weisman

*Writing from the Center,* by Scott Russell Sanders

| JANUARY | FEBRUARY | MARCH | APRIL |
|---------|----------|-------|-------|
| **MAY** | JUNE | JULY | AUGUST |
| SEPTEMBER | OCTOBER | NOVEMBER | DECEMBER |

## MAY 1

Paradigms, maps, and stories: mine are changing, shifting shape. Who would have thought that in my sixty-ninth year I would encounter such a radically challenging, existentially life-changing set of ideas? Not that I thought I knew everything—by no means. But I'm expensively educated (a huge expense of time, if not of money), insatiably curious, an avid reader. If somebody spills words on a page, I'll read them. Climate change isn't new to me, but you'd think I would've bumped into "peak oil" before this year.

Maybe I'm not too far behind the curve, though. The issue of dwindling reserves of cheap, easy-to-get fossil fuels is only just now creeping into the national consciousness, spurred by the current sharp spike in gasoline prices (pushing four dollars a gallon this week). There's a growing assemblage of Web sites, blogs, and books on the subject. Even CNN has been paying attention, with a special last year called "We Were Warned: Tomorrow's Oil Crisis," featuring Matthew Simmons and other peak oil proponents who argue that we're fast approaching—say, in the next five or six years—the peak of accessible, relatively cheap oil. After that, we'll see a growing gap between what we want and what we can get. Or pay for.

But why has it taken so long for us to get to this point? Marion Hubbert came up with the peak oil theory in the late 1950s, and it's been known for decades that America's oil peaked in 1970.

One answer: the oil industry (backed by eight years of the Bush-Cheney administration) has actively suppressed any discussion of energy shortages (except to encourage more drilling) and disavowed any connection to climate change.

*In 1859 the human race discovered a huge treasure chest in its basement. This was oil and gas, a fantastically cheap and easily available source of energy. We did, or at least some of us did, what anybody does who discovers a treasure in the basement—live it up.*

—KENNETH E. BOULDING

*No problem can be solved from the same level of consciousness that created it.*

—ALBERT EINSTEIN

Another answer: Americans live in a culture of denial, fed by cornucopia thinking and exceptionalism. The earth is endlessly abundant, given by God to us to use, spend, waste as we please. Since this is true, divinity will arrange to bail us out. Science will come up with something. And if the obstructionist environmentalists will just go away, we'll find huge oil fields offshore and in the Arctic and we can forget about the problem for another half-century.

A third: Pain and the avoidance thereof. The truth hurts—if not us, then our children and grandchildren, whose standard of living will be substantially lowered (measured by cheap power, easy travel, exotic food) as fossil fuels become expensive or unobtainable.

Since January, Bill and I have been systematically reading the major books about energy depletion and talking about this idea, which intersects with other long-held ideas. For me, the intersecting idea is climate change; for Bill (who decided decades ago not to father children), it's population growth. The planet, he says, is being emptied of everything but human beings.

This is a major issue for us—for Bill and me—and we're starting to take it into account as we think about our own long-term planning. Except that we're not sure what to plan for, or when. Maybe the energy situation will be stable through another decade? Maybe through our lifetimes? Who knows? But the time we live in now, as Churchill said in a different (but equally ominous) context, is a period of consequences.

It doesn't matter that I am just one person, or that we are just one household, or that we don't believe that it—whatever *it* is—will happen tomorrow. There's the Theory of Anyway. We have to do what we can. And what I know, and can do, has to do with food.


MAY 2


So. Gardens. I've been walking around the area I'm returning to garden and thinking about what this garden is, how it's different from vegetable gardens I've had in the past.

This isn't a garden that will feed us this year, although we'll certainly eat everything that grows in it. It's an "R & D" garden, an experimental plot. It's a place to learn what vegetables and varieties will grow in this climate, this soil. (Which means keeping better records than I have in the past.) It's an organic garden, with no chemical inputs, with as few inputs, in general, as possible. A sustainable garden, with open-pollinated plants that will reproduce their own seeds—as opposed to hybrids that don't "come true" or that grow from the brain of a plant geneticist. I've always saved annual flower seeds—marigolds, zinnias, nasturtiums. Now I'm getting serious about saving vegetable seeds.

MAY 3

Bill has been studying our electrical bills and thinks we can save money—the "connect" charge of $20 a month, $240 a year—by rerouting the wiring in the two boxes on the utility pole into a single box. Having two boxes is a historical anomaly that dates back to 1995, when we put Serenity here. Looking back, he calculates that we could have saved more than $3,000 if we had set it up differently. I point out that if we stay here another thirteen years (we'll be here longer, I hope), the rewiring will save us $3,000. We'll break even. He's doing the work tomorrow.

MAY 4

The rewiring was successful, with only an hour's power outage—just long enough for me to make a list of all the things I use electricity for and imagine how much I'd miss it if it went away. Not a pleasant thought.

MAY 5

Lady is gone.

She had a stroke this morning, couldn't walk, couldn't move. The vet put her to sleep in mid-afternoon. I'm bereft, although I'm glad that she's no longer in any discomfort and that the end came so easily. She was always a no-fuss dog.

Lady was three or thereabouts when we got her from the Heart of Texas Lab Rescue. Like all of us, she had her personality quirks. She could hear thunder fifty miles away and began quivering long before storm clouds appeared on the horizon. She loved mealtime, inhaling her food in a flash and then begging Zach and Toro to let her finish theirs. If they were distracted by a fly on the window or the cat coming in, she'd snatch their food. She could demolish chew sticks and pigs' ears faster than we could dole them out.

Lady was accomplished in other ways. She swam like a seal, and if she accidentally got out without a leash or an escort, the lake was the first place we looked. In her early days, before arthritis stole her mobility, she was a champion tennis-ball-and-Frisbee hound. In the house, she was docile and quiet and somehow I always expected her bark to be . . . well, lady-like. It wasn't. It was deep, rich, and authoritative, although she didn't use it often. And she could howl, oh, could she howl! The wildest, most primitive wolf howl—always in her sleep, in the middle of the night. It struck me with terror, that howl, and I would sit up straight in bed with my heart in my mouth, wondering what horrors she had lived through before she came to us and was reliving at night in her dreams.

I once read that we rehearse our own death in every other death we meet. In Lady's, I see an image of my own, and hope it will be as easy.

MAY 6

The yellow flags are blooming along the creek, bold brushstrokes, bright, bright gold among the dark green ferns. They're also wickedly invasive and I'm chagrined at my carelessness: giving them a home where they could flourish without restraint. But it's impossible to get rid of them without resorting to draconian measures. And they are so stunning—sunshine in a blossom—that my distress is mixed with admiration.

The yellow flag has a long history as a healing herb. John Gerard wrote around 1690: "The root, boiled soft, with a few drops of rosewater upon it, laid plaisterwise upon the face of man or woman, doth in two daies at the most take away the blacknesse and blewnesse of any stroke or bruise."

I don't know about black-and-blue bruises, but the sight of the flowers help (a little, plaisterwise) to heal the bruise of losing Lady.

MAY 7

Today, received Molly O'Halloran's first-draft maps for *Together, Alone*. Careful, accurate, artistic, perfect for the book. Looking at them is like looking at photographs, artful images of a place you know well and love deeply, seen and recorded through someone else's eyes. It's the place I know, and yet it's not. A real place, yet it's an imaginary landscape—as the memoir itself is. An imagination of real experiences, a constructed story, but true.

*You have been my friend. That in itself is a tremendous thing. I wove my webs for you because I liked you. After all, what's a life, anyway? We're born, we live a little while, we die. A spider's life can't help being something of a mess, with all this trapping and eating flies. By helping you, perhaps I was trying to lift up my life a trifle. Heaven knows anyone's life can stand a little of that.*

—E. B. WHITE,
*CHARLOTTE'S WEB*

*What I know, finally, and can't shake loose from, is that the bubble breaks for all of us. For me. The beauty of things will go on, but I will not be alive to witness it. When other lives rise on what I was, the familiar light of my awareness will not rise with them. I who hold the world in mind will then be held in the world, without a mind, lost in what I once looked upon.*

—JOHN DANIEL

Reading Sue Bender's *Everyday Sacred: A Woman's Journey Home,* for Reading Circle next week. The book is about the Zen monk's begging bowl, empty, waiting to be filled, as we all are, by experience. Not as complex or subtle a book as I might have wished. Its bowl was hardly empty, though. In 1996, when the book appeared, the publisher laid out a cool $100,000 in ad promotions. Interesting irony here.

## MAY 8

The fall garden is on my mind, but I'm at the desk, working on the sixth Beatrix Potter mystery, *The Tale of Applebeck Orchard.* I began making notes on the book in March and am now trying to pull a story thread out of a knotty tangle of ideas. This is made more difficult by the fact that, while there's a great deal of fantasy in these books (talking animals and even a dragon), there is also a certain amount of reality, and I owe it to Miss Potter to represent her life and the energetic, creative way she lived it as fairly as I can.

So here I sit, surrounded by shelves and stacks of books, including Beatrix's children's books, her journal, her letters. Biographies by Linda Lear (*Beatrix Potter: A Life in Nature*) and Judy Taylor and Margaret Lane. Susan Denyer's *At Home with Beatrix Potter,* with absolutely wonderful photographs and details of the interior of Hill Top Farm. *A History of the Writings of Beatrix Potter* by Leslie Linder, which clarifies the publishing history of the "little books." *A Natural History of the Lake District,* rich with information about the fells, the dales, the lakes, the animals, the birds, the sheep.

The plan for the book is still foggy. But in another couple of months, as I write, read, think, the story lines will come clear, the characters will reveal themselves in all their glory or greed or knavery or kindheartedness, and I will be able to look at what I've written and enjoy it. Not yet. But soon. By the end of August, anyway, which is when the book is due.

## MAY 9

Bill leaves today for a couple of weeks in New Mexico. He planned to go in March but was delayed, and then April came, and he had to be here while I was out and about, doing book talks. Now he'll get some good time to himself out there, working on wood-turning projects in his basement shop. Time apart is good for us—is *necessary* for us.

The Honda minivan he's driving on this trip gets about twenty-three miles a gallon. Thirteen hundred miles there and back (about the same distance I drove last month on my Texas tour), fifty-six gallons, with gas at $3.70—although it's not the cost we're thinking of, it's the consumption.

Discussing this, we remind ourselves that except for book travel and trips to New Mexico, we normally don't drive more than 60 miles a week, compared to the average American weekly commute of 160 miles. A justification? A rationalization?

Then, once again (this is a continuing discussion), we debate the wisdom of having a second house. But both houses are small (together, they are about the size of the average American home) and energy efficient (together, both houses use about half the kilowatt hours consumed by the average American household). Both are mortgage free. More justification? Another rationalization?

The fact that we're thinking and talking about this is evidence that we're in the middle of a substantial paradigm shift. We've built our life around working from home. We've always been frugal. We've always tried to live lightly.

But this is no longer life as usual. Not even life as we lived it just a year ago.

*[T]here can be no health for humans and cities that bypasses the rest of nature. A properly radical environmentalist position is in no way anti-human. We grasp the pain of the human condition in its full complexity, and add the awareness of how desperately endangered certain key species and habitats have become. . . . A culture of wilderness starts somewhere in this terrain. Civilization is part of nature . . . and our souls are out in the wilderness.*

—GARY SNYDER

MAY 11

Not quite through with book travel, although now I'm measuring every mile. This week, I drove (two hundred miles round trip) to Winedale, near Round Top, between Houston and San Antonio. Winedale is a complex of historical structures and modern facilities on 225 acres of wooded countryside. I first went there in the 1970s as a young UT English professor, helping with the Shakespeare at Winedale program. Fun to go back yesterday to a meeting of the Pioneer Unit of the Herb Society of America, where I spoke about the nightshade plant family.

Henry Flowers, the botanist who manages the gardens at nearby Festival Hill, brought an extensive, impressive display of nightshades. Chile peppers, tomatoes, tomatillos, eggplant (the "mad apple" it was called—Europeans were afraid of nightshades and thought they were all poisonous). He also brought a petunia, a nicotiana, and a few other nightshade ornamentals. Potatoes, of course, and a bottle of vodka, to demonstrate that sometimes we drink our nightshades. And a cigarette. Tobacco is a nightshade. Probably—in terms of the number of people it has killed and continues to kill—the deadliest of all plants.

The book travel may be finished for a few months, but book promotion goes on, and on, and on.

A couple of years ago, I came up with the idea for a free weekly herbal e-letter, "All About Thyme." This week, Peggy and I have been working on the May–June mailings. Each e-letter takes me seventy-five minutes or so: writing a short feature article, looking up links, choosing photos. I e-mail everything to Peggy to be formatted and coded. She sends it back, I make corrections, and she e-mails it to the list. The e-letter also contains links to my books (sneaky) and I regularly see a spike in book sales after it's mailed.

Today, Reading Circle in Austin. I'm a little surprised by the enthusiasm for *Everyday Sacred* and wonder what I missed. The group admires exactly what I found most disturbing about the book: Bender's habit of reducing everything—the most complex, intricate, ironic, paradoxical, contradictory—to the simplest level. To my mind, there's a great deal to be said for complexity, density, multiplicity, contradiction. For the multi-layeredness of experience. For including enough complexity in the writing so that the reader can at least trust that the writer herself perceives it.

MAY 13

*With all of the hysteria, all of the fear, all of the phony science, could it be that man-made global warming is the greatest hoax ever perpetrated on the American people? It sure sounds like it.*

—SENATOR JAMES M. INHOFE, 2003

Heat. A week of 100-degree days, constant sunshine. The grass is tinder-dry and we've had no measurable rain since the end of April. May is supposed to be our wettest month, but not this year. The forecast: dry and hot, hotter, hottest.

Air conditioning. I keep the thermostat at 80–82 degrees during the day, a little lower at night, and the new roof is making a difference. But the record-breaking heat has spiked local power consumption to record-breaking highs. We buy our electricity from the Pedernales Electrical Cooperative, which buys it from the Lower Colorado River Authority, which manages six hydroelectric units and four coal- and gas-fired power plants and imports wind-generated electricity from West Texas. More wind energy in the works: a $4-billion proposal for transmissions lines to be completed by 2013. Of course, any transmission line construction will encounter NIMBY opposition and resistance to imminent domain. And projects this large always take much longer than planned. 2020, maybe? In the meantime, will there be enough power to feed the plug-in Priuses and Volts that are coming online?

People talk about watersheds, foodsheds—is anybody talking about powersheds?

**NEWS SUMMARY:** *Tornadoes in Oklahoma and Missouri kill twenty-three. A huge cyclone devastates Myanmar (more than 80,000 dead, a million homeless). Earthquakes in China kill 70,000; 1.3 million downstream dwellers must relocate to escape the flood threat of "quake lakes."*

## MAY 15

The weather, the physical world—in the news this week and frightening, especially the horrible cyclone in Myanmar, its impacts immeasurably worsened by the political situation there, and the loss of so many schoolchildren in China, victims of shoddy building construction.

Here, the blistering heat has been broken, temporarily, by tornadic thunderstorms—two of them, one to the north of us, the other to the south. Don't know if I'm blessed or cursed by the ability to watch these storms on radar (on television and the computer), but there they were, in full color, from eight until midnight, with breathless reports from the weather gurus, tracking them mile by mesmerizing mile.

When things began to look seriously bad, I got ready to seek refuge in Archie Bunker, our storm shelter. Didn't have to. The tornadoes blew past Meadow Knoll and walloped Austin instead: major wind and hail damage. This morning, the local television featured photos of hailstones the size of golf balls, tennis balls, grapefruit. Here, a few downed limbs. That was it—this time.

We invested in Archie Bunker in 1997, after an F-5 tornado leveled part of Jarrell, about twenty-five miles northeast of us. Archie is a concrete box, eight feet by eight by eight with a narrow metal ladder and a metal door, buried in the ground and covered with a mound of earth and tangles of honeysuckle. We stage practice drills every now and then, but we've used it for real only once, on a stormy November evening when the sky was the color of a two-day-old bruise and the radar showed a tornadic thunderstorm with the characteristic "hook echo" the weather people talk about. That tornado missed us by fewer than three miles.

If things look dicey, I gather up my "tornado escape kit": purse, cell phone, the latest flash drive backup from my computer, jacket,

*All across the world, in every kind of environment and region known to man, increasingly dangerous weather patterns and devastating storms are abruptly putting an end to the long-running debate over whether or not climate change is real. Not only is it real, it's here, and its effects are giving rise to a frighteningly new global phenomenon: the man-made natural disaster.*

—BARACK OBAMA

flashlight, cat. Experience (oh, those drills) has proven that Zach, our sixty-five-pound Lab, will never go peaceably down that ladder: he bit Bill the last time we tried. I think I could carry Toro down (he weighs only about forty-five pounds), but I'd damn sure muzzle him first. Lady is no longer an issue, sadly. She hated it, too.

## MAY 16

Don't know whether to smile or cry. The sadly endangered polar bear has finally been listed as a "threatened species"—a belated acknowledgment by the Bush administration that the bear's habitat, in fact, the entire Arctic ecosystem, is melting away. Climate change, which the administration ignores. A criminal, intentional ignorance that our children and grandchildren—and thousands of species, our fellow inhabitants of the earth—will pay for, dearly.

*There will be no polar ice by 2060. . . . Somewhere along that path, the polar bear drops out.*

—LARRY SCHWEIGER, PRESIDENT, NATIONAL WILDLIFE FEDERATION

## MAY 18

*With me, a story usually begins with a single idea or memory or mental picture. The writing of the story is simply a matter of working up to that moment, to explain why it happened or what caused it to follow.*

—WILLIAM FAULKNER

Working on *Applebeck Orchard*. Have drafted a couple of opening scenes, one with a quartet of village animals, another with a pair of village women gossiping over the garden wall while they hang their Monday morning laundry. Both scenes set up the book's central questions: What happens when a farmer decides to close an important footpath that crosses his property? Why does he do it? What happens after that? Who cares? Why? What do they do? What happens next?

It's difficult for Americans to imagine how passionately the British people—especially the rural people—care about footpaths. We travel by roads (paved for autos) and walking is mostly recreational, but in the Lake District, in Beatrix Potter's day, people relied on the paths to walk to work, church, school. Beatrix—a conservationist and preservationist—served on a local footpath committee, ensuring that paths were kept open and that walkers did not abuse the privilege of crossing private lands. The topic is current, as I learned when I began the research. People are still fighting over access to footpaths today, sometimes for daily pedestrian traffic, often for access to what little "nature" is left.

Reading chapters in Lear's *Beatrix Potter: A Life in Nature*. And—for the flavor of the language, for the narrator's knowing and instructive voice, for sheer delight—*The Water-Babies* by Charles Kingsley, the quintessential Victorian children's fable.

When I first imagined the Cottage Tales, Bill and I were still writing our Victorian mysteries. I thought of the Beatrix Potter series in that context and expected to write the books in the same serious tone, with Beatrix as a younger, sprightlier version of the indomitable Miss Marple.

But a couple of chapters into the first book, something happened to change all that. In Beatrix's real life, in October of 1905, when she visited her newly purchased Hill Top Farm, she brought with her a hedgehog (Mrs. Tiggy-Winkle), two rabbits (Flopsy and Josey), and Tom Thumb, a mouse. I was writing a scene in which Beatrix is asleep, her animals in their baskets on the shelf. As I wrote, Mrs. Tiggy-Winkle started to talk, and the other animals joined in. I couldn't shut them up. It was like Luigi Pirandello's play, *Six Characters in Search of an Author*. These animals had a story. They were determined to tell it.

Well. I'm a fairly disciplined writer and I like to think I have a general idea where the story is going. Talking animals were not in my scheme. But I can recognize inspiration when it whacks me over the head. Wherever this idea came from, I wasn't going to tell it to go away.

But Mrs. Tiggy-Winkle and Tom Thumb are Beatrix Potter's characters, and her publisher, Frederick Warne, owns the copyrights. Normally, it would be difficult—or prohibitively expensive—to obtain a license to use the animals. But I was blessedly lucky, or just plain blessed. My publisher, Berkley Books, is owned by Penguin U.S.A., a sister company of Penguin U.K., which owns Frederick Warne. The Berkley lawyers got a license that permits me to use Beatrix's characters. In return, the manuscript and the cover art are read and approved by an editor at Frederick Warne in London—a doubly good thing since she catches most of my errors.

*"I am by nature dramatic" [said Mrs. Tiggy-Winkle]. "My book," she added smugly, bringing the conversation back to herself, "has my name on it. Unfortunately, it's about a silly old washerwoman." She raised the stiff prickles on her back until she looked like a brown clothes-brush. "I do so wish Miss Potter had drawn me as I really am. I am nothing at all like a washerwoman."*

*Josey [the rabbit] chuckled. "Tiggy would rather have been drawn as a duchess with a diamond tiara."*

*—THE TALE OF HILL TOP FARM*

The spirea is blooming, mounds of white blossoms spilling over the creek bank beside the footbridge. I love this plant for the wedding-white purity of its blossoms, the grace of its arching branches. And for its healing properties.

Spirea (like willow and meadowsweet) contains acetylsalicylic acid, the precursor of aspirin, as helpful as it is lovely. Nearby, along the creek, there's a chaste tree (*Vitex agnus-castus*), widely used to treat PMS, and a toothache tree (*Zanthoxylem hirsutum*), supposed to cure an aching tooth.

Standardized synthetic drugs are easier to use—you don't have to brew up a tea or a potion or worry about variable potencies. But I like knowing that these are here. In a pinch, if I had to use them, I could.

**NEWS SUMMARY:** *Barack Obama wins the Oregon primary, Hillary Clinton takes Kentucky. John Edwards endorses Obama, who holds a majority of pledged delegates to the Democratic convention and leads in the popular vote. Clinton stays in the race, despite projections that show she can't muster the votes.*

MAY 21

I'm taking temporary refuge in the writing, away from the tempests of the elections and pundit debates over Clinton's refusal to yield. But it's hard to escape because I'm invested in both Democratic candidates, and just about equally. This is a complex world. I don't accept everything the Dems are pushing, and the latest Dem president (what was his name? oh, yes, Clinton) was an unmitigated jerk who should've resigned and let Al Gore try his hand at governing. But in my lifetime, all sixty-nine years of it, Eisenhower was the only Republican president with real integrity. The Republican Middle has been hijacked by the Republican Right, and there never has been a Republican Left. No place for me in that camp.

I've seen too many elections, feel as though I've lived through an arid desert of presidential politics. In this election, I finally have a sense of hope, an oasis in the desert. Maybe.

MAY 22

Working on *Applebeck Orchard* every day now, from eight until noon, then a break for lunch, a few chores, and back to the book until four-thirty, when Zach and Toro remind me that it's time for their walk, which should naturally be followed by their dinner, and mine.

I'm not writing every minute of the time I'm at the computer, of course. I look things up in books or on the Internet, surf a few Web sites, reply to e-mails. Write. Get up from the computer and do the laundry, sweep the floor, take the dogs out. Then write again. I learned to write as a young mom with three kids, so I'm pretty good at multi-tasking.

The Cottage Tales are more research-intensive than the China Bayles books and the language is Victorian. More complex than slangy, modern English, it does not roll trippingly off my tongue. I have to work at making it sound both out-of-date and natural. I call it work, but it feels like play, most of the time. Playing with words, playing with ideas, characters, dialogue, story lines. Not always fun, but close enough.

*The thing about writers that people don't realize is that a lot of what they do is play. You know, playing around with. That doesn't mean that it isn't serious or that it doesn't have a serious meaning or a serious intention. But it's still play.*

—MARGARET ATWOOD

NEWS SUMMARY: *The number of initial unemployment claims rose by six thousand this week, while the number claiming benefits after their first week of aid hit a four-year high. "These numbers are not good news," said economist Kurt Karl. "We are in an elevated unemployment period because of tight credit, higher oil prices, inflation hurting consumers."*

MAY 23

Learned today that a friend in Maine has lost her job, another (California) has been laid off without any assurance of being rehired, a third (Illinois) given extra, unpaid "vacation." And two mid-list writer acquaintances have lost their contracts. I feel the way I did when I was watching Katrina. So inevitable, so unstoppable, so nothing-anyone-can-do. I wonder how many of us are feeling survivor's guilt.

In Bill's absence, this evening's meal is simpler than usual: sliced fresh zucchini, a fresh tomato, chopped onion and celery, a couple of sliced mushrooms—all sautéed in a little butter, with garlic, fresh parsley, thyme, and piled over hot whole wheat pasta, with a sprinkling of grated parmesan over the top. Nothing to wash but a skillet, a pasta pan, a bowl, a knife, a fork, and the cutting board.

It's not that I don't enjoy cooking—I do. I love trying out recipes, and Bill is an enthusiastic critic. It's just that when I'm by myself, I can think of a great many other things to do than cook a meal and wash up after.

Also in Bill's absence, self-indulgent reading. Reading instead of cooking and washing up. Reading instead of sweeping. Reading instead of writing, although I remind myself that every writer must be a reader first, and that without reading, there's no grist for the creative mill.

Reading, while Bill's gone, light stuff: *Devil's Claw* by J. A. Jance; a pair of memoirs, *Hiking Alone* by Mary Beath and *Forward From Here* by Reeve Morrow Lindbergh (I'm reviewing Lindbergh's book for Story Circle, and we're publishing an interview with Mary Beath); Robert Harris' 1995 novel, *Enigma* (I enjoyed Harris' *Pompeii* very much). Also dipping into *The West Wing Script Book* by Aaron Sorkin.

Heavier, more important, keeping me up late and requiring more of my attention: *Deep Economy: The Wealth of Communities and the Durable Future* by Bill McKibben. And rereading sections of Michael Klare's *Rising Powers, Shrinking Planet: The New Geopolitics of Energy*. Neither is comforting, in any sense of the word, but both are necessary reading, if we are to muster the will to change the way we use energy—as we must. Simply *must*.

## MAY 24

Sometimes readers send me gifts. Poetry, manuscripts, herbs, jars of jam, boxes of cookies. I'm never happy to see an unsolicited manuscript, but I love the other things. Not because I'm crazy about jam or cookies (I'm cautious about eating anything sent by someone I don't know), but because the gift suggests that the books have made a connection, built a bridge, touched someone's heart.

Today, from Jinni Turkleson, Grand Rapids, Michigan: a hand-pieced quilt. The quilt fabric is printed with Beatrix's drawings of animals, with my name and the name of the series (The Cottage Tales) embroidered on it. Stunning, and as a quilter, I know how many hours of work it represents. I've hung it on the wall.

The book, moving forward. Solved a couple of story line problems today but still haven't figured out how much of the real romance between Beatrix Potter and Willie Heelis should be included in this sixth book, how much of it should be put off for the final two. I would prefer to work this out sooner rather than later. (Later means rewriting earlier sections—something I don't much like to do.)

Reading Lindbergh's *Forward From Here*, enjoying the easy pace, the readable prose, the frequent memorable lines. I've read all of her memoirs: this is the best yet. "Funny, tender, compassionate, profound," I write in the review. Yes. Very.

---

*A good book should leave you slightly exhausted at the end. You live several lives while reading it.*

—WILLIAM STYRON

*Simple, cheap, concentrated power lies at the heart of our modern economies. Every action of a modern life burns fossil fuel; viewed in one way, modern Western human beings are flesh-colored devices for combusting coal and gas and oil.*

—BILL MCKIBBEN

*If there's a book you really want to read but it hasn't been written yet, then you must write it.*

—TONI MORRISON

*We live in the ebb and flow of connection and disconnection, moving between tight embrace and full surrender, whether we like it or not. Children nurse at the breast and cling to our hands, and then grow up and leave us. That's their job.*

—REEVE MORROW LINDBERGH

For a blog post, I've been browsing through a book called *Gather Ye Wild Things: A Forager's Year* by Susan Tyler Hitchcock. I've always been interested in wild foraging; it's a way of experiencing the abundant communities of the land.

A couple of years ago, I made a list of the foods here at Meadow Knoll that the nomadic hunter-gatherer Tonkawas who traveled through this area would have found edible—and which I might find edible, if I had to. The plant list is long and surprisingly varied:

| | | |
|---|---|---|
| Agarita | Grape | Prickly pear |
| Cattail | Henbit | Purslane |
| Chickweed | Lamb's quarters | Sumac |
| Chicory | Mesquite | Sunflower |
| Chokecherry | Mulberry | Thistle |
| Dandelion | Orach | Wild onion, |
| Dewberry | Pecan | wild garlic |
| Dock | Plantain | Wild plum |
| Goldenrod | Plum | Yew willow |

*Gathering wild things can become a year-round preoccupation, a way of life. The landscape changes shape when you start noticing which plants grow where, which plants are good for what. Forest underbrush begins to tell a story as intricate as an illuminated manuscript, once one takes the time to read it.*

—SUSAN TYLER HITCHCOCK

For protein, they had fish and game (deer, buffalo, javelina, armadillo, raccoon, possum, squirrel, wild turkey), which were and still are (except for the buffalo and javelina) plentiful. The Indians' lives weren't easy. They must have spent most of their waking hours gathering and preparing food. But they weren't starving.

Recently, I ran across *Edible and Useful Plants of Texas and the Southwest* by Delena Tull. Tull expands my list by adding teas (monarda, limoncillo, salvia, yaupon holly) and spices (epazote, juniper, mustard, peppergrass). She also includes instructions for harvesting and preparing plant fiber and information about making dyes, soap, wax, and rubber.

Yes, rubber. Thomas Edison and Harvey Firestone collaborated to make a set of goldenrod rubber tires, which Henry Ford mounted on his personal Model A touring car. Rubber made from plant hydrocarbons, rather than oil. Imagine that.

*When you come right down to it, living off wild edibles involves a lot of hard work. Finding, collecting, and preparing wild plants consumes a great deal of time and often results in a meager amount of food for the table. The task gives one a greater appreciation for the daily toil of early peoples who relied on wild plants for much of their food.*

—DELENA TULL

NEWS SUMMARY: *More than a quarter million U.S. homes went into foreclosure during March, 65 percent higher than 2007. It's the "worst U.S. housing downturn since the Great Depression," according to Reuters. Many of these are large homes, with large prices, more than a half-million dollars. The losses are affecting local tax bases.*

*Last week, Vallejo, California, a city of one hundred thousand people, filed for bankruptcy.*

## MAY 26

I'd love to put my hands over my ears and shut out the cacophony of bad news (foreclosures, bankruptcies) and just enjoy the spring, the birds, the green countryside around me, the writing. But that's not possible. And not healthy. I have to stay alive to the reality of the world, witness it, try to understand it.

Some (not all) of the mortgage crisis is happening because people want more house than they can pay for. Thinking about the affluent suburbs I saw around Houston and Fort Worth on my trip last month and the luxurious condos on South Padre Island. A half-million-dollar house isn't a home, it's an icon of the consumer society. And it's not just the pain of losing homes that hurts in these foreclosures; it's the pain of recognizing what we have become in our search for more and more. And more.

I'm remembering with a nostalgic pleasure the small houses of my 1940s and '50s childhood, two-bedroom, one-bath bungalows, considered adequate and even spacious—before we began adding on dens and family rooms and media rooms and kitchens with two refrigerators and three-car garages. And massive mortgages.

"We are, to use the very literal vernacular," Bill McKibben says in *Deep Economy*, "living three times as large."

And it's still not large enough.

## MAY 27

A different piece of work arrived today: the first-pass pages of *The Tale of Briar Bank*, which will be published at the end of September. The book is already listed in online bookstores, and I can see that people are preordering it. Amazing how fast things move. In the old days, most people didn't buy a book until they read a review or saw it on the bookstore shelf.

I'm at eighteen thousand words in *Applebeck Orchard* now, keeping at it, still at the point where this is mostly play—"all the playground," as Stephen King says in his excellent *On Writing: A Memoir of the Craft*. Later, as I begin to try to fit all the pieces together, it will become more like work.

Evenings, watching *West Wing*, a show called "In the Shadow of

Two Gunmen," with a flashback to Leo McGarry telling Jed Bartlett why he should run for president. I'm saying amen to Leo's prayer for a literate president, to raising the bar, to a candidate I can care about, somebody I can vote for and feel good about it afterward.

## MAY 28

Manure tea. Not very appetizing, but good for plants. I took a few hours away from the desk and collected a tub of fairly fresh cow manure from the pasture early this morning (when outdoor work is cooler). I'll use it to make compost and (soaked in water) as a drench on the garden beds when they're built next month. Lots of good nitrogen, organically processed from grass, compliments of cow.

I'm sure there's a metaphor here.

## MAY 29

Hot this afternoon—another 100-plus-degree day, but the dogs and I found some delicious coolness along the fence above Meadow Marsh, under Persephone, where I once found a newborn fawn the color of brown leaves and moss, curled up against the tree, waiting for mom.

Long ago, we fell into the practice of naming the important trees here at Meadow Knoll. Persephone is a multi-trunked native pecan with a branch-spread of some seventy-five feet. She was nipped off or burned to the root when she was just a sprout and renewed herself by putting up multiple trunks. We leave her small, sometimes bitter nuts for the squirrels, hoping they'll eat so many that they won't want the larger, sweeter nuts from Bill's grafted trees—a silly hope, of course. What self-respecting squirrel would bother with wild pecans when the domesticated trees are within leaping distance?

The word pecan means "a nut too hard to crack by hand." The Tonkawas planted pecans around their campsites to provide a reliable food source for their children and their children's children. They ground the nuts into a flour for flat cakes and sometimes fermented a mash made from the flour as a ceremonial intoxicant. Explorers marveled at the abundance of the nuts, botanists praised the tree, Thomas Jefferson planted pecans at Monticello. Last year, we harvested some two hundred pounds from Bill's trees. An infinity of pralines, pecan pies, spiced pecans, pecans in coleslaw and green beans, in pancakes and cupcakes.

*There is strength, free-dom, sustainability, and pride in being a practiced dweller in your own surroundings, knowing what you know. . . . You know north from south, pine from fir, in which direction the new moon might be found, where the water comes from, where the garbage goes, how to shake hands, how to sharpen a knife . . . .*

—GARY SNYDER

*We stopped at the place of which we had been told, to eat walnuts [pecans]. These are ground with a kind of small grain [probably amaranth], and this is the subsistence of the people two months in the year without any other thing . . . . The trees are very large and numerous.*

—CABEZA DE VACA
(1553)

*To understand the profound meaning of land—to walk on it with the respect, born of real understanding, of the traditional Amerindian, to see it as sacred—is to be terrified, shattered, humbled, and in the end, joyous. It is to come home at last.*

—SHARON BUTALA

Pecans produce a crop every other year, sometimes every third year. They're taking this year off, apparently. Just looked at a nearby tree, didn't see a single nutlet.

## MAY 30

The Tonkawas left a few of their belongings behind. Not long ago, we found a couple of pieces of chipped flint near the springs where the Indians used to camp. They show unmistakable signs of human workmanship: the "bulb" of percussion at the top of the piece, where a flake was struck off with a hammerstone, probably a rounded stream pebble, perhaps of granite.

The Tonkawas might have brought those pieces of flint from a site near what is now Georgetown, about thirty miles to the east. Toolmakers, they carried flint with them and worked it wherever they stopped, for arrow and spearheads, scrapers, knives, and drills. They also made splinters of bone into needles and awls, to sew leather for moccasins and other clothing. They wove willow splints into baskets to carry what they made. Their tipis were made of buffalo hide.

The springs and the encampment now lie beneath our neighboring lake. The last sad remnants of the tribe, which called itself the Tickanwatic, the "Most Human of People," were exiled to a small reservation near Tonkawa, Oklahoma, in the 1880s.

I think with admiration about these early nomadic travelers passing through this landscape, finding it so rich and varied and hospitable, so generous, so abundant. The people who live in the Hill Country now depend on food and other supplies imported from around the world; on electricity generated (in part) from coal mined in Colorado and Montana; on oil from Saudi Arabia; on natural gas from wells in the Gulf of Mexico; on water wells that are four hundred feet deep.

If these inputs are cut off, we can't survive here. The Most Human of People dwelled in this place in a much deeper sense than we do and without inputs from the other side of the globe. This land was their livelihood, their sacred life, their entire life. Home, in the deepest, richest, most important sense of that word.

## May Reading

*Beatrix Potter: A Life in Nature*, by Linda Lear

*The Botany of Desire: A Plant's-Eye View of the World*, by Michael Pollan

*Deep Economy: The Wealth of Communities and the Durable Future*, by Bill McKibben

*Devil's Claw*, by J. A. Jance

*Edible and Useful Plants of Texas and the Southwest: A Practical Guide*, by Delena Tull

*Enigma*, by Robert Harris

*Everyday Sacred: A Woman's Journey Home*, by Sue Bender

*Forward From Here*, by Reeve Morrow Lindbergh

*Gather Ye Wild Things: A Forager's Year*, by Susan Tyler Hitchcock

*Hiking Alone*, by Mary Beath

*Rising Powers, Shrinking Planet: The New Geopolitics of Energy*, by Michael Klare

*The Water-Babies: A Fairy Tale for a Land-Baby*, by Charles Kingsley

*The West Wing Script Book*, by Aaron Sorkin

| JANUARY | FEBRUARY | MARCH | APRIL |
|---------|----------|-------|-------|
| MAY | **JUNE** | JULY | AUGUST |
| SEPTEMBER | OCTOBER | NOVEMBER | DECEMBER |

## JUNE 1

The bees are having a glorious week. The mesquite trees sing with energy, ambition, purpose from dawn to dark. Each mesquite catkin, the heart's desire of every bee in Burnet County, is made of hundreds of tiny five-petaled flowers. Each flower holds a single drop of seductive amber-colored nectar in its throat, powerful enough to lure the lascivious pollinator deep inside. From the sun's earliest light to the last sunset spark, delighted, drunken bees and insects lurch from one catkin to another. With all this sexual energy, there'll be an abundance of mesquite pods in another couple of months.

*[Mesquite] comes as near characteristic of the whole Southwest including much of Mexico, as any species of plant life known to the region. It is as native as rattlesnakes and mocking birds, as characteristic as northers, and as blended into the life of the land as cornbread and tortillas.*

—J. FRANK DOBIE

## JUNE 2

And on the other side of the yard, the chaste trees, another sweetly alluring destination for bees, butterflies, and delirious hummingbirds. We have a dozen, all daughters (grown from cuttings) of a single tree we planted two decades ago, now a lovely lilac-flowering hedge, some eight feet high.

The name tells a part of the story. In ancient Rome, the chaste tree (*Vitex*) was supposed to inhibit sexual desire, and cooks in medieval monastic kitchens were in the habit of adding a handful of the spicy berries to the soup. Monk's pepper, it was called. A dual-purpose spice.

No inhibitions as far as the birds and the bees are concerned, as they join the divine dance. And when the news is full of unnecessary war, rocketing oil prices, earthquakes in China, typhoons in the Pacific, genocide in Darfur, and other natural and unnatural tragedies,

*The seeds [of the chaste tree] were once held in repute for securing chastity, and the Athenian matrons in the sacred rites of Ceres used to string their couches with the leaves.*

—MAUD GRIEVE (1929)

it's pure joy to look up and see the trees buzzing, blooming, beautiful, benevolent.

For just this brief moment, the whole wronged world seems entirely right.

## JUNE 3

Bill is back from New Mexico. I've enjoyed the silence, but I'm glad for the company again, the long conversations. Focused now on the book, writing, writing, writing from nine to five every day, with a little time off for household chores and lunch. *Applebeck Orchard* is up to about twenty-eight thousand words, and although the story isn't very well developed yet, I can see where it's going. Sort of. If I were a new writer, or if this were a first book in a new series, I might be panicking. But I'm not and it isn't, and I'm okay. The book will pull itself together, when the time comes. I hope.

Took a couple of days away from *Applebeck* to finish the production process of *Together, Alone*: print the typescript (two copies, plus a floppy containing the e-file), assemble the maps, review the checklist. Tomorrow, the project goes back to the Press. Looking through the pages, I remember once again just how hard it was to write the book, to recover the personal history of a couple of decades of our marriage, to describe the uncertainties of those early months, the first years of the writing work, the times I wanted to chuck the whole damned thing and start over somewhere else. Hard remembering, hard writing. I'm glad I did it—for myself. No idea whether it will find an audience.

## JUNE 4

Having lunch with your editor: a prime privilege of the writing life. On this beautiful day, I drive into Austin, thinking the whole way about what an extraordinary day this is, how fortunate I am. Thirty years ago, in 1978, the University of Texas Press published my first academic book, a reworking of my dissertation, with the scintillating title of *Stylistic and Narrative Structures in the Middle English Verse Romance*. I've edited two other books for them, both anthologies: *With Courage and Common Sense* (2003) and *What Wildness Is This* (2007). Now, *Together, Alone*. My first academic book, my first memoir. Bookends for a writing life. There's a nice symmetry to that.

The Press is off campus, on the east side of I-35. I find a park-

*Wildness matters not because it alone is sacred but because it arouses in us the sense of sanctity that makes visible the sacredness of everything else in life.*

—PAUL GRUCHOW

*[W]riting a novel is a process. It is an experience that evolves. The novel is its own experience and its subject is always the evolving of consciousness . . . that of the reader, the author, the characters . . . the world itself.*

—JOYCE CAROL OATES

*We write to expose the unexposed. If there is one door in the castle you have been told not to go through, you must. Otherwise, you'll just be rearranging furniture in rooms you've already been in. Most human beings are dedicated to keeping that one door shut. But the writer's job is to see what's behind it, to see the bleak unspeakable stuff, and to turn the unspeakable into words—not just into any words but if we can, into rhythm and blues.*

—ANNE LAMOTT

ing space in the shade (another 100-degree day), lug the heavy box of typescripts up the stone steps, and there is Theresa May, my editor, wrapped in smiles and lively enthusiasms. Lunch at Eastside Café is nonstop chatter about books, the economy, the primaries, Theresa's upcoming trip to Italy, the price of gasoline, the cost of energy and resource depletions, the blistering heat, books and more books, yadida-yadida. Good talk, good food, good friendship, a book finally finished. An extraordinary day.

The book isn't finished, though. That's a lie. I'll see the copyedited manuscript in September, the page proofs in February. And I need to start thinking about the Web site. Some months ago, Theresa and I debated whether to include photos in the memoir; we agreed that black-and-white photographs wouldn't do the landscape justice, that color photos would be too expensive, and that it would be better all around to post photos and additional text on a Web site.

The world has changed in thirty years.

*Books are never finished, they are merely abandoned.*

—OSCAR WILDE

NEWS SUMMARY: *Clinton concedes. Barack Obama is the Democratic nominee.*

JUNE 5

Amazed. Astonished. Incredulous. Profoundly proud. The way I've felt all year, as I watched this nomination process unfurl. A black man and a woman, both superlative candidates for the presidency. Two winners, as far as I am concerned. America is already a winner, with these two people as candidates.

Oddly, the fact that Obama is black hardly matters now—to me, although I know that race matters enormously to the millions of black voters out there and to a racist minority of voters. What matters more: the striking intelligence, the calm focus, the ability to make an argument that holds together and deliver it so well that I want to listen to every word. So well that I *care* about what he's saying.

I've never been a political junkie, but this year, I've joined MoveOn .org's e-mail campaign. No point in trying to do anything here in our red-party, rural county, in George W. Bush's home state, where the pro-gun, pro-war, and anti-abortion lobbies flood the media and contribute every dollar they can (and then some) to political campaigns. But online, I might be able to help. And I can donate.

**NEWS SUMMARY:** *Oil rose to nearly $140 a barrel this week. In the United States, gasoline spiked to $4 a gallon, increasing recession fears. President Bush flew to Saudi Arabia to discuss the situation with King Abdullah. The Saudis later announced plans to increase production by three hundred thousand barrels a day.*

## JUNE 6

The oil situation: increasingly, alarmingly serious, not something that can be ignored. What's becoming clear is that any natural or geopolitical disruption (an accidental pipeline explosion in Nigeria, hurricane threats in the Gulf, war threats in the Caspian) has an effect on the availability and the price of oil and gasoline—and an effect on everyone here in America. On *us*, on Bill and me, remote as we are from the centers of power.

Happier matters: sweet potatoes. A few weeks ago, I started some sweet potato slips by sticking toothpicks into a sweet potato and suspending it in a mayo jar filled with water. When the slips were about four inches long, I snapped them off and put them in water, where they've grown marvelous masses of curling roots. This week, the slips will go in the ground—in the rose garden, since the vegetable garden is still under construction. I've never grown sweet potatoes before, but Texas is a big producer of sweet potatoes. They should do well here.

Reading: Janice Emily Bowers, *A Full Life in a Small Place* and *The Mountains Next Door*. Rereading: Wendell Berry, *The Gift of Good Land*, feeling grateful for Meadow Knoll, for the garden, and for writers like Bowers and Berry, who remind me that to live in a place—any place—mindfully and with care is to live richly, completely.

*I pick up my journal again. A white-winged dove calls from the telephone wire, its voice throaty and muffled. He sounds as though his head is buried beneath a pillow. The watermelon vines silently plot to take over the backyard. Tiny blue butterflies spark from the zucchini plants. The scutter of an invisible bug under fallen leaves brings the cat to attention. If these ordinary miracles aren't enough, that's too bad, because this garden—this here and now—is all I've got. It's more than enough for a full life in a small place.*

—JANICE EMILY BOWERS

**NEWS SUMMARY:** *The Senate Select Committee on Intelligence today issued a report stating that President Bush, Vice President Cheney, Secretary of Defense Rumsfeld, and Secretaries of State Powell and Rice repeatedly exaggerated evidence that Saddam Hussein possessed nuclear, chemical, and biological weapons of mass destruction and misled the American people about ties between Iraq and al-Qaeda.*

## JUNE 7

Reading about the Intelligence Committee report (the full document is available online, but I don't have the heart to read it), I remem-

*And what we've seen recently that has raised our level of concern to the current state of unrest . . . is that [Saddam Hussein] now is trying, through his illicit procurement network, to acquire the equipment he needs to be able to enrich uranium—specifically, aluminum tubes.*

—DICK CHENEY
(SEPTEMBER 7, 2002)

*Facing clear evidence of peril, we cannot wait for the final proof—the smoking gun—that could come in the form of a mushroom cloud.*

—GEORGE W. BUSH
(OCTOBER 7, 2002)

*I can't say if the use of force would last five days or five weeks or five months, but it certainly isn't going to last any longer than that.*

—DONALD RUMSFELD
(NOVEMBER 14, 2002)

ber being in Canada for a month during the run-up to the Iraq invasion. We were staying in a cottage at Johnston Harbor on the Bruce Peninsula, with access to both American and Canadian media. The American media, toad-like, stuck out its tongue and swallowed every exaggeration that buzzed out of the White House, the Pentagon, the State Department, then spit it out to the country. The Canadian media wondered, probed, questioned, criticized, tried to get at the facts behind the claims. For an American, the differences between the American and Canadian media were as embarrassing as the exaggerations themselves.

JUNE 8

Nearly four weeks now without rain, and more record-breaking heat. Early morning—between 6:30 and 8—is the only decent time to be outdoors. The rest of the time, I'm inside, keeping cool, working on *Applebeck Orchard*, reading Hannah Hinchman's *Little Things in a Big Country*.

The extreme heat is good for something, though. Yesterday afternoon, the compost pile registered a toasty 140 degrees on the nifty new thermometer Bill gave me—a point-and-click gadget with a digital readout. Not all solar heat, of course: when compost is rich with nitrogen, it cooks. But the sun undoubtedly helps.

I pity the polar bears.

JUNE 9

What I saw when I was out with the dogs this morning, just as the sun came up:

—the Zepherine Drouhin draping pink blossoms across the trellis
—a patch of coreopsis along the creek, bright as spilled sunshine
—the last bluebonnet, bravely blue among the parched grasses
—a single purple martin looping elegantly against a bright blue sky
—a Cooper's hawk swooping low
—an Inca dove perched on a wire, singing his dawn song, low and throaty
—a painted bunting showering the world with melody

A June morning here in the Hill Country, nothing special, nothing exciting or thrilling, just simple, ordinary everyday beauties. Lucky, lucky me.

Later, drove to Austin for the monthly Story Circle Reading Circle—this month, *The Memory Keeper's Daughter* by Kim Edwards. A strong story (if slow) about an impulsive choice, made in a moment but lived with for a lifetime, told in lovely, lyric language. There were eight or nine women in our group; the discussion was thoughtful, perceptive, moving. For me, there's no pleasure like the joy of a good book, shared.

Also reading: *Little Heathens: Hard Times and High Spirits on an Iowa Farm During the Great Depression* by Mildred Armstrong Kalish. Direct, detailed, authentic, funny. Love its homely comforts.

*We read to know we are not alone.*

—C. S. LEWIS

## JUNE 10

The Honda Civic's windshield has been cracked for some time and we thought it might be a good idea to replace it. The young man who came out to do this did a good job, but he thought it was okay to take the TX Tag (one of those electronic gizmos that allow you to zip like Batman and Robin in their Batmobile through the toll plaza without stopping to feed the greedy meter man) off the old windshield and glue it onto the new.

No. Not.

Peeling the tag off the window deactivates the silly thing.

Three e-mails, two phone calls, some language difficulties (I don't speak Spanish), a lost TX Tag envelope, and a few harsh husband-wife words later, we now have a new TX Tag on our new windshield and are good to go through the toll plaza, zip-zip.

The moral of this story: do not replace your windshield, no matter how bad that crack looks. It is not true that the glass will fall into your lap or shatter across your face. All those tags and seals and certificates and parking permits pasted across it will hold it together and keep it from breaking. You and your windshield will live forever.

## JUNE 11

I took an hour's break from writing (*Applebeck* at thirty-five thousand words, not quite half-finished) to pull a wheelbarrow-load of weeds from the cottage garden. No better way to clear the mind, in my opinion, than to clear a flower bed.

Before today's wheelbarrow-load, there have been several others, each representing an hour's hot, hard labor. There's goldenrod (which qualifies as a weed when it starts bumping into the roses) and

*Many gardeners will agree that hand-weeding is not the terrible drudgery that it is often made out to be. Some people find in it a kind of soothing monotony. It leaves their minds free to develop the plot for their next novel . . .*

—CHRISTOPHER LLOYD

bluebonnets (no, not a weed, but finished blooming and ready for the compost pile), several square yards of dried-out southernwood, and some migrant Engelmann daisies that wandered in from elsewhere. And Johnson grass, that alien scourge that has some sort of biological agent in its roots and rhizomes that is said to kill its neighbors.

I don't mind weeds, in the natural course of things. As long as they keep their heads down and don't call attention to themselves, they can hang around. I've never been comfortable with sanitized, orderly gardens, anyway. I love flowers tumbled and jumbled all together, the artemisia happily rubbing shoulders with the Jerusalem sage, the daylilies creeping through the daisies. The wild bunch.

But there's a limit. Weeds bother me when they get big and boisterous, like middle school bullies with no manners. Today, they're off to a new beginning, a new life on the compost heap. The cottage garden looks a little cleaner, and I like to think that some of the less robust plants—the red bee balm that came from a friend in Indiana, and the lovely perennial marigold—are happier because the Johnson grass isn't poisoning their roots and the goldenrod isn't breathing down their necks.

JUNE 12

My mother would have been ninety-nine today.

She was born Amber Lucille Franklin in Sullivan County, Missouri, the second daughter of a family of nine children, all raised on a small subsistence farm. In 1929, she left the farm and went to Chicago, where she worked throughout the Depression as what was called a "mother's helper." She married my father in 1938 and put up with him until his death a half century later. I've never known whether she didn't leave him because she loved him or because she couldn't imagine life without him.

In her heart, Mom never left the farm. She was happiest (or so I remember) during the years we lived in the country, where she raised chickens, a milk cow, a large garden. She learned those skills from her mother, Mary Susan Jones (1881–1977), who learned them from her mother, Sarah Elizabeth Tolbert (1859–1930), who learned from her mother, Mary Ann Coldiron (1840–1920), who learned from her mother, Joanna (born around 1810 in North Carolina), who was said to be full-blood Cherokee—five generations of countrywomen, all deeply connected to the land.

None of the women of my motherline had much formal education. Mother left school to work when she was fourteen; her mother was married at sixteen; her grandmother was married at seventeen. They were strong women with a practical, earthy wisdom. They knew how to make do or do without, cheerfully. They were the mainstays of their families.

Mom died in 2000. Every year I celebrate her gifts of strength and courage by planting something. This year, I planted the rosemary cutting I've been nurturing on the kitchen windowsill.

Here's rosemary, Mom. That's for remembrance.

NEWS SUMMARY: *Earlier this month, the jobless rate saw its biggest monthly increase in twenty-two years, from 5 percent to 5.5 percent. Part-time summer work is almost impossible to find.*

## JUNE 14

My garden helper is available again, and we've started work on the vegetable garden, getting ready for fall planting. Miles' back and arms are younger and stronger than mine, and his help is welcome. Besides, he needs the work. The credit crunch is quickly morphing into a job crunch.

Bill and Miles took the ranch truck up to the old corral and rounded up a load of twenty-year-old eight-foot landscape timbers—sufficiently weathered that the chemicals used to treat the wood are no longer a hazard. Miles and I stacked them, two timbers high, around five raised beds, one four-by-sixteen feet, the others four-by-eight. That's about half the size of my previous vegetable garden, but these are experimental plots, designed to be intensively planted and managed, so I can select for the vegetables and the varieties that do best. There's space for containers because some of the things I want to grow will do better in pots. Oh, and between the beds: thick layers of newspaper, covered with mulch from our cedar trees.

There was topsoil here a century ago when this land was covered with mid-grass prairie, its thatch decaying, the overgrowth periodically burned off, the roots maintaining the soil moisture. But cotton and overgrazing destroyed the grasses and during the droughts of the 1930s and 1950s, the soil dried to a fine powder and blew away. But the soil in the garden area is in good condition: Bill double-dug it for me when we made our first garden here more than twenty years ago, and it's been primed with bushels of compost and chicken manure. Miles is digging it again, about twelve inches deep, and topping it off with eight inches of a mix of sand and compost.

*It takes 500 years for nature to replace 1 inch of topsoil. Approximately 3,000 years are needed for natural reformation of topsoil to the depth needed for satisfactory crop production. . . .*

—DALE ALLEN PFEIFFER

*To take part in the intricate and endlessly interesting process of providing for our sustenance is the surest way to escape the culture of fast food and the values implicit in it: that food should be fast, cheap, and easy; that food is a product of industry, not nature; that food is fuel, and not a form of communion, with other people as well as with other species—with nature.*

—MICHAEL POLLAN

## JUNE 15

File this under "They Live Here Too." Zach had a close encounter with a pair of young skunks when we were out for a walk this morning. The skunks did what their mama told them to do, and Zach was much less exuberant when I got him home. Bill stirred up a potent mix of hydrogen peroxide, baking soda, and dish detergent and we gave Zach a good scrubbing. It eliminated most of the stinky smell. Maybe he won't be quite so interested in baby skunks from here on out.

I wish the lesson would transfer to baby bunnies. A silly (or a very inexperienced) mother rabbit scooped out a shallow depression beside the dog kennel fence and deposited three babies in it. I've surrounded the nest with bricks and put a board over the top to give the babies some shelter, and we're keeping Zach and Toro on the leash outdoors. They'd kill the bunnies if we let them.

But at the rate those little rabbits are growing, they'll be ready to leave the nest and start eating my lettuce and beans sometime in the next hour.

*It begins to make me dizzy even trying to think of taking a census of everybody [plants and animals] who lives here; and all of them seem to have certain claims to the place that are every bit as good as and perhaps better than mine.*

—SUE HUBBELL

NEWS SUMMARY: *In a five-to-four ruling, the Supreme Court found that prisoners at Guantánamo Bay have a right to challenge their detention in federal court. It is the third judicial decision against the Bush administration's detainee policy.*

## JUNE 16

It's not that I don't want them to go unpunished—those men locked up in Cuba. I want them to be held accountable for whatever they've done. But even more, I want *us* to be accountable: accountable for fairness, for justice, for humane treatment of those in our custody, for respect for human rights. For adherence to the rule of law. An administration that makes its own laws is a threat to every citizen.

## JUNE 17

*North Americans now devote 40,000 square miles to lawns, more than we use for wheat, corn, or even tobacco.*

—ROBERT FULFORD

Bill has mowed a path to the creek across the meadow in front of our house between the front porch and the pasture fence: the space we'd call a lawn, if we lived in suburbia. He could probably mow the whole thing—the firewheels and yellow daisies and bluebonnets and paintbrush have already bloomed and gone to seed. But we're waiting

AN EXTRAORDINARY YEAR OF ORDINARY DAYS

for the monarda (also known by the unlovely name of spotted bee balm), which will bloom in another week or two, in the company of the basket flowers and (if we're lucky) our lovely Texas bluebells—the gentians. Of course, if we lived in suburbia, we'd have to mow now or face the ire of our neighbors. Been there, done that, both of us, veterans of countless hours on the business end of a mower.

But out here, nobody's watching, nobody's taking notes or names, there are no lawn police. We're free to let the firewheels and paintbrush go to seed, wait for the monarda and the basket flowers, hope for bluebells.

*Applebeck Orchard*: moving ahead, into Chapter Eleven.

## JUNE 18

A native Rio Grande turkey has been stopping by mornings and evenings for the past week. She walks up from the wild woods and open meadows to the south. She stalks through the grass, unhurried, unflustered, not bothering to look up when I come out onto the porch to take her picture. Breakfast has her full attention.

We were lucky enough to see the gobbler the other morning, just after sunrise, his distinctive red wattle like a bright necktie at his blue throat. More often, we hear him gobbling, that high-pitched, fluttery gabble that makes me chuckle but no doubt warms the heart of his ladylove—or -loves, plural. He is such a splendid fellow that he undoubtedly has a harem.

Once, in another year, we saw a pair of turkeys coupling, two brown shapes in the shadows of the tall grass. Male turkeys (like most birds) have the same plumbing as females—except that his orifice squirts semen and hers doesn't, in something called a "cloacal kiss." I love Barbara Kingsolver's rollicking description of a pair of inexperienced turkey lovers in *Animal, Vegetable, Miracle*:

> *Paradise arrives when a fellow has kneaded his lady's erogenous wing zones for a long, long time with his feet, until she finally decides her suitor has worked himself up to the necessary fervor. Without warning, quick as an eyeblink, she flips up her tail feathers and reaches upward to meet him. Oh, my gosh! I gasped to see it. It was an air kiss. They really did miss. Mwah!—like a pair of divas onstage who don't want to muss their lipstick.*

Wild turkeys may be more dexterous than their domesticated cousins—or maybe they just get more practice. Last year, a hen brought

*I wish the bald eagle had not been chosen as the representative of our country; he is a bird of bad moral character; like those among men who live by sharking and robbing, he is generally poor, and often very lousy. The turkey is a much more respectable bird.*

—BENJAMIN FRANKLIN

the consequence of her cloacal kiss to this same unmown meadow, where the chicks, poults, darted here and there on lightning feet, feasting on grasshoppers. I came too close, and they rattled up from the grass, five little poults and their mother, and flew off in a noisy clatter and whirr of wings.

The Texas Rio Grande turkey population was nearly annihilated by hunting and habitat destruction through the early part of the last century. It took a vigorous protection and restocking program to restore the turkey's numbers. Larger and louder than a canary in a coal mine, they're an indicator of the well-being of the prairies and woodlands that surround us here.

## JUNE 19

Making steady progress in *Applebeck Orchard*. The story lines are beginning to come together, but I'm still not sure how to handle the central narrative: the romance that led to Beatrix Potter's marriage—at the spinster-ish age of forty-seven—in 1913.

Beatrix's fiancé, Norman Warne, died in 1905, just before she completed the purchase of Hill Top Farm in Near Sawrey, in the Lake District. In the next few years, she met and formed a close friendship with Willie Heelis (I've called him Will in the books), a solicitor who lived in the nearby market town of Hawkshead. The friendship was forbidden by Beatrix's parents, just as they had resisted her earlier engagement.

I've shown Beatrix and Will meeting in the first book, set in 1905, and drawing closer in Books Two through Five. *Applebeck Orchard* is set in 1911, and it's time something happens to bring them to some sort of declaration, perhaps even an exchange of pledges.

I'd better encourage Will to declare himself in this book. He's very shy; I wonder how he'll manage.

*When I got engaged last June I was quite of a mind to wait . . . but there was a good deal of bother—they [Beatrix's parents] were very silly they would not let Mr. Heelis come to the house for ever so long—and I think the opposition only made us more fond of one another . . . . We have every prospect of happiness—if it pleases Heaven.*

—BEATRIX POTTER
TO FANNY COOPER
(OCTOBER 1913)

NEWS SUMMARY: *Citing dependence on foreign oil, President Bush urged Congress to act by July 4 to rescind a 1990 law (passed by the first President Bush) that prohibits offshore oil drilling.*

## JUNE 20

Gas is $4.10 a gallon and more, everywhere. It's the top of every news story, and the political arguments go on and on: *drill, don't drill, do, don't, yes, no.* Drivers are cutting back because they can't afford to fill up their suvs and pickup trucks—a knee-jerk reaction to spiking prices. The minute prices at the pump go down, consumption will shoot up again. And the Bush administration's warning about "dependence on foreign oil" is code for "we have already run out of oil here at home" and a rationale for "drill, baby, drill."

On the book, I'm bogged down with fiddly rewrites, which happens when I can't find the thread that draws the story forward. I've been through this often enough to recognize the symptoms: I'm afflicted with the "middle-of-the-book syndrome." In this case, it's complicated by the fact that I'm still not clear about Will's romantic intentions. I've done more rewriting than I usually do, trying first one approach, then another. So far, nothing's clicked. I'm stuck.

So I allow myself to be easily distracted. Bill and Miles are painting the house and every fifteen minutes, I run outside to see how the job is coming. I answer e-mail. Shop for seeds on the Internet. Read (currently, John Graves' *Hard Scrabble*, about a Texas homestead a lot like this one). Clean the bathroom—the toilets, even (gasp!). I tell myself that I'm not killing time; I'm just letting the story stew. But the real truth is that when I reach the midpoint of almost every book I've ever written, the daily business of life becomes enormously attractive. Middle-of-the-book syndrome.

I need to get past this.


JUNE 21

The summer solstice yesterday, midpoint of the year. After this, shortening days, lengthening nights. Midpoint of this journal, too.

While avoiding Beatrix and Will, I took photos of eight swallowtail caterpillars on the fennel. These stripy guys are the reason I grow this herb. I'm not crazy about the taste of fennel, but I love the look of its ferny leaves and especially love this bronzy variety, which the caterpillars adore, too. Adore to death, actually. In a day or two, they'll have the plant chewed down to bare stalks. Okay by me, guys. Go for it.

Unfortunately for the caterpillars, there are also red wasps in the neighborhood, and they have an appetite for caterpillars. An example of nature's grand plan: caterpillars chowing down on the fennel; wasps nibbling on the caterpillars (truly—they seem to eat them, alive, a bite at a time); and swallows, bluebirds, martins feeding on the wasps.

I'm hoping, though, that the wasps will find another little something to eat, so a few of these fennel fans survive to become butterflies.

*It starts with this: put your desk in the corner, and every time you sit down there to write, remind yourself why it isn't in the middle of the room. Life isn't a support-system for art. It's the other way around.*

—STEPHEN KING


*I find it difficult at times to accept nature as it is. Investigating a flapping noise in a patch of weeds, I was sickened to see a praying mantis devouring a butterfly headfirst as the butterfly's wings beat the air. . . . I felt anguished for the butterfly, although it would have been as logical to rejoice for the mantis.*

—JANICE EMILY BOWERS

Today: my youngest child's birthday.

Michael is raising a second family (his first child, a daughter, graduates college this year) in Juneau, Alaska. Both Michael and his wife Sheryl are schoolteachers, but he's taking a few years off to be an at-home dad to Becky, six, and little Michael, four. Both children are autistic, Michael Jr. mildly so, Becky moderately. Both are lucky, born to child-oriented parent-teachers who give them the structure and the guidance they need.

Michael is also taking a twentieth-century American history class at the university and e-mailed me, asking about my experiences during the feminist movement of the sixties and seventies. He was looking for a firsthand report from the field.

I told him that what I remembered most about those chaotic years was the enormous effort it took to juggle three elementary school kids, a part-time teaching appointment, graduate classes, a doctoral thesis, and a serious boyfriend. I didn't burn my bra because one was all I had; I might actually want to wear it again.

Did you think of yourself as liberated? he asks.

I thought of myself as busy, I reply. Incredibly busy.

But I *was* liberated, I think now: freed from old ways of thinking, from constrained ambitions, diminished dreams. I'd left a marriage, moved from the conservative Midwest to the radical West, and set my sights on a doctorate—a challenging target for a small-town girl. I still have the bumper sticker somebody gave me: *Only she who attempts the absurd can achieve the impossible.* In those days, most of the time, I merely felt I was attempting the absurd and that the impossible was just that. Liberation didn't have a helluva lot to do with it.

Another generation, and it's Michael who is liberated, staying home with the children by choice and writing a newspaper column about the experience. He's also doing an ambitious full-scale remodel on the home they've just bought, using carpentering skills he's taught himself.

Times change. Gender responsibilities are reevaluated, rethought, renegotiated. This is a good thing.

Happy birthday, Michael.

*Before modern feminism, stories of female ambition were silenced or erased; even now, they are told with apology ("Yes, it's a great honor to be a Nobel Prize laureate, but really, what I love best is staying home and being a mother to Kevin and Annie").*

—HARRIET GOLDHOR LERNER

## JUNE 23

Summer's here, with another 100-degree day.

But the indigo bunting doesn't care—he's just glad for the open sky, the sun, the tallest twig. This morning, just after dawn, I saw him, brilliant blue, and heard him pouring out his scrambled melody from the very top of the willow tree in the pasture by the lake. I've read that indigos return to their breeding grounds throughout their lives and that the male's song is unique to the neighborhood where he grew up. He shares this song, more or less, with other males of adjacent territories, while neighbors a few miles away carry a different tune. For him, song and place are inextricably bound up together, song bound to earth's body. When these buntings migrate, they plot their course by the stars, having learned the constellations as young birds. Ah, all that wisdom of song and celestial navigation, of native ground and native music, hardwired into that tiny brain!

Yesterday evening, Bill and I watched both the male and the female indigos foraging for insects. I imagine their nest nearby, a tidy cup of woven grasses lined with leaves and milkweed fluff, fastened to a low shrub with the elastic lashings of spider webs. Imagine the bunting chicks gazing up out of this soft cup at the stars, learning how to find their way home from places they have not yet visited, mooring their yet-to-be-learned songs to the stars.

NEWS SUMMARY: *A leatherback turtle nest has been found on South Padre Island, the first since the 1930s.*

JUNE 24

Good news amid this week's tumble of markets, the death rattle of the banks. The turtle rescue folks on South Padre scored a big one: a leatherback turtle crawled out of the water and into the dunes, where she dug a nest and laid her eggs. They were retrieved before they could be destroyed by predators and will be hatched. Lucky little leatherbacks.

A turtle here at Meadow Knoll wasn't quite so fortunate. I saw her—a large snapping turtle—laying a cache of eggs in the creek bank beside Turtle Pool last week. (Not the first snapper we've seen there: that's why we call it Turtle Pool.) I watched her at this age-old task, depositing her eggs in the hole she'd dug in the creek bank, scratching the dry earth over them to discourage predators. A couple of days later, I found the nest completely dug out and leathery egg shells scattered across the rocks at the head of the pool. A raccoon, likely, enjoying turtle eggs as a midnight snack. I'm sorry there won't

*Indigo buntings are small but emphatic birds. They believe that they own the place, and it is hard to ignore their claim. The male birds . . . belt out their songs, complicated tangles of couplets that waken me first thing in the morning. . . . One day, walking back along the edge of the field, I came upon a young indigo bunting preoccupied with song practice. He had not yet dared to take as visible a perch as his father would have chosen, but there he was, clinging to a bare twig and softly running through his couplets, getting them all wrong and then going back over them so quietly that had I not been within a few feet of him I would not have heard.*

—SUE HUBBELL

be any baby turtles from that nest, but raccoons have to eat and feed their young, too. Another evidence of the way of the earth.

As the Inuit say, "All our food is souls."

## JUNE 25

*Applebeck* has come unstuck, although I still haven't solved the Beatrix-Will problem. Found another story line—the badgers, those helpful animals—to carry the narrative forward, at least for a couple of chapters.

I'm reading *Overshoot* by ecologist William R. Catton. Reading it slowly, because it's a difficult, painful statement of the predicament that population growth and our striving for "progress" have gotten us into. Reading it with a reluctant fascination, because it's another paradigm-shifting book. We're no longer that minor species, *Homo sapiens*, Catton says. We are living in the "Age of Exuberance," have become *Homo colossus*. We have created technologies that have supersized us, so that we have grown beyond ("overshot") the carrying capacity of our planet:

> *The more potent human technology became, the more man turned into a colossus. Each human colossus required more resources and more space than each pre-colossal human. . . . The more colossal man's tool kit became, the larger man became, and the more destructive of his own future.*

*Overshoot* was written in the late 1970s. Catton's arguments were compelling then, but much more powerful now. The tool kit is larger. There are more of us. And we are even more colossal than we were when he was writing.

## JUNE 26

On the lighter side, I've been reading about kitchen gardens in a little book called *Kitchen Gardening in America: A History* by David M. Tucker, a comprehensive look (the only one I know of) at the history of growing family food: Native American gardeners (beans, corn, squash, Jerusalem artichokes), Thomas Jefferson's experimental gardens at Monticello, the seed catalogs of the nineteenth century, the Victory Gardens of the First and Second World Wars, and the community gardens of the 1970s and beyond.

*We must alert and organize the world's people to pressure world leaders to take specific steps to solve the two root causes of our environmental crises: exploding population growth and wasteful consumption of irreplaceable resources. Overconsumption and overpopulation underlie every environmental problem we face today.*

—JACQUES-YVES COUSTEAU

*We must learn to live within carrying capacity without trying to enlarge it. We must rely on renewable resources consumed no faster than at sustained yield rates. The last best hope for mankind is ecological modesty.*

—WILLIAM R. CATTON

Victory gardens seem to be making a comeback, judging from the number of Web sites devoted to them. Economic hard times, uncertainty about energy supplies, misgivings about industrial agriculture, growth of the locavore movement—it all adds up to an urgent, growing interest in growing our own food. I'm glad to be one of the many.

*Applebeck* is moving along more easily: fifty-eight thousand words.

NEWS SUMMARY: *The Supreme Court struck down the District of Columbia ban on handguns, ruling five to four that the Second Amendment protects an individual's right to possess a gun. Writing for the majority, Justice Antonin Scalia wrote that this "is not a right to keep and carry any weapon whatsoever in any manner whatsoever and for whatever purpose." It does allow individuals to have guns for lawful purposes, such as hunting and defending themselves and leaves it to the states to regulate gun ownership.*

*Growing our own food would save money and cut inflation by reducing the demand for commercial food. Increasing and decentralizing our stockpiles of preserved foods could provide a safety net against supply-system breakdowns that could leave whole communities vulnerable to shortages. And consuming local food would reduce the enormous environmental impact of our fossil fuel–dependent food production and transportation systems.*

—PHILIP S. WENZ, *SAN FRANCISCO CHRONICLE* (APRIL 12, 2008)

JUNE 27

Guns (owning, using, locking up) are a continuing topic of discussion at our house, and we waited for the court's ruling with interest. Bill is a trained marksman and a gun owner. I favored the D.C. ban and sympathize with urban police who are losing the war against crime to a better-armed enemy. Another five–four ruling, another demonstration of the power of this administration's judicial legacy.

But here in the country, being armed is a question of necessity because we are isolated and because the nearest Mountie may be on the other side of the county when we need him (or her). So I am glad to accept Bill's guns, at the same moment that I wish that guns had never been invented. Consistency is not one of my virtues.

*A foolish consistency is the hobgoblin of little minds, adored by little statesmen and philosophers and divines.*

—RALPH WALDO EMERSON

JUNE 30

Live in a place long enough, watch patiently enough, and you'll see plants at their prettiest. The prairie flameleaf sumac, for instance, is in spectacular flower this week, to the delight of the sweet-toothed insects feasting on the nectar.

Hundreds of these small trees grow wild in a wilderness corner of

*To make a sumac gargle, gather ripe berries as early as possible, coax them off the stem, and steep them in boiling water, about four cups water to a cup of sumac seed. The tea will turn deep red. Strain it through a couple of layers of cheesecloth. . . . Then keep it in your medicine chest—it won't go bad—for daily use as a wild mouthwash.*

—SUSAN TYLER HITCHCOCK

our thirty-one acres, and the females (the lovelier of the species) are covered with creamy flower clusters that ripen into conical reddish-brown fruits, a mainstay winter food of raccoons, possums, deer, and birds. Native Americans steeped sumac fruits in water to make a tart drink that white settlers called Indian lemonade. They also used the bark, leaves, roots, and fruits for a wide range of medicinal treatments, from toothache to tuberculosis.

The sumacs at their finest, the glorious blossoms busy with insects, the dawn-washed air fresh and cool, a blue sky arching overhead, the dogs—only two, now that Lady is gone—eagerly sniffing scents left by coyotes and armadillos that traveled this way in the night.

Such abundance, such beauty, such grace grown from a generous earth. What else can I be but grateful, even as I try to be aware—to *stay* aware—that the beauty I see here, all beauty everywhere on this planet, is threatened?

## June Reading

*A Full Life in a Small Place and Other Essays from a Desert Garden,* by Janice Emily Bowers

*The Gift of Good Land: Further Essays Cultural and Agricultural,* by Wendell Berry

*Hard Scrabble: Observations on a Patch of Land,* by John Graves

*Kitchen Gardening in America: A History,* by David M. Tucker

*Little Heathens: Hard Times and High Spirits on an Iowa Farm During the Great Depression,* by Mildred Armstrong Kalish

*Little Things in a Big Country: An Artist and Her Dog on the Rocky Mountain Front,* by Hannah Hinchman

*The Memory Keeper's Daughter,* by Kim Edwards

*The Mountains Next Door,* by Janice Emily Bowers

*Overshoot: The Ecological Basis of Revolutionary Change,* by William R. Catton

| JANUARY | FEBRUARY | MARCH | APRIL |
|---------|----------|-------|-------|
| MAY | JUNE | **JULY** | AUGUST |
| SEPTEMBER | OCTOBER | NOVEMBER | DECEMBER |

## JULY 1

Armadillos.

In *Hard Scrabble*, Texas author John Graves remarks that dillos have "rather dim brains and their eyes and ears are not alert to danger." But as they bumble through the world, nose to the ground, they can do a fair amount of damage to seedlings and plants. They've been rooting in the unfenced rose garden, where I planted a dozen sweet potato slips. The plants are flourishing and I was determined not to let the dillos dig them up, so I surrounded them with rocks. That worked, because the dim-bulb dillos aren't bright enough to push the rocks aside. But now there's a different problem.

Deer.

There are at least two herds in our area, six or eight in each. Fun to watch in the evenings and early mornings—as long as they stay on their side of the fence. But last night, some of them visited the rose garden, browsed the roses, and ate every last sweet potato leaf.

Looks like my sweet potato experiment is over since there's not time for another crop. Sweet potatoes will have to wait until next year. And the vegetable garden will certainly need a deer fence.

The deer population is definitely growing. Their only predator (excluding hunters) is the mountain lion, which has extended its range from South Texas into the Hill Country and beyond. A few years ago, a big cat was struck by a truck on the highway about twelve miles away. They're here, but there aren't enough of them to keep the herd size down. Yet.

**NEWS SUMMARY:** *The Dow Jones Industrials fell by 10 percent in June as many large banks announced stock offerings in an effort to raise cash to meet billions of dollars in losses from subprime mortgages.*

## JULY 2

On TV, a drumbeat of economic bad news accompanying the cacophony of election news, with both candidates on the campaign trail from pre-dawn to after-dark.

*Applebeck*: sixty-two thousand words, about 70 percent finished. It's time to start rounding up the vagrant story lines and corralling them into a coherent ending—not all that easy, because Will still hasn't summoned the courage to declare himself. However, the mutually happy futures of Captain Woodcock and Miss Nash, two continuing characters in the series, have been assured, and I may be able to tie the two romance story lines together.

Next week, a trip to the dentist and jury duty. Also next week, Bill goes back to New Mexico. Uncertain when I'll go—around the first of August, maybe. I want to have the book substantially finished. Worried about Zach, though. He still enjoys his daily walks, but he's not tempted by the chicken and beef I cook for him. I'm not sure that an eleven-hour drive and a change in altitude (from 600 to 7,500 feet) will be good for him.

> *The moment comes when a character does or says something you hadn't thought about. At that moment he's alive and you leave it to him.*
>
> —GRAHAM GREENE

**NEWS SUMMARY:** *From the Pentagon: June was the bloodiest month for U.S. and coalition troops in Afghanistan since 2001. There were 45 reported fatalities, bringing this year's American dead to 123; 872 over the course of the war. Also from the Pentagon: a 700-page report on Iraq, saying that while the U.S. Army was capable of deposing Saddam Hussein, it was not equipped or staffed to rebuild Iraq into a functioning country.*

## JULY 4

Writing, working in the garden on this Fourth of July, struggling to get past the policy blunders of the current administration, its denials of human rights, and feel properly patriotic.

And then, late in the evening, I saw a clip of Marian Anderson in her unforgettable 1939 concert on the steps of the Lincoln Memorial, after the Daughters of the American Revolution refused permission for her to sing to an integrated audience in Constitution Hall. *That* reminded me of what this day is about.

And also reminded me of something a priest friend said to me once: "Don't confuse God with the church."

Don't confuse the current administration and the conduct of its wars with the United States of America.

## JULY 5

*[I]n our family, we'd decided if we meant to eat anything, meat included, we'd be more responsible tenants of our food chain if we could participate in the steps that bring it to the table. We already knew a lot of dying went into our living: the animals, the plants in our garden, the beetles we pull off our bean vines. . . . [W]e'd settled on a strategy of giving our food a good life until it was good on the table.*

—BARBARA
KINGSOLVER

Miles finished fencing the garden, using recycled hog wire and wire netting salvaged from my chicken project of the mid-1990s. In those days, I raised four dozen chickens a year for the freezer and kept a dozen free-range hens and a rooster for eggs and entertainment. I was careful not to get attached to the chicks because they were destined for the dinner table. But I was fond of the hens. Enjoyed taking care of them, collecting their eggs, watching them chase bugs, take dust baths, make chicken whoopee with their rooster.

The fence isn't high enough to keep out the deer, so we're adding several strands of barbed wire. Looks like a garden gulag, Miles observes. Recalling the sweet potato episode, I tell him that this is exactly the idea. Plants on the inside, deer and armadillos and rabbits on the outside. Also chickens, if I decide to have them again. (Thinking about it. Thinking seriously about it.)

Got a letter from our publisher, requesting contract amendments for all our books (mine, as well as the books that Bill and I wrote together), so they can be published as e-books. No hesitation here. It's a good move, and we're glad to agree.

## JULY 7

Jury duty today, my second jury in four or five years.

The earlier jury—we were more enlightened than I'd expected—found the defendant guilty of attempted jailbreak but not guilty of assaulting an officer. Pure Keystone Kops. The defendant (jailed for smoking pot) skipped out of the prisoners' dayroom, dashed down the stairs, and bolted straight into a closet. (He mistook it for the front door.) When the closet door was opened, the prisoner allegedly attempted to hit one of the four cops who were waiting for him.

After we rendered our verdict, the jurors told the county prosecutor that the fact that the prisoner came out of the closet swinging did not (as far as we were concerned) constitute "assault." It would have helped, we said, if there'd been some evidence that his swing connected. And if the prisoner himself had not ended up with a black eye, a smashed lip, cuts, and bruises, which made us think that he just might have been the one assaulted.

Today's jury was even more assertive. The defendant, a twenty-five-year-old restaurant bartender, was accused of selling beer to a minor. He'd been on the job for three weeks. He was the only bartender on the evening shift, the bar was crowded, the restaurant was jammed, he was servicing seven waitpersons, the music was loud. And he was set up. It was a sting. The two minors who bought the beer were employed by the police. The two officers gave conflicting testimony. So did the beer-buying minors.

It took less than ten minutes for the jury to render a not guilty verdict. In the debriefing, we told the prosecutor (the same one who prosecuted the earlier assault) that the police work was sloppy and the case badly presented and that this was an instance when a warning, not an arrest, would have been in order. (The word "arrogant" might even have been used once or twice.) Moreover, we were unanimously unenthusiastic about the use of minor children as undercover agents in a sting operation.

I left the courthouse with the feeling that we had done our civic duty. And then some.

JULY 9

The button bush is blooming beside the creek, and the hummingbirds and native bees (we're not seeing many honeybees this year) are swarming over it. There's not much else in bloom right now—a few straggly brown-eyed Susans, blue ruellia, and some early sunflowers. Between the drought and the blistering heat, the wildflowers are pretty well baked, broiled, or fried. The creek is dropping fast, and the emerging silty shoals are pocked with coon tracks, fresh ones every night: they're feasting on stranded bluegills, sunfish, and crawfish. The baby bunnies have graduated from their nest to my garden, and Mother Rabbit has already started on her next family, judging from the erotic hanky-panky we've witnessed in the front yard. No cloacal kisses there.

Hot, yes, hot. The mornings are muggy, the noon sky shimmers, the afternoons are loud with singing cicadas. Summer moves along, in all its lively, lovely moods.

*I like to think of the landscape not as a fixed place but as a path that is unwinding before my eyes, under my feet. To see and know a place is a contemplative act. It means emptying our minds and letting what is there, in all its multiplicity and endless variety, come in.*

—GRETEL EHRLICH

Doing housework, catching up on the e-mail, cleaning off my heaped-up desk—even unearthed the book I misplaced a couple of weeks ago. Getting Bill off to New Mexico took some time, but I've managed to work a couple of days this week. *Applebeck Orchard* is at seventy-two thousand words. I absolutely have to start tidying up the loose story threads and mend the gaping hole in the main mystery.

My major achievement for the week: resolving the Beatrix-Will problem. He's proposed, she's accepted. Getting the tone right was difficult, but I'm pleased. Not passionately romantic (this pair is middle-aged and supremely Victorian), just sweet love and affection with a touch of pragmatism. I think Beatrix would approve.

Looks like I have maybe two more weeks of work on the project, so I'm planning to follow Bill to New Mexico in about three weeks—if Zach's appetite improves.

Reading *Coming Home to Eat: The Pleasures and Politics of Local Foods* by Gary Paul Nabhan. I appreciate Nabhan's philosophy and politics and admire his commitment to renewing the knowledge of desert wild plant foods. Need to learn more about this, about the how-to of cooking and eating wild plants.

Also: rereading Maureen Murdock's *Unreliable Truth: On Memoir and Memory.* "The deepest memoir is filled with metaphor," she says. In Murdock's early life, it is the nun's habit that clothes her world. For Terry Tempest Williams, in *Refuge: An Unnatural History of Family and Place*, the central metaphor is the Great Salt Lake. Food writer Ruth Reichl (*Tender at the Bone*) tastes life through food.

We all taste life through food, don't we? And it's more than a metaphor.

*Most of the desert's edible plants still persisted somewhere in small patches, but ancient knowledge about how to harvest, prune, or cook them had already wilted and withered. The time-tried ways of gaining a livelihood within this austere landscape had nearly faded from memory.*

—GARY PAUL NABHAN

NEWS SUMMARY: *In 2007, the Supreme Court ruled that the Environmental Protection Agency, under the Clean Air Act, has the authority to impose new rules regulating the emission of greenhouse gasses. This week, the EPA refused to act. More regulation would "represent an unprecedented expansion of EPA authority," according to EPA executive, Stephen Johnson. "There can be profound consequences across all sectors of our economy and every individual living in their homes or where they work or driving cars."*

JULY 11

Profound consequences. Damn right.

But it looks like any action resulting in profound consequences has to wait until the next administration—assuming that the American people elect a president who cares about consequences.

JULY 12

The full, ripe beans are dropping from the honey mesquites (*Prosopis glandulosa*), to the joy of the raccoons, rabbits, possums, deer, coyotes. I've read that mesquite beans make up something like 80 percent of a coyote's midsummer diet.

Good for wildlife, bad for ranchers, who say that mesquite competes with grass for limited water. It's invasive, too. Back in the days when cows were rounded up by real cowboys on real horses, you could lose half your herd in a thorny mesquite thicket.

But there's not a lot of cattle ranching in Burnet County these days, and it's harder than it used to be to object to mesquite. Honey made from mesquite flowers is the best you'll ever spread on your cornbread. Dried and ground, the beans make a nutritious flour, which the natives turned into bread and booze. Gathered green, they make a good jelly. The thin branches are prized for grilling, and Bill turns larger chunks on his lathe, making them into beautiful vases and bowls. These days, mesquite has sex appeal.

At the eastern edge of the arid West, the mesquite is a metaphor for the life that's lived here. Twisted trunks, pale green canopies, feather-light against the blue of the sky, bee-rich flowers in late spring, clusters of beans in early summer. A Texas tree, a tree that belongs in these open spaces, under these wide skies, on these prairies.

A rancher neighbor gave me this recipe for mesquite jelly.

You start by making your juice. Collect two pounds of well-dried beans from your mesquite trees—the beige ones, or the ones with red stripes (they're sweeter). Don't use green pods—too bitter. Wash off the bugs and the dust and put your pods in a pot. Add enough water to cover them a couple of inches. Get this boiling good, then simmer for an hour until the water looks like dark clover honey. Drain it into a good big kettle. Take a potato masher and smash up the beans, add some more water, and boil until it looks like tea. Strain that into the kettle and set it on the fire to boil again. You're aiming to get seven cups of juice.

To make the jelly: while your seven cups of juice are getting to boiling in your kettle, mix up ¼ cup sugar and 3 teaspoons pectin. Some folks put in lemon juice, 3–4 tablespoons. When the juice is boiling, add 2½ cups sugar. Get it boiling again and skim off the foam best you can. Stir in your sugar-pectin mixture. Boil it for a minute. Pour it into clean, hot pint jars and screw on the lids. Turn them upside down on a tea towel until they cool off. Click the lids to be sure they're sealed tight. Real good, sweet, mild jelly.

NEWS SUMMARY: *The housing and credit crisis intensified with the federal seizure of Los Angeles mortgage bank IndyMac in the second largest bank failure in U.S. history. On another front, the Treasury Department proposed to invest billions of dollars in Fannie Mae and Freddie Mac, companies that either own or guarantee half the mortgages in the United States.*

JULY 13

Out here in the country, it's too easy to ignore what's beyond our horizons, to try to escape by ignoring the rest of the world. But every day makes me more deeply aware that this is a globalized world in which all of us live in the context of others, not in isolation.

After 9/11, I remember shaking my head at the idea that duct tape and plastic was sufficient protection against anything more dire than an early frost. (Was this like the duck-and-cover mantra I used to hear when I was a schoolgirl, instructed to kneel under my desk to save myself from an A-bomb blast?) I'm shaking my head again, and thinking that no matter where you are or who you are, we'll all have to face these issues. Economic crisis, climate change, species extinction, energy depletion—there's no getting away. And no amount of duct tape or duck-and-cover will save us.

JULY 14

Still thinking these thoughts, I drive to Austin for the Reading Circle, to discuss Barbara Kingsolver's locavore memoir, *Animal, Vegetable, Miracle*. Fascinating discussion, but not in the way I hoped. And in some ways, wildly ironic.

For one thing, we met in the community room at Central Market, one of Austin's most upscale food emporiums. We were surrounded by acres of shelves and bins and refrigerated cases and deli displays of high-end food: imported, out-of-season, heavily processed, ready-to-serve, expensive. In fact, most of the products on the shelves probably wouldn't qualify as food if you used Michael Pollan's rule of thumb: "Don't eat anything incapable of rotting."

For another, I was the only one of the group—all of whom I count as friends—who seemed to share Kingsolver's urgencies about food security. In fact, most wanted to avoid her basic argument: that our industrial-based, fossil-fueled food culture is about to become a thing of the past. That it *must* become a thing of the past, if the planet is to survive. That if *we* are to survive, we need to reconstruct a food culture that grows out of the place we live, out of its soil, its climate. Maybe Kingsolver knows many people who are "waking up" to the "troublesome truth," but they weren't in this group of readers.

Like Kingsolver, I'm beginning to feel like a "dweeby ant in a grass-hopper nation." When the discussion was over, I left our circle feeling profoundly isolated, out of step, out of synch, in conflict with my culture, even with my friends—perhaps the price to be paid for seeing the world and its resources in a different way.

I didn't go shopping.

*A lot of people at once are waking up to a troublesome truth about cheap fossil fuels: we are going to run out of them. Our jet-age dependence on petroleum to feed our faces is a limited-time-only proposition.*

—BARBARA KINGSOLVER

JULY 16

*Applebeck*: seventy-five thousand words. Now that Beatrix's and Willie's romantic destiny is settled, I can untie some of the other knots in the book. Also, working on the recipes, one of the (to me) interesting features of the series. Most come from cookbooks of the period, like *Mrs. Beeton's Book of Household Management*, which Beatrix asked for (and got) as a wedding present, so she could cook for her new husband—a definite break from the custom of women of her social class, who always had a full domestic staff.

Once married and settled on her farm, Beatrix had a large garden, worked in it herself, and ate what she grew. She would have understood Kingsolver's efforts. I think she would have been dismayed at the sight of that supermarket—of any supermarket.

Mrs. Beeton's Best Soda Bread: To every 2 lbs. of flour allow 1 teaspoonful of tartaric acid, 1 teaspoonful of salt, 1 teaspoonful of carbonate of soda, 2 breakfast-cupfuls of cold milk. Let the tartaric acid and salt be reduced to the finest possible powder; then mix them well with the flour. Dissolve the soda in the milk, and pour it several times from one basin to another, before adding it to the flour. Work the whole quickly into a light dough, divide it into 2 loaves, and put them into a well-heated oven immediately, and bake for an hour.

## JULY 17

Gardening here at the edge of the arid west may be a challenge, but I'm looking at wild food.

This morning, the mustang grape vine (mustang comes from the Spanish word *mesteño*, meaning wild or untamed) is heavy with tart, purple-red fruits, shining with a silvery sheen. The raccoons have stripped the grapes they can reach, but there's plenty for everybody. The juice makes a tart jelly, very good. I've read that it also makes an interesting wine.

Nearby, a clump of prickly pear cactus, brash with spines, thriving in this summer's drought. Boiled or grilled, the pads (*nopales*) are a tasty, nutritious vegetable. The fruits (*tunas*, which ripen in September) make a splendid jelly.

All around, the ubiquitous mesquites, also drought-tolerant, with their hefty crop of beans. Red mulberry, chokecherry, Mexican plum, all fruiting now. In another three months, pecans.

Wild fruits, native abundance. No cornucopia, but there's food here for people who know what to look for, how to use it.

## JULY 18

Another item filed under "They Live Here Too." From a prudent distance, Zach was paying absorbed attention to something in the corner of his backyard dog kennel yesterday. When I investigated, I found a diamond-backed water snake. Looks like a rattler, but nonpoisonous. Zach got some intensive anti-snake training from Bill a few years ago. I'm glad to see that some part of that training apparently lingers in the depths of his doggy brain.

This is rattlesnake territory. One night years ago, Bill took our then-dog, Val, out to his kennel. Knowing what was good for him, Val planted his feet and steadfastly refused to go in. Investigating, Bill found a six-foot rattler curled around Val's water bowl.

But this diamond-backed water snake holds no such terrors. Zach came when I called him. The snake went on about her (or his) business. Nice bit of wild life entertainment on a hot summer afternoon.

To be on the safe side, the dogs are vaccinated against rattlesnake venom.

## JULY 19

Miles and I finished the raised garden beds and laid a thick pad of newspapers on the paths between them. Then we covered the paper with cedar chips from the pile I've been saving for mulch.

The trees on our thirty-one acres shed a great many dead limbs, topple over in windstorms, and choose inconvenient places to grow, all of which requires a fair amount of cutting down and cleaning up. Come winter, when it's cool enough for extended outdoor muscle-work, there's a big pile of wood to split and stack for the fireplace, put through the chipper for mulch, or burn in our annual solstice bonfire.

The wood chips under my feet: the splintered bones of splendid trees, returning to the soil where they were born.

*We all travel the Milky Way together, trees and men . . . trees are travelers, in the ordinary sense. They make journeys, not very extensive ones, it is true: but our own little comes and goes are only little more than tree-wavings— many of them not so much.*

*—JOHN MUIR*

## JULY 20

For the past several months, I've been working long-distance with my daughter Robin, designing a couple of bookmarks and a flier. The bookmarks arrived this week—beautiful.

Also arrived: Robin's birthday.

The year she was born, in those faraway fifties, we lived in east-central Illinois, just outside of Danville. It was summer, and the pick-them-yourself strawberries were ripe. I was big-bellied with Robin, but she wasn't due for a couple of weeks and I wanted strawberries for the freezer. In fact, I was absolutely fixated on getting those strawberries. Her father and I drove to the field, picked forty quarts, and drove back home, where I washed, stemmed, sliced, and bagged them for the freezer, moving more urgently toward the end. Robin was born that night. I never smell a fresh strawberry without thinking of her.

What a wonderful baby she was. I woke up this morning remembering the purest pleasures of nursing her, sweet and milky, all contentment. She smiled early and never stopped smiling—until it was time to brush her cornsilk hair, so fine that it tangled in the lightest breeze. Brushing it out for school in the morning was a tearful trial for both of us. There were other trials, too. Robin was the middle child, a sweet-natured girl between an older and a younger brother,

*Suddenly, through birthing a daughter, a woman finds herself face to face not only with an infant, a little girl, a woman-to-be, but also with her own unresolved conflicts from the past and her hopes and dreams for the future.*

*—ELIZABETH DEBOLD AND IDELISSE MALAVE*

and came in for too much teasing. And then there were the usual disagreements between teenage daughter and mother—we were both pretty hard to live with in those days, I think. But we grew out of it and into a deep, affectionate friendship.

She's too far away—in the mountains of Colorado—her children (Amy in Alaska, Jason in Colorado) far off, too. She's worked in advertising for years, now works for a local hospice organization and edits the *Story Circle Journal* and other newsletters. She and husband Jeff are both active volunteers for the Boy Scouts: they give hundreds of hours a year to various programs. I'm amazed by her commitments, her organizational skills, her competencies.

And she never stops smiling. Maybe it was those strawberries.


JULY 21

When Bill is home, I usually join him in front of the television for an hour or two in the evenings. He's away, so I'm spending the evenings reading.

Inspired by Kingsolver's and Nabhan's books to think about food in the larger context of the changing American diet, I'm reading more about the history of American food preparation. Some favorites from earlier reading: *Perfection Salad: Women and Cooking at the Turn of the Century* by Laura Shapiro, and her later book, *Something from the Oven: Reinventing Dinner in 1950s America*. Fascinating for me because I learned to shop and cook in the fifties, without a very clear idea of the way food was prepared in earlier decades—except for what I saw in my grandmother's kitchen. Reading, thinking back, I can see that the food on Grandma Franklin's table was almost all pre-industrialized, home-raised vegetables, meat, milk, and eggs. How lucky I am to remember that.

Just finished *Kitchen Literacy: How We Lost Knowledge of Where Food Comes from and Why We Need to Get It Back* by Ann Vileisis, which is more academic than its title suggests. On my to-be-read stack: Barbara Haber's *From Hardtack to Home Fries: An Uncommon History of American Cooks and Meals*, and Harvey Levenstein's two books, *Revolution at the Table: The Transformation of the American Diet* and *Paradox of Plenty: A Social History of Eating in America*. And for fun, M. F. K. Fisher's classic *How to Cook a Wolf*, which saw its first printing in 1942 when wartime shortages were at their worst. Some recipes: Green Garden Soup, Polenta, Sausage Pie, War Cake, Tomato Soup Cake.

Should be enough to keep me busy while I'm keeping a weather eye on Dolly.

**NEWS SUMMARY:** *Tropical storm Dolly was named upon its formation in the Gulf of Mexico because it skipped the tropical depression phase: the storm already had tropical storm-force winds. This marks the earliest times a fourth name storm has formed since the 2005 season, which holds the record. Seventeen people dead in Guatemala, one in the Yucatán. The storm is aimed at South Texas.*

JULY 22

No rain since May. The fields are dry, dry, dry. But Dolly has formed in the Gulf. I'm not hoping for a hurricane, mind you, just praying for rain. If Dolly will only curve a little to the north . . .

The summer solstice tomorrow. Fireflies tonight, erratic brilliance dancing in the July dark, under a platinum moon. Remembering, as a child on Grandma Franklin's Missouri farm, reaching for them, leaping for them, watching them, antic stars, in a bottle-lantern.

> *Many a night I saw the Pleiads, rising thro' the mellow shade/Glitter like a swarm of fireflies tangled in a silver braid.*
>
> —ALFRED, LORD TENNYSON

JULY 24

Dolly romped in as a Category One hurricane between Brownsville and Corpus Christi. No serious damage. One of the wraparound rain bands brought us a half-inch of rain. Not enough. Not nearly enough.

The garden and I are spending a great deal of time together. The planting beds are finished, the paths are in, the fence is up. Rain on the way (maybe?), I put in a couple of rows of carrots, some pinto beans, southern peas, and green beans. I've also planted some tomatoes—Heat Wave and Silver Fir, open-pollinated "early" tomatoes (50–55 days)—in homemade self-waterers contrived from three-liter plastic soda bottles with a wick torn from an old flannel shirt. The tomatoes go under grow lights, along with cabbage and broccoli seeds in newspaper plant pots. With luck, the seedlings will be ready to move to the garden when I get back from New Mexico at the end of August.

Rereading parts of Catton's *Overshoot* and listening to the presidential candidates talk about "becoming independent of foreign oil."

> *We set out our own tomatoes . . . for early yields, Silvery Fir Tree and Siberian Early, two Russian types that get down to work with proletarian resolve, bred as they were for short summers.*
>
> —BARBARA KINGSOLVER

Thinking that it's not just foreign oil but oil itself—our dependence on irreplaceable fuels—that's the problem. And more drilling (McCain's agenda) is only a short-term fix. "Human self-restraint, practiced both individually and especially collectively, is our indispensable hope," Catton says.

Live modestly. Live at human scale. Hard to do in a culture that encourages people to constantly want more of everything, an economy that is based on the principle of perpetual growth.

## JULY 25

*Applebeck Orchard*, nearly done. Deleted a story line I'd neglected to develop (maybe I'll use it in the next book), compressed a couple of scenes in the early chapters, expanded several scenes toward the end. By the close of the book (I'm at eighty-five thousand words now), I usually find that some of the early scenes need adjustment—sometimes they get moved, sometimes expanded, even deleted. (How the devil did writers do this before the computer?) The last chapter is yet to be written, anticipating the first chapter in the next book. I'm mindful of John O'Hara's instruction: Life goes on, and for the sake of verisimilitude and realism, you cannot positively give the impression of an ending: you must let something hang. A cheap interpretation of that would be to say that you must always leave a chance for a sequel. People die, love dies, but life does not die, and so long as people live, stories must have life at the end.

## JULY 26

Zach's just back from a trip to the vet. He's alarmingly anemic, and I'm instructed to dose him with an iron-and-mineral tonic that's sold for anemic horses. I hope it improves his appetite. It's getting harder to convince him that he needs to eat, but he's always at the door, tongue lolling, tail wagging (even if only a little), when it's time to go for a walk. We don't walk far, and we don't walk fast: just far enough to give him some exercise and slow enough to let him lead.

The book's nearly done, and I'm wanting a change of scene. I've told Bill to expect the three of us—Zach, Toro, and me—on the first Monday in August. After a couple of months of torrid temperatures here, I'm yearning for the mountains.

There won't be three of us going to New Mexico next week.

Our vet—a kind, good man, and a friend—came out to our house this morning and put Zach to sleep. Cushing's is hard to treat and Zach is an old dog, so we knew that his chances of recovery weren't good. Still, he had fairly good energy until last week. Yesterday, he started spitting up blood, just a little, but this morning, much worse. Bill and I (via phone, and in consultation with the vet) decided that today was the right day to help him end his journey.

Zach was around two when he came to us, so in human years, he lived into his nineties—a ripe old age for a grand old dog, unfailingly loving, gentle, joyful, and amenable to most suggestions, although not all, since he was also a dog who knew his own mind. He loved going on walks, especially when the grass was wet and ripe with smells for sniffing; riding in the car; breakfast, dinner, and treats; petting, hugs, and tummy rubs; and his bed. He didn't like snakes (smart fellow!), was not impressed by armadillos (he tasted one once), and was not a natural-born swimmer (although he could be coaxed once or twice into the water with a tossed stick). He ignored the cats, tolerated Lady, and learned to like Toro. He adored Bill and considered him the Alpha Dog: I wasn't even in the picture when Bill was around.

How do you say goodbye to someone you've loved and lived with for a dozen years?

*[W]e are caught by the old affinity, a joyfulness—his great and seemly pleasure in the physical world. Because of the dog's joyfulness, our own is increased. It is no small gift. It is not the least reason why we should honor as well the dog of our own life, and the dog down the street, and all the dogs not yet born. What would the world be like without music or rivers or the green and tender grass? What would this world be like without dogs?*

—MARY OLIVER

## July Reading

*Coming Home to Eat: The Pleasures and Politics of Local Foods*, by Gary Paul Nabhan

*From Hardtack to Home Fries: An Uncommon History of American Cooks and Meals*, by Barbara Haber

*How to Cook a Wolf*, by M. F. K. Fisher

*Kitchen Literacy: How We Lost Knowledge of Where Food Comes from and Why We Need to Get It Back*, by Ann Vileisis

*Overshoot: The Ecological Basis of Revolutionary Change*, by William R. Catton

*Paradox of Plenty: A Social History of Eating in America*, by Harvey Levenstein

*Perfection Salad: Women and Cooking at the Turn of the Century*, by Laura Shapiro

*Revolution at the Table: The Transformation of the American Diet*, Harvey Levenstein

*Something from the Oven: Reinventing Dinner in 1950s America*, by Laura Shapiro

*Unreliable Truth: On Memoir and Memory*, by Maureen Murdock

| JANUARY | FEBRUARY | MARCH | APRIL |
|---------|----------|-------|-------|
| MAY | JUNE | JULY | **AUGUST** |
| SEPTEMBER | OCTOBER | NOVEMBER | DECEMBER |

## AUGUST 1

A lost sort of week, without enthusiasm or pleasure. Finished the *Applebeck* historical note, added the bibliography, assembled the recipes. Put away Zach's toys and dishes, washed his beds (several, in various corners: he occupied them according to whim or some secret schedule), and swept the black Lab fur fuzz bunnies out of the corners. I performed the same sad chores after Lady died; it somehow feels cruelly unfair that this must be all done again, and so soon. But there's no unfairness or fairness about death, only finality.

Toro is bewildered. He missed Lady after she died, but Zach kept him company. Now Zach is gone, too, and the emptiness is large and heavy. He asks to go outside more often—I think to look for his buddy, hoping he's just gone off somewhere and will come trotting back, eyes bright, tongue hanging, tail wagging. Somehow, even in the worst times, Zach's tail never quite stopped wagging. I'm resisting the temptation to let Toro sleep with me. It would be a comfort for both of us, although Bill would not find three-in-the-bed a comfortable combination when he's back home. But it's lonely, especially on our morning and evening walks.

Now, there are just the two of us—not five, or four, or three, just two.

*It's so curious: one can resist tears and behave very well in the hardest hours of grief. But then someone makes you a friendly sign behind a window, or one notices that a flower that was in bud only yesterday has suddenly blossomed, or a letter slips from a drawer . . . and everything collapses.*

—COLETTE

*When you are sorrowful look again in your heart, and you shall see that in truth you are weeping for that which has been your delight.*

—KAHLIL GIBRAN

## AUGUST 3

With Zach gone, there's nothing to keep Toro and me from joining Bill in New Mexico. I love the silence here, and the solitude, but it's too hot to work in the garden, the creek has stopped flowing, the landscape has a parched, high-summer look. And the book is finished, except for one last editing pass.

So I'm packing knitting projects and books, buttoning everything up, and making arrangements for a neighbor to water outdoor plants and check the livestock. Toro dances along beside me as I haul boxes and bags to the Element, loading it for the trip. For him, glorious fun. On-the-road-again, ride-in-the-car-again *fun*. His happy enthusiasm buoys me, and I join him in a little jig.

He's right. It's time to move on.

## AUGUST 5, COYOTE LODGE, NEW MEXICO

*In three words I can sum up everything I've learned about life: it goes on.*

—ROBERT FROST

*It seems as if the right words can come only out of the perfect space of a place you love. In canyon country they would begin with three colors: blue, terra-cotta, green. Sky, stone, life. Then some feather or pelt or lizard's back, the throat of a flower or ripple of sunlit river, would enter the script, and I would have to leap from three colors to uncountable thousands, all in some exquisite combination of Place, possessed by this one and no other.*

—ELLEN MELOY

Moving on but not forgetting.

I've never driven to Coyote Lodge without three dogs in the back of the van. It was a cozy fit, but they rarely bickered, never nipped their buddies (unlike some children of my acquaintance). The roadside rest stops, easier with only Toro, were poignant reminders of happier, more hectic times, when I had my hands full with three excited dogs eager to stretch their legs and exercise their sniffers.

Enough of that.

Moving on, we arrived here in New Mexico last night, and *here* is good, fine, splendid. The mountains are heartbreakingly beautiful, the morning sky indescribably blue, lucid, translucent, a blue for drowning in, a sky deeper than any terrestrial ocean. August is monsoon season; sun every morning, rain every afternoon, so much rain that Bill's outdoor work (cleaning, preserving, staining the logs, which weren't properly treated when the house was built) has been delayed. He's understandably frustrated: rain here; no rain at all in Texas.

But the rain here means that the valley below is a windblown sea of lush grass, green waves curling high up the sides of the mountain, black Angus cows riding the waves up into the higher meadow, under the green trees. The breeze feels as if it's sweeping down from the Arctic, and not (as it does in Texas right now) radiating up from the infernal tropics. Yes. I'm glad to be here.

## AUGUST 6

Left behind: summer-brown Texas hills and parched trees along the creek, the late-blooming blue ruellia and brown-eyed Susans. Here, forest-green mountains, Ponderosas and lodgepole pines, and along the road, a dazzling ribbon of color: sunflowers, head-high; towers of mullein; swaths of purple verbena, red clover, white clover, and yarrow; spills of purple asters.

Left behind: Eduardo, a ragtag hurricane that sputtered into a tropical storm—nothing, not even a few drops of rain, for us. And Zach, a difficult leaving that will only be steadied by time.

## AUGUST 7

Wonderful being with Bill again: lover, friend, partner, intellectual companion. Long conversations, usually early in the morning, when we're just waking up, and over breakfast. We're doing a great deal of reading. I'm into Ellen Meloy's *The Anthropology of Turquoise*. Bill and I are currently sharing *The Long Descent: A User's Guide to the End of the Industrial Age* by John Michael Greer. Greer is right when he says that modern societies can't turn on a dime. It'll be two or three decades before there's enough alternative energy to keep things going as oil and gas become less available—and only if the investments are made *now*. As in today.

The impacts are sobering. I'm thinking of our dependence on fossil-fueled agriculture, on food; Bill is thinking of transportation, the economy. He has a dark view, feels that things are likely to go to hell all of a sudden, and sooner, not later. I'm of the view that the situation will get bad (slowing economy, credit crunches, job losses, recession), then better (but not as good as before), then worse again, slowly enough to give at least some people—those who are watching the situation, who are flexible—time to adapt to new ways of living and making a living. Bill thinks: when things get bad, there'll be widespread social unrest, violence. I think (or rather, hope): people will pull together, try to find common solutions. He says I'm overly optimistic; I say he's too pessimistic.

But we do agree on this: that we were born into extraordinary times and that the extraordinary energy resources at our disposal have given us extraordinary privileges. That we (not just *we*, but citizens of developed nations, wealthy nations) have not appreciated these gifts or used the resources and the privileges wisely. That the inevitable depletion and global climate impacts that are the consequences of our ignorance will be borne by following generations. And that we—Bill and I, Americans, everyone on the planet—have to make changes in the way we live.

Not a heartening topic for two people on vacation. But there's some comfort in being realistic, in talking to one another about it, even if we're not of the same mind. We agree on the essentials. And since there's nobody else to share this stuff with, it's drawing us closer together.

## AUGUST 8

Re: discussing the situation with others. In *The Long Descent*, John Michael Greer poses an interesting argument. Suppose, he says, that it is 1700 and a resident of a rural English village somehow knows that the Industrial Revolution is on the way, and that within a century, the village's way of life will have been destroyed by new fossil-fueled, capital-based industries, by factory labor, and by the Enclosure Acts, which permitted the transformation of the commons into privately owned lands. Imagine that this person tries to warn his neighbors and that (improbably) they listen. They begin to believe. "What should we do?" they ask, deeply concerned. "How can we keep this from happening?"

Greer's answer: nothing. "It's clear," he says, "that nothing the villagers could have done would have deflected the course of the Industrial Revolution even slightly." And so it is in this case, he concludes. What we are facing—this life-altering confluence of climate change, resource depletion, population growth, runaway capitalism—is a predicament to which there is no solution. There are responses, but nothing we can do will change what's about to happen, any more than the village could have altered the forces that were shaping its destiny.

Bill agrees with Greer. We've reached a tipping point. From here, it's all downhill. His "dark side" position, as he calls it.

I agree, too. But I can't leave it there. I can't.

NEWS SUMMARY: *Russian tanks and soldiers entered South Ossetia, an independent province in Georgia, after Georgian soldiers and South Ossetian separatists began to battle. Fighting between the two has been sporadic since the 2004 election of pro-Western Mikheil Saakashvili, who declared his intention to bring the province back into Georgia. Russia moved troops into Abkhazia and launched airstrikes on Tbilisi, the capital of Georgia.*

No television here, and radio reception is spotty, although we can usually pick up a signal from KUNM-FM, the National Public Radio station from Albuquerque. This morning, we heard an NPR report on the real issue behind the Russia-Georgia conflict: an eleven hundred–mile oil pipeline through Georgia. The oil comes from Azerbaijan (which holds the world's third largest reserves) to the Mediterranean Sea, where it's pumped into tanker vessels headed for the West—and the United States.

Bill and I look at each other and shake our heads, thinking of our conversations. I'm remembering what I read months ago in Michael Klare's book, *Rising Powers, Shrinking Planet* about the intensifying competition for energy. The world seems suddenly small, interconnected, and very fragile.

AUGUST 10

After a few days getting settled (remembering where I'd put things, saying hello to neighbors, stocking up on groceries), I'm back at work on *Applebeck*, doing one absolutely, utterly final edit, trying to mop up the superfluous *shrugs, smiles, twinkles*, etcetera. I could invest weeks in this edit, but I'm forcing myself to work fast, thirty pages a day, so that I don't spend the entire month camped in front of the computer.

Reading *High Noon for Natural Gas: The New Energy Crisis* by Julian Darley, a dark book, as suggested in the ironic sunniness of its title. A couple of years ago, perhaps even last summer, I would have preferred fiction, would have found Darley's serious book dull, boring. Now, I find it topical, important, challenging.

Years ago, when I was a graduate student, I read Thomas Kuhn's *The Structure of Scientific Revolutions* and was struck by his definition of a paradigm: a pattern of thought—in the larger sense, a world view—within which scientific theories and conclusions are developed. In a more general way, each of us makes sense of the world within our paradigms, which have enormous stability. Now, I'm in the midst of a personal paradigm shift, which Kuhn describes as a revolution in which "one conceptual world view is replaced by another." A metaphoric moment. The equivalent of an intellectual earthquake. "A conversion experience," in Kuhn's words.

The reading I've been doing, these books, these writers—they're transforming my paradigms, realigning my understanding of the

*To enhance their competitive stances vis-à-vis one another, energy-deficient countries may forge strategic partnerships with friendly energy-rich states, often cementing these arrangements with massive arms transfers, new or revived military alliances, and troop deployments to unstable energy-producing regions. Such moves, which are already visible on the political landscape, are a recipe for all sorts of conflicts.*

—MICHAEL KLARE

*By having too many people using too much technology, we have outstripped the planet's capacity to deliver its billion-year store of sunlight ever faster to suit an economic system designed for an expanding universe, but not a spherical, finite planet.*

—JULIAN DARLEY

planet and our human place on it. I feel as if I'm living in two worlds: the ordinary world of everyday life, where everyone lives within the old paradigms of endless bounty and infinite growth; and another world, almost another universe, where humans will have to learn to live modestly, with much fewer resources.

AUGUST 11

But we still live in the ordinary world. Bill couldn't locate the paint and the ten-foot stepladder he needs in Las Vegas and wanted to drive to Santa Fe. We debated the trip (ninety miles each way) and decided it's a necessity. A gorgeous drive on a break-your-heart-beautiful morning.

*The Battle of Glorieta Pass, fought from March 26–28, 1862, in northern New Mexico Territory, was the decisive battle of the New Mexico Campaign during the American Civil War. Dubbed the "Gettysburg of the West" by some historians, it was intended as the killer blow by Confederate forces to break the Union possession of the West along the base of the Rocky Mountains. . . . In the end, the dreams of a Confederate stronghold in the Southwest were impractical; New Mexico did not provide enough food or sustenance for any prolonged Confederate occupation.*

—WIKIPEDIA.ORG

We're following the route of the Santa Fe Trail, which staggers up the wooded, craggy eastern flank of the Sangres and over the top at Glorieta, seventy-five hundred feet. The pass was the site of a bloody Civil War battle in March 1862. Filled with ambition, the zealous Rebels aimed to seize southern sections of New Mexico and Arizona and gain access to the mines of California and Nevada: they needed the gold and silver to finance their cause. They marched up the Rio Grande Valley, captured Santa Fe, and were on their way to take Fort Union when they ran into the Union Army at Glorieta. After a couple of days of hard fighting, the Yankees stumbled across the Rebels' supply wagons and burned them—a lucky find that turned defeat into a larger victory than the soldiers could have imagined. The Confederates retreated to Santa Fe and eventually to San Antonio. Nevada's silver and California's gold went to support the North, not the South, and helped to finance the Confederate defeat.

We buy Bill's ladder, grab a quick lunch, and get lost getting on the freeway, making a long loop through an affluent suburb of huge air-conditioned homes surrounded by irrigated landscapes and past a mall—a palace of conspicuous consumption—of astonishing size, encircled by acres of suvs.

At last, we find the freeway and head back home over the pass, where nearly a hundred men died to keep the Confederacy from reaching the resources that might have enabled it to win the war.

AUGUST 12

Gave a book talk last night at Tome on the Range, the independent bookstore where (last January) I stumbled on the book by William deBuys that completely upended my understanding of New Mexico. Tome is only a block from Las Vegas' Old Town Plaza, where in 1846, during the Mexican-American War, Stephen W. Kearny claimed the territory of New Mexico for the United States. Old Town was the Spanish Colonial heart of this small settlement, and the buildings were constructed around the Plaza to defend it in case of attack.

Didn't help. Kearny took it anyway—part of the U.S. westward expansion, driven by the seemingly boundless, limitless promise of a "manifest destiny," an idea that still drives us, unsustainably.

## AUGUST 13

Every August, we host a birthday party for Bob Goodfellow, who lives just up the mountain. Bob and his partner Don were guests at our wedding in 1986. After they bought a house here in 1997, we drove out to visit. One thing led to another, and here we are. It's all their fault.

And here, come 'round again, is Bob's birthday. We celebrate with a dozen neighbors, a store-bought cake, and rousing choruses of "Happy Birthday" and "For He's a Jolly Good Fellow" (of course). My excuse for store-bought: I'm on vacation. But the truth is that while pies are no problem, I haven't yet managed to turn out a decent cake at seventy-five hundred feet. I need more practice before I subject a cake to social scrutiny—although our neighbors here aren't really the scrutinizing sort. They're kind, helpful, generous with gardening suggestions and local lore. One neighbor offers a ladder, which Bill is glad to accept. His theory: when one is painting one's house, one can never have too many ladders.

## AUGUST 14

Just e-mailed the electronic file of *Applebeck Orchard* to New York. Often as I've done this, it should be old hat by now. But it still feels like black magic, hocus-pocus, a now-you-see-it-now-you-don't sleight of hand. Anyway, the book is now officially delivered, so I can spend more time reading, knitting, walking.

And thinking. At the party, the subject of energy came up, and I advanced some of my concerns about what may happen when there's not enough oil to go around. This group's response made me feel as alienated as I felt when the reading circle discussed Kingsolver's ideas for producing the food we consume. People don't want to hear things they're happier not knowing.

Gray, drizzly, so Bill took a break from painting and the two of us drove down the valley, up a ridge and through the village of Ledoux, named for a French trapper, one of the many who plundered the area for beaver pelts until the animals were gone. Then over another ridge and down to the village of Mora.

Mora was settled by land grant in 1835, burned by Texas freebooters in 1843, burned again by federal troops in 1847. But the settlers, mostly Hispanic, persisted, growing vegetables and grain, and raising cows, sheep, and goats in the fertile valley. After nearby Fort Union was established, they sold meat and produce there. By 1900, Mora was thriving. It lost its commons in a land sale in 1916, an act that stripped land grant holders of the right to pasture their animals on land held by the village—a tragic end to a self-sustaining, sustainable way of life.

Now, Mora has a grocery store, several gas stations, a farmers' market, a café, and Tapetes de Lana, a weaving center that processes local wools—churro, angora, alpaca. It also offers weaving and spinning classes and sells handspun yarns, apparel, and rugs. The center is closed today, and I'm sorry. I'd like to see the weaving. I keep promising myself to spend some time with my rigid heddle loom. What I need is inspiration. Some hand-dyed churro might help, too.

*The Sangres between Santa Fe and Taos were the first mountains in the Southwest—and among the first in the entire West—to be ransacked for beaver. . . . The year's gross sales [1823–1824] represent the skins of about two thousand animals. Two thousand may not be a great many gnats or cabbages, but it is a tremendous lot of beaver.*

—WILLIAM DEBUYS

AUGUST 18

This morning, Bill and I walk down the road to visit a neighbor's garden. Behind a fence, on a shelf of deep, rich soil, Marge and Dick have planted neat rows of beans, peas, lettuce, corn, carrots, strawberries, potatoes, tomatoes. The growing season is short here: the last frost comes in mid-June, the first in mid-September. But long enough for an abundant garden, when there's rain. This summer, there's been plenty, and the garden is lush, a delight. We come away with a bag of lettuce and another of fresh peas, which I shell and cook with mushrooms and green onions for supper.

I'm wondering now how my garden back home is doing—especially the seedlings, coming up under the lights, in their homemade self-waterers, on their own. Wondering whether they've survived, what I'll find when I get back.

NEWS SUMMARY: *In Warsaw, U.S. Secretary of State Condoleezza Rice and Poland's Foreign Minister Radek Sikorski sign an agreement for an American missile defense base in Poland, scheduled to be operational by 2012. Rice: the system is "defensive" and "aimed at no one."*

## AUGUST 20

Without TV, with only morning and evening NPR news, the disconnect from the rest of the world feels sharper than usual. Which is why I have to laugh at the idea of building a missile system "aimed at no one." We've spent more than $100 billion on a system that hasn't yet been demonstrated to work. Given the operational speeds, critics say, it'll be like aiming a bullet at another bullet. With all the other issues facing the country, this is what we're spending money on? But that's okay, because it's "aimed at no one."

I carry these thoughts as Toro and I set off for a walk along our gravel road. The sunflowers and mullein are tall and bright on either side, the sun setting behind a stained-glass painting of red-gold clouds, violet shadows darkening the valley and climbing the mountain. Behind us, to the east, is Cerro Pelón, its rounded top glowing pink in the sun's last light. Ahead, to the west, nestled against the flank of the Sangres, Rociada.

This half-mile-wide valley was once the home ranch of Jean Pendaries, who emigrated from Gascony in the 1870s. The ranch went to Pendaries' daughter, Marguerite, and her husband, Don José Baca. Among the Baca children was a girl named Consuelo, who grew up to marry a Pulitzer Prize–winning author named Oliver La Farge.

La Farge wrote about the ranch and the valley in *Behind the Mountains*. The 1951 book contains some fine descriptions of Rociada and the ranch when Consuelo was a girl, in the early twentieth century. On a still day, he wrote, "when the mill on the . . . lower ranch was running, one could hear the dull clack of the wooden water wheel from the ranchhouse." The mill and its wooden wheel still stand, less than a mile away from here on Rio Manuelitas, which spills now, even as it did then, down the flank of the mountain and across the rich grass.

Standing still in the gathering shadows, I imagine that I hear the clacking wheel, dulled by the decades that have gone since the Pendaries and the Bacas lived here with their sleek cattle and fat sheep and fine horses in the splendid isolation of their beautiful valley. Somewhere on the mountain above me, an owl calls, and then, much

*Visitors to New Mexico do not go to Rociada, . . . Broadly speaking, the name Rociada covers two villages, the embracing ranch, and the valley in which they lie. The valley is high, long, and irregular, walled by the higher mountains of the Sangre de Cristo range. . . . Behind the crests of the first rugged walls, shaggy with spruce and fir and pine, are the main peaks, with the brown, domed, pure rock of El Ermitaño [Hermit's Peak], snow-powdered until midsummer, as a monument and guardian notching the western sky.*

—OLIVER LA FARGE

farther away, a coyote, and another and another, their changing, changeless voices carried by the wind that is like a river, like the river that spills down the mountain and across the landscape of time.

And on the other side of the world, we are spending 100 billion of our tax dollars to build a defensive system aimed at no one.

## AUGUST 21

*The reality is that interest in local food is growing, and so is interest in food production, as food prices skyrocket and quality falls. And the best news is that this is a case where grassroots action not only can work, but it is the only thing that ever has worked. . . .*

—SHARON ASTYK

Drove to Las Vegas yesterday, to the farmers' market, which on this cool, misty morning has attracted some two dozen vendors and a crowd of buyers. The beds of pickup trucks and the trunks of cars and a few tables display heaps and mounds of locally grown garden vegetables, greens, melons, fruits, flowers, and herbs, as well as cheeses and honey and fresh-baked breads, pastries, tortillas. A heartening abundance. I bought sweet corn, lettuce, tomatoes, radishes, and onions. Bob Goodfellow came for supper and we feasted on tostadas.

But my corn tortillas were a fiasco. I'm fine with flour tortillas, but something went wrong with this first batch (for me) of corn. Good thing I had some store-bought tostada shells in the pantry. Good thing that store-bought is okay, especially when loaded with the tastiest of fresh tomatoes. Good thing my friendship with Bob is well past embarrassment at a minor culinary misadventure.

Later: reading, in the quiet of the evening, Donald Hall's *Unpacking the Boxes: A Memoir of a Life in Poetry*. A favorite poet whose work I encountered in college and have treasured since, now in his eighties, a former poet laureate. The memoir: a long, quiet look at the landscape of a poet's life.

## AUGUST 22

Big job, done well and with dispatch. We've had the driveway reengineered by a hard-working local father-son crew who showed up this morning with a Bobcat front-end loader and three dump truckloads of road base. Bill had them relocate one end of the drive so we can more easily park the car under the deck to keep it out of the snow in the winter.

What seems like a small change—the relocation of the one end of the drive—represents a big shift in our thinking. We were planning to build a free-standing garage and remodel the existing basement garage into more living space, spending something like fifty thousand dollars on the project. But talking seriously about the changes that may lie ahead, we've scrapped this idea. We'll hunker down, enjoy what we have—which is surely sufficient, beyond sufficient—although this will not bolster the economy. To do that, we would have to spend, to consume.

Well, we are spending—we're just not spending fifty thousand dollars or consuming a mountain of construction materials. The reengineered drive cost a thousand dollars, most of which went into the pockets of two local guys, hard workers.

Not exactly a tough economic choice.

*Small is beautiful.*

—E. F. SCHUMACHER

## AUGUST 23

We took Toro and drove this morning to Morphy Lake, some fifteen miles down the valley, across the ridge and through the villages of Ledoux and Guadalupita, up and up through a narrow, twisting valley to the twenty-five-acre lake, cupped in the mountains at eight thousand feet. The clear water is home to rainbow and brown trout and kokanee salmon, and the surrounding pine forest is home to squirrels, which we met, as well as porcupines, coyotes, deer, and black bear, which we didn't.

Toro waded into the crystal water and lapped it up, then romped gaily along the shore, scattering drops, trailing rainbows in the sunshine. We followed more slowly, holding hands, looking at small stones at our feet, at green-gray lichens, at a perfect gray feather. At the picnic table, we feasted on chicken salad sandwiches, deviled eggs, and chips, lounged and laughed, talked and walked again, feeling happy, alive, blessed, even though (or perhaps because) we have not forgotten that the future is so desperately uncertain.

Blessed.

*When you arise in the morning, think of what a precious privilege it is to be alive—to breathe, to think, to enjoy, to love.*

—MARCUS AURELIUS

**NEWS SUMMARY:** *Barack Obama announced his vice presidential choice: Delaware senator Joe Biden. Biden brings to the ticket foreign policy experience, Senate and congressional experience, and years of working to combat domestic violence.*

## AUGUST 24

Well, damn. I was hoping for an Obama-Clinton ticket. She has legislative experience, she's ready to step into the job if she has to (God forbid), she's mustered a strong constituency among women and the working class. I wanted to see the two of them—Obama and Clinton—together.

But there's Bill. Bill the Wild Card.

So it's Biden. Not the best choice, in my view, but a good one, if he can keep his lip zipped.

Up early this morning for another day trip, to Coyote Creek, fifty miles to the north, between Mora and Angel Fire. The drive took us north past the Victory Alpaca Ranch, where a couple of years ago I nearly bought an entire alpaca fleece. Oh, I was sorely tempted, but settled instead for a small bag of brown alpaca wool—soft as cashmere, fine and very strong—which I carded and spun and knitted into a soft brown hat. I think of this as we drive past a herd of plump, placid alpacas, heads down in the green grass, and wonder which of them shared her brown wool with me.

Coyote Creek winds through Guadalupita Canyon, between the Rincon Ridge to the west and the Ocate volcanic field to the east. Wildflowers: sunflowers, storksbill geraniums, red penstemon, purple asters, flax as blue as chips of sky, lacy white yarrow. Toro, leashed, pulls us along the path, where chokecherries hang like jewels around the slender necks of willows and tiny fish catch the light like silver darts in the glittering shallows.

Lunch under an aspen above the creek, the mountain beyond: ham and Swiss sandwiches, carrots and celery, boiled eggs.

This, I think, is what happiness is, must always be: the natural world, at every moment giving us what is necessary, what is lovely, what is all too brief.

## AUGUST 25

*To have the mind of an alchemist is to know that there are forces that change life, and the earth, too, and the universe at the core of which is always, one's own heart.*

—DIANA KAPPEL-SMITH

Packing, getting ready to leave for home tomorrow. Bill is staying, hoping for a few dry days to finish working on the logs. I take one last walk through the quiet meadow, feasting on the sight of asters and fleabane and yarrow and plush, purple thistles, oh, and sunflowers, each of which hosts a foraging alchemical bee, pollen baskets loaded with grains of pure gold to be changed to amber honey. I'm sad to be leaving the mountains and the sky and the cool wind that rushes up the valley to brush my face and lift my hair. It'll be hot in Texas, and the air will be thick as syrup with Gulf moisture. But I'll be at home there, too.

That will be good.

Too.

AUGUST 27, MEADOW KNOLL, TEXAS

Arrived at Meadow Knoll after dark last night to—unbelievably—rain! Nearly a half-inch in the gauge. This morning, the air is sweet and clean, the temperature reasonable (75 degrees), the grass green, cows sleek and contented, garden flourishing. The pole beans, tendriled and unruly, need staking, so my first chore (after unloading, unpacking, putting things away) is to cut poles from the stand of cane on the other side of the creek to serve as bean tripods. My second is to check the tomato, cabbage, and broccoli plants left under lights (on a timer). I am surprised—astonished, really—to see them strong and healthy and eager to go into the garden when I get an extra hour—maybe tomorrow.

Home in time to see the report that tropical storm Gustav is stirring up the eastern Caribbean. Too early to know whether it's headed for Texas, but that hasn't been ruled out.

And home in time to watch, spellbound, as Barack Obama stands before a roaring crowd in a packed football stadium in Denver to accept the Democratic nomination. I remember once when I was nine or ten: my father, a racist (as were many white men of his generation), spotted me roller skating on the sidewalk near Garfield School with Louie, a black boy in my class. He forbade me to do that again, *ever*. I watch Obama, listen to him, am extraordinarily, unspeakably proud, and hope that wherever he is, Louie is watching and listening, too.

Home in time.

NEWS SUMMARY: *John McCain names Sarah Palin, governor of Alaska, as his pick for vice president.*

AUGUST 28

Sarah who? Alaska governor for two years, six-year mayor of a town of fifty-five hundred, a hockey mom, an anti-abortion, anti–gun control Pentecostal conservative.

*What is he thinking?*

Thinking of shoring up support among the Republican faithful who worry that he is too liberal, not anti-abortion enough, not born again. He's thinking that he'll get the hockey mom vote. He's thinking that her youth will balance his age, her vivacity will enhance his solidity.

Home is all-embracing, a continuous inclusion of all events: this too and this too and this too. Home en route. Home is the place from which I have come and to which I return. Home is where I always am.

—DIANNE CONNELLY

Four years ago, I stood before you and told you my story—of the brief union between a young man from Kenya and a young woman from Kansas who weren't well off or well known, but shared a belief that in America, their son could achieve whatever he put his mind to. It is that promise that has always set this country apart—that through hard work and sacrifice, each of us can pursue our individual dreams but still come together as one American family, to ensure that the next generation can pursue their dreams as well. That's why I stand here tonight.

—BARACK OBAMA

The difference between a hockey mom and a pit bull? Lipstick.

—SARAH PALIN

I've questioned some of McCain's positions. I've never questioned his judgment.

Until now.

## AUGUST 29

*Today our food travels an average of 1500 miles from farm to table. The process of planting, fertilizing, processing, packaging, and transporting our food uses a great deal of energy and contributes to the cause of global warming. Planting a Victory Garden to fight global warming would reduce the amount of pollution your food contributes to global warming. Instead of traveling many miles from farm to table, your food would travel from your own garden to your table.*

—WWW.REVIVEVICTORY GARDEN.ORG

Did some e-mail campaigning this morning. Now that Palin's on the ticket, there's a great deal more active opposition. I'm not the only one questioning McCain's judgment.

In my surfing around the Internet this morning, I found several Web sites calling for the return of the Victory Garden as a response to industrialized agriculture, climate change, energy depletion. The University of California has a "Victory Grower" blog and a page on Facebook, urging gardeners to "Pick up a hoe and go." FoodShed Planet has a Victory Garden drive and a motto: "One person. One seed. Where will it lead?" And the blog "Red, White, & Grew" (Pam Price's blog—Pam lives in San Antonio) is subtitled: "Promoting the Victory Garden Revival and other simple, earth-friendly endeavors as bipartisan, patriotic acts in an age of uncertainty."

Yes.

## AUGUST 30

*This is the real deal, not a test. For everyone thinking they can ride this storm [Gustav] out, I have news for you: that will be one of the biggest mistakes you can make in your life.*

—RAY NAGIN, MAYOR, NEW ORLEANS

Gustav crossed the western tip of Cuba as a Category One hurricane and, within eighteen hours, exploded into a Category Four storm. Must be the fastest-growing hurricane on record. The track is shifting east and the weather gurus are telling people in New Orleans to prepare for a hard hit.

In 1979, my first year as dean of Newcomb College in New Orleans, Hurricane Frederic blew in along the Mississippi-Alabama border as a Category Four. This was before the new generation of weather satellites gave weather forecasters much to go on, before the days of major mandatory evacuations. I worried that the storm might shift to the west, so I moved some of the Newcomb students to a safer dorm on a neighboring campus—turned out to be completely unnecessary. I took a lot of heat from the local people for that call. Some, straight-faced, dead-serious, told me that New Orleans was hurricane-proof. Even after Katrina, some people were still saying the same thing.

But most got the message. And now, here's Gustav, and they're listening.

**NEWS SUMMARY:** *One day after the third anniversary of Hurricane Katrina, two million people have fled New Orleans in one of the largest evacuations in U.S. history.*

## AUGUST 31

They're evacuating New Orleans. Contra-flow lane reversals, seven hundred buses for those with no transportation (they can bring pets, this time), and eight thousand National Guard troops are getting ready. Katrina taught them a thing or two, looks like.

No storms here and 102 yesterday. In the garden, I've planted snap beans, peas, carrots. The transplants (tomatoes, broccoli, cabbage) are in the ground, shaded from the fierce sun. The squash have plenty of blossoms, but most are male—researching on the Internet, I learn that the squashes are waiting for cooler weather to produce female blossoms and fruit. I don't blame them. Sex in this heat doesn't appeal to me, either.

Rereading an old (1994) favorite—*Solar Gardening* by Leandre and Gretchen Poisson, full of information about intensive gardening: interplanting, succession planting, crop rotation. "We are solar creatures," the Poissons write. Gardeners need to be "married to a place and to its finite resources, dedicated to extracting life's essentials from the sun and to reestablishing the biosphere and occupying a nondestructive place within it."

Yes. Coming in from watering the garden, hot, sweaty, tired, happy, a solar creature, married to a place, and to its limited, finite resources.

*I am . . . a creature of the garden, happy to invest my sweat here, to watch daily for nearly invisible increments of growth in our lettuce or green beans and breathe the mingled scents of herbs. Here I can feel the active love of attachment, the work of place making.*

—DEBORAH TALL

| JAN | FEB | MAR | APR | MAY | JUNE | JULY | **AUG** | SEPT | OCT | NOV | DEC |
|-----|-----|-----|-----|-----|------|------|---------|------|-----|-----|-----|

## August Reading

*The Anthropology of Turquoise: Reflections on Desert, Sea, Stone, and Sky*, by Ellen Meloy

*High Noon for Natural Gas: The New Energy Crisis*, by Julian Darley

*Lights Out: The Electricity Crisis, the Global Economy, and What It Means to You*, by Jason Makansi

*The Long Descent: A User's Guide to the End of the Industrial Age*, by John Michael Greer

*Petrodollar Warfare: Oil, Iraq and the Future of the Dollar*, by William R. Clark

*Reinventing Collapse: The Soviet Example and American Prospects*, by Dmitry Orlov

*Solar Gardening: Growing Vegetables Year-Round the American Intensive Way*, by Leandre Poisson and Gretchen Vogel Poisson

*Unpacking the Boxes: A Memoir of a Life in Poetry*, by Donald Hall

| JANUARY | FEBRUARY | MARCH | APRIL |
| MAY | JUNE | JULY | AUGUST |
| **SEPTEMBER** | OCTOBER | NOVEMBER | DECEMBER |

## SEPTEMBER 1

Mayor Nagin was wrong about the "real deal," which may affect the way people respond to the next call for evacuation. Gustav dodged New Orleans, made landfall in a relatively unpopulated area to the west of the city, and stormed across Louisiana and East Texas and into the Midwest, spinning off a couple of dozen tornadoes and dumping twenty inches of rain here and there. Landfall was only about two hundred miles away from us, but we were on the "dry" side of the storm. Didn't get a drop of rain. Not one drop. Fourteen months since we've had anything significant. The weather gurus are now talking about a "severe" drought for Central Texas.

With Bill still in New Mexico, I'm doing some felting, using wool fleece I've carded and dyed. I love playing with the textures, colors, shapes, but the work takes so much space—the dining room table, the kitchen counter—that I can't do it when Bill's home. Mostly I content myself with hand-spinning (on wooden spindles) and knitting. Neither takes up any more room than I do, sitting down, and I can think about the next book while I'm knitting easy, small, quick stuff. Socks, a hat, a scarf, for Christmas presents.

On the reading stack: *The Knitting Way* by Linda Skolnik and Janice MacDaniels. Two wonderful books of Mary Oliver's poems: *Winter Hours* and *White Pine*. A fine, feisty study of Native American foods by food historian, anthropologist Sophie D. Coe: *America's First Cuisines*—what was eaten, by whom, why, how it was prepared. A memoir for Reading Circle (*Eat, Pray, Love* by Elizabeth Gilbert). On the top of the stack, handy whenever I sit down: *The Orchard*, written in the 1930s by Adele Crockett Robertson. During the Depression, Robertson gave up her city job and went home to try to save the fam-

*Knitting is not just something you do, it is a place that you can go. The mind needs a safe and secure space for thoughts and dreams— a place of resting that settles the spirit and refreshes the brain. . . .*

—LINDA SKOLNIK AND JANICE MACDANIELS

*It is not a crime or a sin to know about and think about what you are eating. The origin of the bean, or of the potato, should be part of the landscape of everybody's mind, so that eating is not just an automatic process.*

—SOPHIE D. COE

ily farm. She didn't—it had to be sold. But something in me, maybe the part of me that moved out here to these empty Hill Country acres twenty-five years ago, admires that kind of reckless courage.

NEWS SUMMARY: *The Pentagon reports that seven civilians and thirty-five Taliban were killed in last month's airstrike by U.S. troops on a village in Afghanistan. The United Nations and the Afghan government say that as many as ninety Afghan civilians, sixty of them children, died.*

SEPTEMBER 2

Doesn't matter what the Pentagon says, or even what actually happened. What matters is what the rest of the world believes. Feels to me like Vietnam all over again, with civilians the losers.

NEWS SUMMARY: *Half a million acres of dryland cotton have been lost on the South Plains as heat and wind rob the soil of an inch of moisture a day. Even irrigated cotton is threatened because blowing sand is damaging plants. "It's a whole different scenario than we've ever seen as far as the potential loss," said Travis Miller, Texas Agri-Life Extension Service drought specialist. "This thing came on us with a vengeance."*

SEPTEMBER 3

*The distinguishing climatic characteristic of the Great Plains environment from the ninety-eighth meridian to the Pacific slope is a defiency in the most essential climatic element—water. . . . This deficiency . . . conditions plant life, animal life, and human life and institutions. In [it] is found the key to what may be called the Plains civilization.*

—WALTER PRESCOTT WEBB

The drought is serious and getting seriously worse—not just here but all across Texas. For our county, here on the ninety-eighth meridian, the level has been raised by the USDA from "severe" to "extreme." Pecan Creek stopped running in June and the herons and raccoons, nocturnal visitors, have fished out the last few puddles of water. I see their tracks in the cracked, dried mud, along with a scattering of fish and crayfish carcasses. Only the third time in our twenty-five years here that the creek has gone completely dry.

I'm watering just the vegetable garden now; the roses and native perennials will have to survive on their own. Problem: the electric pump on our four-hundred-foot well quits after ten minutes or so. Solution: trudge to the pump house, thump the well's pressure gauge, flick the switch. Repeat as necessary.

Bill (consulted via telephone) diagnoses the culprit as a sticky gauge, or maybe a dirty switch, most likely the switch. Fire ants by the hundreds, fatally attracted to the electrical current, crawl into electrical switches and die. Their fried corpses short the switch, which trips the breaker. No kidding. Texas spends $140 million a year just to fix traffic signals shorted out by fire ants, fried in search of a buzz.

Or maybe the problem goes deeper. Switches and gauges can be fixed, but there's nothing to be done about the dropping water levels in our aquifer, the Trinity, where, some four hundred feet below the surface, the water flows through a layer of porous, permeable limestone and sandstone. Even in wet years, our section of the Trinity isn't very "productive," meaning that there's not a lot of pressure. In drought years, the pressure drops even more. My problem may not be a repairable gauge or defeatable fire ants. Maybe there's just not enough water down there.

Drought is a painful reminder of human limits. Electricity came to Burnet County in 1939, the year before I was born. Until then, there were no electricity-powered pumps and no wells deep enough to reach the aquifer, except in the few places where the aquifer reached the surface. No electricity, no well, no water, no garden. And no living here, either.

We'd have to live somewhere else.

## SEPTEMBER 4

It's official: June, July, and August were tied (with 1998) for the hottest three-month period on record: an average of 86.7 degrees at Camp Mabry in Austin, where official records are kept. Another significant number: forty-nine 100-degree days, third highest on record.

I'm thinking about temperatures right now, because I'm still adding a few plantings in the garden, even though the soil is too warm for some seeds to germinate. But not beans. As far as beans are concerned, the hotter the better. And this warm weather may go on through the first of November, which means I could still get a snap bean harvest. Maybe. Or maybe not. Worth a try.

Also thinking about travel. My high school graduating class is celebrating its fiftieth anniversary with an early October reunion, and I'm planning to drive to Illinois. Other than that, though, and an end-of-the-year trip to New Mexico, I'll be here at home.

At home. Feels right.

*Global warming is one of those things, not like an earthquake where there's a big bang and you say, "Oh, my God, this has hit us." It creeps up on you. Half a degree temperature difference from one year to the next, a little bit of rise of the ocean, a little bit of melting of the glaciers, and then all of a sudden it is too late to do something about it.*

—ARNOLD SCHWARZENEGGER

*I rejoice in the voices of the women in this book [What Wildness Is This], almost a hundred, raising our voices in celebration or warning, the words echoing off the canyon walls and the border fences, whistling through ocotillo wands. This body of work expresses what so many people most deeply feel and most clearly believe: gratitude for the gift of this place; astonishment at what each moment presents—peach jelly on the table, rain in the wind, fear in a standing wave, ghosts in the soil; an abiding love for this sere and mysterious patch of earth; and the terrible understanding that we cannot wreck this place without destroying also ourselves.*

—KATHLEEN DEAN MOORE

Good news, for a change.

*What Wildness Is This: Women Write about the Southwest* won the 2008 Willa Literary Award for Creative Nonfiction from Women Writing the West. I was the lead editor on the book, an ambitious multi-year project with contributions from nearly a hundred women writers. One of those once-in-a-lifetime projects, the kind you'll never do again after you've done it the first time and discovered just how much work it is. Now I have the pleasure of telling the other editors—Paula Yost, Susan Hanson, and Jan Seale—that the book has won, and Theresa May at the University of Texas Press (editor/publisher), and the contributors, and the women at the Story Circle Network, which sponsored the project. And Kathleen Dean Moore, who wrote such a fine introduction to the book.

Oh, and *Spanish Dagger*, my 2007 China Bayles novel, was a finalist in the Contemporary Fiction category. A double honor.

NEWS SUMMARY: *The U.S. Treasury has placed giant lending institutions Fannie Mae and Freddie Mac into conservatorship. Between them, they hold more than half of the mortgages in this country. The Bureau of Labor Statistics reports that the jobless rate in the United States hits 6.1 percent. Eighty-four thousand people lost jobs in August.*

SEPTEMBER 6

Gustav is history, but here comes Ike, with Josephine in his wake. Josephine isn't a problem for the Gulf, the weather folks say. But Ike is headed in this direction and may make landfall somewhere on the Gulf Coast by the end of next week. We're far enough inland not to worry about hurricane winds; it's the rainfall and flash flooding that can be dangerous—although at this point, fourteen months into this drought, any rain at all would be welcome.

Reading the news about the subprime lending situation, I am once again grateful that we don't have a mortgage. Our house may be small and architecturally undistinguished, but we don't owe a dime on it. But with the drop in the Dow, our 401Ks (vestiges of past formal employment) are deflating fast. Others have similar stories of loss. A friend in an Austin suburb reports that houses in her neighborhood have lost more than thirty thousand dollars in value in the past year, with many foreclosures. An acquaintance in New Jersey writes to say that her husband lost his job in July; she lost hers last week. No savings, no job prospects, a sizeable mortgage, payments on two cars, credit cards, college tuition. Tough times.

## SEPTEMBER 8

Austin today, annual mammogram and biannual bone density scan early in the morning, Reading Circle at noon, then grocery shopping.

The mammogram and scan were both routine, except for the fact that there's a huge sprawl of construction around the clinic and I got lost in the fifteen-acre parking lot. Seriously lost. Came out of a different entry and hadn't a clue to where I'd parked the car. Took a half hour to find it. Not routine. Not a senior moment, either. I ran into another woman who was looking for her car, and she was younger by at least thirty years.

For Reading Circle: *Eat, Pray, Love* by Elizabeth Gilbert. Exuberant, intelligent, witty, easy to read, occasionally insightful—although the narrative was . . . well, chaotic. The other readers liked it more than I did.

I try to keep Austin trips to a minimum, once a month or so. Depending on how far into the city I have to go, it can be a 130-mile round trip, half in heavy traffic. Today, 100 miles, with the price of gas at $3.85 (spiking because of the threat of Ike and the lingering effect of Gustav on the Gulf's oil rigs and pipelines). The drive seems shorter because I'm listening to a powerful book: *American Theocracy* by Kevin Phillips, which predicts the current market apocalypse. When he wrote it (2004–2005), Phillips must've been looking into a crystal ball.

## SEPTEMBER 9

Today, my brother's birthday. John is eighteen months younger than I am, and I've always played Big Sister to him—a little more difficult now that we're in our sixties, but old habits are hard to break.

A happy memory: John, four, and I, five, sitting together on the back steps at the Indiana farm where we lived during the last year of the Second World War. Mother had given us each a bowl (mine, I remember, was blue) of bread and milk, a standard snack in our wartime household. I made short work of mine, but John was slower. Too slow. The big white gander came up behind him, stuck his long

I've spent so much time these last years wondering what I'm supposed to be. A wife? A mother? A lover? A celibate? An Italian? A glutton? A traveler? An artist? A Yogi? But I'm not any of these things, at least not completely. . . . I'm just a slippery antevasin— betwixt and between—a student on the ever-shifting border near the wonderful, scary forest of the new.

—ELIZABETH GILBERT

The financialization of the United States economy over the last three decades—in the 1990s the finance, real-estate, and insurance sector overtook and then strongly passed manufacturing as a share of the U.S. gross domestic product—is an ill omen in its own right. However, its rise has been closely tied to record levels of debt and to the powerful emergence of a debt-and-credit industrial complex.

—KEVIN PHILLIPS

neck over John's shoulder, and gobbled up the bread and milk. John sat there holding his empty bowl, wailing.

Ah, different days, different world. No electricity in that farmhouse, no central heat, no indoor plumbing. We pumped water by hand from a shallow well in the yard and visited the privy out back. Mother had chickens and a garden and milked a brown cow named Daisy—the milk in my blue bowl was fresh and unpasteurized. Dad worked as a farmhand on a neighboring farm and (because we had no car) walked there and back every day, along the railroad track. For trips to the grocery (far fewer, in those days of rationing), Dad borrowed the farmer's truck. No radio, no television, no Internet, no books—except for my mother's Bible and a 1909 encyclopedia we called "the big brown book." With these cultural "deprivations," it's maybe a little surprising that John and I both grew up to be published writers.

Hoping to see John and his wife Jean in December, when we may be able to get together in New Mexico for a few days and talk about books, and the days when we ate bread and milk on the back steps.

## SEPTEMBER 10

Ike (Category Four) damaged 80 percent of the homes in the Turks and Caicos, crossed Cuba yesterday (Category Two), and is now barreling across the Gulf of Mexico, with an enormous wind field that (in the satellite images) covers the entire Gulf. Not clear yet where this huge storm may make landfall, although the bookies are betting on the Texas coast. If it comes in around Corpus Christi, we'll likely get tropical storm winds here, power outages, ten to twelve inches of rain (I wish!). Farther north, nearer Houston, and we'll be on the dry side again. No rain, not much wind.

Bill drove home from New Mexico, and we're buttoning up. Checked our supplies: extra water, batteries for the emergency weather radio, gas for the generator that runs the freezer and the fridge when the power's off, oil lamps and lamp oil. Plenty of food, other necessities.

Intermittently Ike-watching (on television), I'm also working on the copyedited manuscript of *Together, Alone: A Memoir of Marriage and Place*, which arrived from the University of Texas Press yesterday. The copyeditor, Sally Furgeson, did a beautiful job, without a murmur of rebuke for my botch of the endnotes. Bless her.

## SEPTEMBER 11

Just watched Charlie Gibson's ABC-TV interview with Sarah Palin. McCain had his pick of qualified, articulate, politically gifted women—there are plenty in his party. Too bad he didn't choose one.

## SEPTEMBER 12

Ike is aimed at Galveston.

The west end of the island was evacuated yesterday, although many—40 percent or so of the population—say they're staying put. They've got to be crazy. Or maybe they remember what Mayor Nagin told the citizens of New Orleans about Gustav's being the "real deal," which it really wasn't. Nevertheless, the Hurricane Center is sounding exceptionally stern. Certain death. That would scare the hell out of me.

The rest of Galveston's citizens evacuated today, together with residents of the low-lying parts of Houston, along the ship channel. We briefly debated making a trip to Houston to fetch Bill's mother, Freda, who lives in a nursing home on the southwest side of the city. We gave up the idea. We're seeing the traffic jams on television—they're not as bad as the evacuation traffic before Rita in 2005, but they're bad enough. It wouldn't be hard to get into the city, but nearly impossible to get out of it. Bill calls and talks to Cindy, the nursing home administrator. She's confident that they'll weather the storm. We'll have to take her word for it.

*All neighborhoods and possibly entire coastal communities will be inundated during the period of the peak storm tide. Persons not heeding evacuation orders in single family one- or two-story homes will face certain death.*

*—NATIONAL WEATHER SERVICE*

## SEPTEMBER 14

Galveston was smashed. Cleaning up and rebuilding will cost billions of dollars and years of people's lives. Many of the city's buildings are either flooded or demolished by the storm surge. The houses on the Bolivar Peninsula are gone; if people stayed behind, they're gone, too. No report yet on damage to oil refineries and offshore rigs. The power lines are down, landlines and cell phones are out, so there's no word from Bill's mother or from our Houston friends. Ike's rain and wind are wreaking havoc as far north as Canada today: Quebec got more rain (some three inches) out of the storm than we did. Bone dry here and windy, but cooler—some relief, at least.

Picked beans for supper, thinking about the people in shelters. If

The link between changes in the temperature of the sea's surface and increases in North Atlantic hurricane activity has been quantified for the first time. The research—carried out by scientists at University College, London—shows that a 0.5°C increase in sea surface temperature can be associated with an approximately 40 percent increase in hurricane activity.

—SCIENCE NEWS (JANUARY 31, 2008)

I lived in Galveston, I'm not sure I'd go back to live there, with other hurricanes—next year, the years after that—ominous on the eastern horizon. Scientists are saying that the tropical Atlantic is growing more active, a trend that's related, in part, to the increase in ocean temperatures. And with sea-level rise coming over the next few decades, a beachfront house isn't the attractive property it used to be.

I'm cooking the beans with bacon and onions, the way Mom used to do, and we're having meatloaf baked in the slow cooker. Comfort food.

NEWS SUMMARY: *The Dow Jones Industrial Average dropped more than five hundred points, or 4.4 percent, amid concerns over a global financial crisis. It was the worst one-day loss since the September 11, 2001, terrorist attacks.*

## SEPTEMBER 15

Bill and I drove to Austin, he for errands, I for my regular doctor's appointment. I like my doctor (I've known her for more than a decade), but there's nothing enjoyable about lying on my back, mostly naked, my feet in metal stirrups, to be probed in several directions. Bill was waiting out front: this time, I exited the right door and didn't get lost in the parking lot. Then across town to the Press, where I turned in the finished copyedited manuscript of *Together, Alone*. To celebrate, we went to our favorite Indian restaurant, the Taj Palace. I love their naan and battered, fried spinach. Oh, and rosewater-flavored rice pudding. Delicious, delicious.

Grocery shopping, home by three. Turned on the television to see that Lehman Brothers has declared bankruptcy (not too big to fail, apparently). Stocks took a swan dive, the worst day since 9/11.

Reading: Nancy Pickard's very fine mystery, *The Virgin of Small Plains*, a compelling story with likable characters and a strong setting. Like the way Nancy manages the present story and the back story. Also enjoying *The Black Swan* by Anne Batterson and rereading an old favorite, E. F. Schumacher's *Small Is Beautiful: Economics as if People Mattered*, with all my underlinings and notes from the 1980s. And *A Century of War: Anglo-American Oil Politics and the New World Order* by William Engdahl. Illuminating, unsettling. Makes a clear connection between the decline of energy resources and the Bush administration's efforts to control the Middle East. Arguments not to be read quickly, taken lightly.

The prospect of a sudden, unexpected global peaking of present oil and gas supplies, perhaps before the end of the [first] decade [of the twenty-first century] . . . would indeed explain Washington's mood of obsessive determination for war.

—WILLIAM ENGDAHL

**NEWS SUMMARY:** *Ike was blamed for at least 186 deaths: 74 in Haiti and 112 in the United States, with 26 people still missing. Ike caused devastation from the Louisiana coastline to Corpus Christi, Texas, as well as flooding and significant damage along the Mississippi coastline and the Florida Panhandle. Behind Andrew (1992) and Katrina (2005), Ike was the third costliest Atlantic hurricane of all time, with damages estimated at $24 billion in the United States alone.*

## SEPTEMBER 16

Bill finally managed to connect by phone with Freda's nursing home. All safe, no serious damage, plenty of food and water, a generator for lighting, but still no power for air conditioning. The weather there has been cooler than usual (in the eighties), but the idea of some three hundred elderly people, many requiring nursing care, living without air conditioning in Houston is nothing short of terrifying.

I can see from online and television photos that Galveston is disastrously uninhabitable. It will be weeks before there is power, water, sewer. People aren't permitted to go back home until next week, even if they have homes to go to. That means another week out of work, added to the cost (financial, physical, psychological) of evacuation—*if* the office, retail outlet, service operations still exist. There may not be any work to go back to.

People love to live by the sea, and yes, Galveston is a beautiful place. But shouldn't somebody be asking whether this city ought to be rebuilt? It was destroyed by a hurricane once before, in 1900. It's constructed on a barrier island that is environmentally fragile and naturally unstable, even sinking. A recent geohazards study recommended that new development be halted west of the seawall (it wasn't). And the likelihood of another powerful storm is high. Nevertheless, the mayor is asking Congress for $2.3 billion to rebuild.

I'd have a hard time saying yes.

I suspect that this is a politically incorrect opinion.

*Barrier islands tend to be even riskier places to live than coastal areas, because they bear the brunt of any approaching storm impact. "If you think about their location, they're basically lonely sentinels that serve as barriers for the mainland," said Clark Alexander, a marine geologist at Georgia's Skidaway Institute of Oceanography. "The lifespan of a typical house is something like sixty years. But if you live on a barrier island, you can't guarantee you'll have land under your house in sixty years. It's trying to put something permanent in a place that's very dynamic."*

*—FOXNEWS.COM
(SEPTEMBER 15, 2008)*

**NEWS SUMMARY:** *The U.S. House passed legislation allowing offshore drilling for oil within fifty miles of the coast if all adjacent states agree, and regardless of a state's disagreement, if the drilling takes place one hundred miles off the coast.*

## SEPTEMBER 17

Drill, baby, drill.

But the more oil we have available, the more $CO_2$ we'll produce. Isn't it time we started using less of the stuff?

Reading *A Thousand Barrels a Second: The Coming Oil Break Point and the Challenges Facing an Energy Dependent World* by Peter Tertzakian and thinking about electricity for our well, for the air conditioning in Freda's nursing home—thinking how *invisible* electricity is, until it stops working and everything else stops, too. Bill and I can make do without a lot of things here in the country, but electricity to power the water pump is absolutely essential. And in Freda's nursing home, life literally depends on electricity.

Same thing is true for oil. We see what it does (powers the cars), but we don't really *see* it until we can't get it; witness the long lines at gas stations in Atlanta when Hurricane Gustav disrupted oil shipments to the Southeast.

We've built a society entirely dependent on vulnerable supply lines, diminishing resources.

And disruptions are the new normal.

*Every time we flick on a light switch, turn up the heat, or start up our car, a vast and complex energy supply chain kicks into gear. To fuel and power our lifestyles, the world in 2005 draws from these supply chains to consume 85 million barrels of oil, 240 billion cubic feet of natural gas, 14 million tons of coal, and 500,000 pounds of uranium every single day.*

—PETER TERTZAKIAN

## SEPTEMBER 18

More manageable matters: seed potatoes. A couple of days ago, I cut them into planting pieces and set them aside so that the cut sides could dry—maybe reduces rotting. This evening, I planted the pieces in "potato towers": cylinders made of hog wire, which I will fill with compost and grass clippings as the plants grow up. I've never grown them this way, but garden space is limited right now and this seems like a good idea.

Researching online, I've found a solar water pump that's powered by photovoltaic panels and will handle the depth of our well. Adding it to my wish list of energy-saving (energy-*replacing*?) purchases for next year, to lessen our dependence on the grid.

## SEPTEMBER 19

Just got off the phone with the district ranger of the Texas Parks and Wildlife Department. The absentee landlord who owns the lot to the west of us has set up a deer feeder and deer blind so that he's shooting into our picnic area, the paths where I walk the dogs, and the pasture where our cows and sheep graze.

I did some online research in the TPWD codes and found a code called "Discharge of Firearm Across Property Line," making it illegal to shoot across your neighbor's fences. The ranger called this "trespass by bullet": the shooter can be charged with "deadly conduct." We'll write a letter to the man who intends to hunt and include a copy of this TPWD code and a drawing of the properties. We're hoping he'll move the feeder or the blind, or both. But we're not holding our breaths.

The joys of life in the country.

NEWS SUMMARY: *Lehman Brothers investment bank filed for bankruptcy, the largest filing in U.S. history. The Treasury Department is asking for authority to buy up to $700 billion in bad mortgage assets from private investment companies, the largest bailout in U.S. history.*

## SEPTEMBER 20

The sky is falling. Not our personal sky (except for our 401Ks). The entire country's financial sky. The subprime mess has boiled over. $700 billion. 700 *billion*!! Hard to get my mind around that number. Hard to see the potential for much long-term improvement, given the co-occurrence of the subprime debacle, the energy problem, climate change. A perfect storm of converging catastrophes.

But the sky will just have to fall by itself. Nothing I can do to shore it up. I'm abandoning this cacophony of mixed metaphors. Heading out to the garden, where there's plenty I can do.

*Do not be daunted by the enormity of the world's grief. Do justly, now. Love mercy, now. Walk humbly, now. You are not obligated to complete the work, but neither are you free to abandon it.*

—TALMUD, ATTRIBUTED

## SEPTEMBER 21

The fall equinox and our wedding anniversary, both today. We were married on a bright, sunny equinox twenty-two years ago, with a passage from Wendell Berry as part of the ceremony. Bill's family was there, my brother and his family, my three children, and a crowd of our friends—all gathered in Zilker Park in Austin. Afterward, everyone came to our house for a buffet lunch, catered by the bride and groom. Then Bill and I piled all the dirty dishes into the dishwasher, climbed into Amazing Grace (our antiquated RV), and drove off on an extended honeymoon to Nova Scotia.

Twenty-two years. In that time, we have homesteaded Meadow Knoll; added on to the initial five acres to make it thirty-one; collected dogs, cats, cows, sheep, chickens, ducks, peacocks, geese, and guinea fowl; acquired a getaway place in New Mexico; and built a writing career that allows us to work wherever we are. We've said hello and welcome to new daughters- and sons-in-law, new grandchildren and a great-grandson. We've said goodbye to three parents, a brother, and too many friends and animal companions. We've grown gardens and mown hay and cut trees and split firewood and dug trenches and fixed fences. We've written more than a hundred books and driven a million miles and lived together 24/7 for twenty-two years. Remembering Berry: "One who returns home—to one's marriage and household and place in the world—desiring anew what was previously chosen, is neither the world's stranger nor its prisoner, but is at once in place and free."

My anniversary present from Bill: a solar oven.

My present to him: a fourteen-inch band saw.

A team, equipped to face the future. I can cook it, he can cut it up. Whatever *it* is.

## SEPTEMBER 23

The electricity is on at Freda's nursing home, and they now have air conditioning. But three quarters of a million customers—one in four Houstonians—are still in the dark, as well as everyone who stayed behind on Galveston Island. In the *hot* dark, since temperatures are in the nineties. They probably don't even know that the sky is falling since they can't turn on their televisions and watch Treasury Secretary Henry Paulson and Fed Chairman Ben Bernanke plead with Congress to dish out $700 billion to save the banks from utter ruin, or go online and check out their foundering 401Ks. When their power comes back on, days or weeks from now, they'll find that more than a hurricane has blown through the neighborhood.

NEWS SUMMARY: *In September, so far 110 civilians killed in suicide bombings in Yemen, Islamabad, Syria, Baghdad. Thirty in car bombs in India. Six in a killing spree in Alger, Washington, twenty-four in a commuter train wreck in Los Angeles (the engineer was texting on his cell phone).*

Feeling enclaved here, with ugliness and violence and carelessness all around. Is this just my feeling, or do others feel like this? The more I hear from the world out there, the more I treasure the world right here.

Walks are a delight these days. Only sixty degrees when Toro and I went out this morning, the breeze chilly enough for a sweater. The native big bluestem grasses are nearly shoulder high along the path through the east meadow, and the fields are bright with goldenrod, eryngo, white heath aster, snow-on-the-prairie, frostweed, and broomweed. The cypress trees are turning a bright russet-orange. The color is too early, though, and sadly unhealthy. Accustomed to having their roots in the running creek, the trees are stressed by the drought.

Back home, I eat hot oatmeal with raisins at the computer, catching up on the news. More big chunks falling out of the sky, and Congress and the Bush administration have not yet come to terms (can they? will they?) on how much it will cost to shore it up. Galveston has ended its "state of emergency." The refugees can go home, but the city is considering declaring a "state of disaster" for the next twelve months (well into the 2009 hurricane season). A quarter of a million people in Houston don't have drinking water.

Suicide bombings, shooting sprees, train wrecks. Maybe it's time I got started on the next murder mystery. Killing people in fiction is easier on the soul than reading and thinking about the real-world news, which I find myself, as a citizen of the world, required to consider.

It's also much easier than listening to interviews with some of the candidates for high office.

SEPTEMBER 26

The next book on the schedule is a China Bayles mystery called *Holly Blues*. If I'm going to finish it by Christmas, I need to get started on it soon. But the reunion trip (to Illinois) will eat up all of next week, so it's probably a good idea to put the book off until I get back. Which means it won't be done by Christmas. Not a tragedy, I suppose—it isn't due until the end of March. I've got this thing about finishing early, though, in case of family emergencies.

According to the polls, Barack Obama won the first presidential debate, held at the University of Mississippi. According to me, it was a big win, hands-down. He says the right words about energy depletion and climate change. Wasn't clear until the last minute that John

McCain would participate. He suspended his campaign and went to Washington to have a say in the bailout discussion, although as it turned out, the people making the decisions had already settled the matter without him.

**NEWS SUMMARY:** *Government regulators seized Washington Mutual, the country's largest savings and loan. It is the largest bank failure in U.S. history.*

## SEPTEMBER 27

September is a month for record-breaking bad news. Until this year, bank failure was something I associated with the Great Depression. Is that where we're headed?

I don't think about this stuff *all* the time. We're spending evenings this week watching season five of *West Wing*. The political situation there is at least comprehensible. And every episode has not only a beginning and a middle, but also an end. Anticipation begins, suspense builds, tension is released, conclusion. Aristotle would love it. Nothing that simple with this political campaign or the bad news cycle that never seems to end. Just anticipation, suspense, tension, and then again, and more. No release, no conclusion.

*Leo McGarry: "If we're going to walk into walls I want us running into them full speed. We're going to lose some of these battles, and we might even lose the White House, but we're not going to be threatened by issues. We're going to bring 'em front and center. We're going to raise the level of public debate in this country, and let that be our legacy."*

## SEPTEMBER 28

Experimenting with the solar oven Bill gave me for our anniversary, basically an insulated metal box with a glass lid and reflecting wings. You set it up and point it toward the sun, so that the solar energy heats the oven—this afternoon, to 350 degrees.

So far, I've cooked potatoes, fresh green beans, rice, chicken, cornbread. Baked lasagna yesterday, with a meat-and-tomato-and-mushroom sauce, layered with mozzarella and cheddar, lots of oregano, basil, thyme from the herb garden. Through the years we've lived here, I've made it a practice not to bake in the summer because the oven heats up the kitchen. Now, we can have lasagna even when it's 110 degrees outside. Maybe especially when it's 110 degrees outside—means faster cooking.

The zucchinis have begun producing joyfully, multitudinously, so today I baked a chocolate zucchini cake—outside, in the solar oven.

Used my grandmother's angel food cake pan (banged up, because I played with it when I was a child) and was delighted with the rich, chocolaty flavor and dense, moist texture. Bill liked it too: a triumph, for he does not suffer zucchinis gladly.

Chocolate Zucchini Cake
2½ cup flour
½ cup cocoa
2½ teaspoons baking powder
1½ teaspoons baking soda
1 teaspoon salt
½ teaspoon nutmeg
1 teaspoon cinnamon
¾ cup shortening
2 cups sugar
3 eggs
1 teaspoon vanilla extract
2 teaspoons orange extract
2 teaspoons grated orange rind (can be omitted)
2 cups coarsely shredded zucchini
½ cup milk
1 cup chopped pecans

Preheat oven to 350 degrees. Combine flour, cocoa, baking powder, soda, salt, nutmeg, cinnamon; set aside. Beat together the shortening and sugar until smooth and fluffy. Add eggs one at a time, beating after each. Stir in extracts, orange rind, and zucchini. Alternately stir in the dry ingredients and the milk, adding nuts last. Pour the batter into a greased and flour-dusted 10-inch tube pan or bundt pan. Bake for about 50 minutes or until a wooden pick inserted in the center comes out clean. Cool in pan 15 minutes; turn out on wire rack. Drizzle glaze over cooled cake. Makes 10–12 servings.

Glaze: Mix 2 cups powdered sugar, 3 tablespoons milk, 1 teaspoon vanilla, 1 teaspoon orange extract. Beat until smooth.

SEPTEMBER 29

Our bois d'arc tree—we have only one—is dropping its fruit now: solid green balls the size of softballs but heavier. When I was a kid, we called them hedge apples. They made dandy weapons. I recall being hit by one, squarely between the shoulder blades. I can still feel it.

Hedge apple trees were everywhere in rural Illinois when I was growing up. In the 1930s, they were planted across the Great Plains as hedgerows and windbreaks to protect the soil from erosion—and to make work for those out of a job. The hedgerows themselves are gone now, bulldozed by farmers who plow every available inch of soil to "maximize profits." The roadsides are mowed and sprayed in the name of safety.

Such a shame. Such *loss*. I remember the hedgerows and rural roadsides as rich with native plants—trees, shrubs, vines, wildflowers—and a haven for small animals, birds, bees. Our bois d'arc is a reminder for me of all that. A reminder of what's gone.

NEWS SUMMARY: *The U.S. House rejected the bailout plan, 228 to 205. Reacting to the news, the Dow Jones Industrials dropped 778 points in one day, its biggest point decline ever.*

## SEPTEMBER 30

Getting ready to drive to Illinois for my class reunion, thinking back over this momentous month. Ike wreaked havoc on Houston and Galveston, and the storm in the credit and equities markets will be even more widely destructive than the hurricane, and world-wide. People are frightened. I'm hearing the terms "global recession," "global depression." And comparisons to the Great Depression.

Not a heartening thought. The next book in the Cottage Tales series, *The Tale of Briar Bank*, comes out tomorrow, and I'm wondering how book sales will be affected. This isn't an academic question. Independent bookstores were barely hanging on before this current credit crisis. The bookstore chains—Borders, Barnes & Noble—depend on profits from holiday sales to carry them through the year. Tough times for the book business, and for authors.

But maybe that's not all bad. Maybe recession, painful as it is, will shrink our growth-addicted human enterprise. Maybe it'll reduce our greenhouse gas emissions and buy us a little more time to develop alternative energies before oil gets so expensive that it bankrupts everyone. Maybe we'll learn how to make do with less: less house, less money, less credit, less horsepower, less stuff. Maybe we'll even learn how to turn less into more, transform the contraction into a deeper contentment with what we have or can make or can grow, into greater individual and family self-sufficiency, into stronger communities.

*The condition of the land as it was when we came to it is the only possible measure of our history. Only by knowing what it was can we tell to what point or result it has been changed. As we felled and burned the forests, so we burned, plowed, and overgrazed the prairies. We came with visions, but not with sight. We did not see or understand where we were or what was there, but destroyed what was there for the sake of what we desired.*

—WENDELL BERRY

*No one can possibly have lived through the Great Depression without being scarred by it. No amount of experience since the Depression can convince someone who has lived through it that the world is safe economically.*

—ISAAC ASIMOV

Maybe it will teach us to be more modest in our ambitions and more humble about our place as only one of the many species on this very small planet.

Maybe, maybe, maybe.

I'd love to be optimistic about the possibilities.

*In a world where energy and all other nonrenewable resources are likely to get progressively more scarce and expensive, it's time to learn again how to think small— and that process will be much easier if we say farewell to Utopia and focus on the things we can actually achieve in the stark limits of time and resources we still have left.*

*—JOHN MICHAEL GREER*

## September Reading

*American Theocracy: The Peril and Politics of Radical Religion, Oil, and Borrowed Money in the 21st Century,* by Kevin Phillips

*America's First Cuisines,* by Sophie D. Coe

*The Black Swan: Memory, Midlife, and Migration,* by Anne Batterson

*A Century Of War: Anglo-American Oil Politics and the New World Order,* by William Engdahl

*Eat, Pray, Love,* by Elizabeth Gilbert

*The Knitting Way: A Guide to Spiritual Self-Discovery,* by Linda Skolnik and Janice MacDaniels

*The Orchard: A Memoir,* by Adele Crockett Robertson

*Small Is Beautiful: Economics as if People Mattered,* by E. F. Schumacher

*A Thousand Barrels a Second: The Coming Oil Break Point and the Challenges Facing an Energy Dependent World,* by Peter Tertzakian

*The Virgin of Small Plains,* by Nancy Pickard

*White Pine,* by Mary Oliver

*Winter Hours,* by Mary Oliver

| JANUARY | FEBRUARY | MARCH | APRIL |
|---------|----------|-------|-------|
| MAY | JUNE | JULY | AUGUST |
| SEPTEMBER | **OCTOBER** | NOVEMBER | DECEMBER |

## OCTOBER 6

Back home, after an enormously satisfying reunion trip to Illinois. I went into this with a feeling of . . . well, obligation. A few of my classmates—Byron, Karen, Phil, Marjie—got bitten by the reunion bug, and I felt I had to do my part. It was, after all, our fiftieth.

As my contribution to the event, I helped to set up a reunion Web site: photos from the fifties and bios and current photos of almost everyone in the class, including several teachers—a good way of getting people involved before the event. We'll leave it in place, with the idea of keeping in touch and getting together another year.

Bismarck was a small rural high school—I count thirty-nine in our cap-and-gown graduation photo. As in most class groups, it was the people who stayed behind who kept in touch with everyone else. Many left for a larger life: small towns weren't as attractive in the sixties as they are these days, and family farms were being sold. Some of our classmates had died and some were hard to track down, but in the end, we accounted for all but six. Twenty (plus spouses, our English teacher and band director, and friends from neighboring classes) came to the reunion, from as far away as Arizona, Colorado, Florida—and Texas.

The usual reunion activities, the usual nostalgia, but it was all very real, and genuinely moving. The Homecoming parade with vintage cars and the queen's float, the streets of the small town lined with kids and parents; a tailgate party at the football game (cold and windy—I'd forgotten how cold it can be in October in Illinois); Saturday breakfast at a local coffee shop, with good, gooey cinnamon rolls and coffee; Saturday night banquet at the Boat Club, overlooking Lake Vermilion,

*Those truly linked don't need correspondence. When they meet again after many years apart, their friendship is as true as ever.*

—DENG MING-DAO

163

where my handsome soon-to-be-husband taught me to ice skate the magical winter I turned eighteen. Oh, young, young, we were so very young.

For me, threaded through it all, a strong sense of "this is who I am, this is where I came from, these are people I knew and cared about during an important time in our lives." No matter that most of us had been away for fifty years. No matter that we hadn't all liked each other very much when we were teens or that some of us had sometimes felt—and were treated—like outsiders. It was Homecoming (with all that this word means) and we were together, and we were friends.

I had a little free time, so I gave a couple of Illinois library talks (Danville and Marshall) and did a book signing at an antique shop in Covington, Indiana. The turnouts were good, book sales encouraging. Saw Eleanor Mackey, my cousin, in Marshall and traded genealogical information. Gave her the black darning egg that our mutual great-grandmother, Jane Jackson Turnell, brought from England when she immigrated in the early 1870s. Jane no doubt darned a great many family socks on that durable egg.

Take-along books for evening reading on the trip: Sharon Astyk's *Depletion and Abundance* and John Dunning's mystery, *The Sign of the Book*. For listening in the car: *The Forgotten Man: A New History of the Great Depression* by Amity Shlaes.

NEWS SUMMARY: *The Senate and House approved and President Bush signed the bailout package. On the following trading day, British stocks had their worst-ever day, and the Russian market dropped by nearly 20 percent. In Iceland, the stock exchange suspended trading, and the government nationalized three major banks. The Dow closed below 9,000 for the first time in five years.*

OCTOBER 7

More crises on the national scene, international, global. Thinking of turning off the TV, tuning out the news, but ignorance is no answer—not for me, anyway. I'd be happier not knowing, but the slow-motion train wreck would still be happening. I'm mesmerized, compelled to try to understand it, rather than try to ignore it.

Here at home, though, life is nicely normal. I'm unpacked, the house is straightened, the dog-fur bunnies banished, the grocery shopping done. In the garden, the potatoes are healthy, the lettuce

*My bet is that change will come soon to some of us, later to others, but the changes I'm worried about are now essentially already in motion. Whatever happens, we're probably never going to be quite as comfortable or privileged or ready as we are today. . . . We may believe that these things are crises, but life is still going on, so it is hard to imagine that so much change could happen. . . . We're still caught between the life we live now and the life we will live in the coming years, and it can be damned hard to navigate that distinction.*

—SHARON ASTYK

eager to be picked, and the snow peas are starting to bear. Not so the squash, which was attacked by a horde of marauding green worms that reduced a mat of green leaves to tattered lace in a day or two—according to Bill, who witnessed the debacle but didn't know what to do about it. He feels responsible since it happened on his watch.

After ten minutes of Internet research, I identified the invaders as "melon worms" with a special affinity for squash, cucumbers, melons. BT (*Bacillus thuringiensis*) might have helped, if we'd had any, and if it had been applied in time. But we didn't and it wasn't and the squash are goners. The survivors: one butternut, one large spaghetti squash, and three or four forlorn zucchini. Locking the garden gate after the bugs have made off with the squash, I've ordered some BT.

*On every stem, on every leaf . . . and at the root of everything that grew, was a professional specialist in the shape of grub, caterpillar, aphis, or other expert, whose business it was to devour that particular part.*

—OLIVER WENDELL HOLMES

**NEWS SUMMARY:** *Vice presidential candidates Biden and Palin debated on October 2. The second presidential debate between candidates Obama and McCain (October 7) was dominated by the economic crisis. The Labor Department reports that 159,000 jobs were lost in September. Total job losses so far this year: 760,000.*

OCTOBER 8

Biden is reported to have won the VP debate (happened while I was traveling, so I saw only clips). One poll found that viewers thought Palin was more "likable" than Biden (54 percent to 36 percent), but Biden seemed more capable of fulfilling the VP's duties (87 percent to 42 percent). Glad to know that debate watchers can discriminate between likability and capability.

I did watch last night's town hall presidential debate, moderated by Tom Brokaw. Both candidates stayed safe and played it cool, neither said anything new or put any of their standard arguments in a new way. They're tired and look it: this has been a long process—for them and for us. The CNN post-debate poll gave a clear win to Obama, 54 percent to McCain's 30 percent. CBS: 40 percent Obama, 26 percent McCain. The polls for the general election seem to be trending toward Obama. The poll-of-polls shows Obama at 49 percent, McCain at 43 percent, with Obama leading in the electoral college, where it counts. I'm hoping for a *decisive* win, not another president chosen (disastrously) by a five to four vote in the Supreme Court.

*"By 5–4 we decided enough is enough and we put an end to it and I think the vast majority of citizens in the country were grateful that we did that," Justice Antonin Scalia said of the court's decision, which ended the Florida recount.*

—ASSOCIATED PRESS

*Although we may never know with complete certainty the identity of the winner of this year's Presidential election, the identity of the loser is perfectly clear.*

—JUSTICE JOHN PAUL STEVENS, IN HIS DISSENTING OPINION IN *BUSH V. GORE*

Back to the writing desk, feeling urgent about starting *Holly Blues*. Not that I've been procrastinating—there are plenty of good reasons for starting a couple of weeks later than usual. I'm teaching an online class for Story Circle ("Personal Maps and Place as Story") and helping with the online class program. Both of these projects are taking a lot of time, especially now that the student papers are coming in— one a week for six students for the next six weeks. And there's no getting around it: the garden really does cut into my writing time.

But there's something inside me that feels a little like an oyster cooking, as Sophy Burnham puts it in *For Writers Only*—although it's hard to separate the anxiety and tension I feel about the book and my feelings about the election, the economy, and all the rest of it. I'm on edge, uncomfortable. The other-shoe feeling.

Since *Wormwood* was set away from Pecan Springs, *Holly* has to be a Pecan Springs book, with the standard Pecan Springs cast. I've been thinking about it off and on all summer, thinking about another "split-screen" book, with McQuaid carrying part of the narration, as he did in *Nightshade*. Now I'm back at the computer, with the Word file open on the screen in front of me. I usually start with a general sense of the story. Sometimes I even know where/how to begin—but rarely have any very clear idea of the conclusion or the way the story will work itself out. Every writer is different. Toni Morrison, for instance: "I always know the ending; that's where I start."

Over the decades I've been writing, I've learned to depend on that unconscious—or semi-conscious—sense of direction. I have a notion that I need to go to a place that lies, shall we say, to the north of here. I have a compass (a sense of what the characters are likely to do) that keeps me headed in the right direction. But I don't have a map that would show me what roads to take, or where to cross the rivers, or which cliffs might be dangerous.

So all I can do is take a deep breath and head for the first scene. By the time it's finished, I usually see where the second scene ought to begin—and so on, moving through the story. I don't pretend to understand the unconscious process that governs this complicated business, or how all the plot business seems to sort itself out somewhere around eighty-five thousand words. I find myself agreeing with E. L. Doctorow, who said that writing a novel is like driving a car at night. "You can see only as far as your headlights, but you can make the whole trip that way."

When I relate Doctorow's remark to Bill (a former small plane pilot), he has another take on it. When you're making an emergency

*Beginning is the hardest part. You roam the house, your rooms, the streets. You are jerked on the leash of your unease. Everything is calling to you—plants, children, animals, or worse, the need to make money: weed me, water me, feed me, pay me, clean me, tend me, buy me; while inside anxiety and tension curl like the edge of an oyster cooking.*

—SOPHY BURNHAM

*The story chooses you, the image comes and then the emotional frame. . . . I think a story ideally comes to the writer; the writer shouldn't be casting the net out, searching for something to write about.*

—RAYMOND CARVER

*You may wonder where plot is in all this. The answer—my answer, anyway—is nowhere. I won't try to convince you that I've never plotted any more than I'd try to convince you that I've never told a lie, but I do both as infrequently as possible.*

—STEPHEN KING

166   AN EXTRAORDINARY YEAR OF ORDINARY DAYS

landing at night, he says, you turn on your landing lights and look ahead as far as you can. If you don't like what you see, you turn the lights out.

## OCTOBER 10

Happy day. The reviews of *The Tale of Briar Bank* are uniformly good—including the all-important *Publishers Weekly* review ("Readers will delight in Albert's special blend of fact and fiction")—and I'm getting positive letters and e-mails. The people who like the Cottage Tales really *like* them. I've long ago given up the hope that the books in this series might sell in large numbers, but sales are "respectable" (my editor's judgment), librarians call it a "classic," and one reviewer even suggests that the series "will be as beloved as Beatrix Potter herself."

There are some things that numbers just don't count.

But I am counting numbers. As of quitting time today, there are thirty-three hundred words in the *Holly Blues* file, and I've got a draft of the first chapter. I'm happy to be writing about Texas again, and about Pecan Springs, a fictionalization of San Marcos as it was in the early seventies, when I first came to Texas—before it became suburbanized, a satellite of Austin. I feel as if I've known the place, and other small towns like it, my whole life. Feels like home. Feels like where I ought to be.

*Here I am, where I ought to be. A writer must have a place where he or she feels this, a place to love and be irritated with. One must experience the local blights, hear the proverbs, endure the radio commercials. . . . . Location, whether it is to abandon it or draw it sharply, is where we start.*

—LOUISE ERDRICH

## OCTOBER 12

Bill called me to follow him into the woods yesterday evening to see an extraordinary sight: a chokecherry tree full of monarchs. This is the butterflies' migration season, and we're lucky to live along their flyway. In the spring, the adult females lay their eggs on the milkweed plants in our meadows. In the fall, when the temperatures up north begin to drop, a new generation flies south to a winter home in Mexico, to a place they've never seen, a tiny, sixty-square mile space on the face of our planet, navigating (scientists think) by the angle of the sun.

For the past few days, the woods have been full of drifting patches of bright colors, sifting like cheerful autumn leaves through the branches. Now the butterflies—delicate, fragile, yet powerful enough to fly two thousand miles—are asleep in the chokecherry tree, hanging silently and motionless, orange wings folded, clustered thickly as if for protection or solace. An oddly moving sight, so many vulner-

*I have read about butterfly trees, these ancient inns that mark the migration routes of the monarchs. . . . The butterflies hanging on for dear life . . . have never seen the Michoacán mountains, and they probably never will. And yet, that one high valley in Mexico is their alpha and omega, the reason for and the meaning of their brief tenure on earth. Chances are they will never know why they do what they do, or how their part fits into the whole. Just like us.*

—ANNE BATTERSON

able creatures clinging together. I think of the perils they've survived already: agricultural chemicals, BT-laced corn pollen drifting onto the milkweed they eat, the moving vehicles they collide with. I think of the long journey ahead of them and measure that almost incomprehensible distance against their fragility, their tiny size, and am awed.

## OCTOBER 13

Reading Circle in Austin today. An anthology, edited by Victoria Zackheim: *For Keeps: Women Tell the Truth About Their Bodies, Growing Older, and Acceptance.* Good book, lively discussion, fast-paced, and deep. Plenty to think about here. Did some quick shopping and headed home. Spent what was left of the afternoon working on e-mail, then put in a couple of hours in the evening marking essays written by the students in my online class, strong writers with something to say.

Reading. *The Forgotten Man* was such a fascinating introduction to the 1930s that I've started another book: *Daily Life in the United States, 1920–1940: How Americans Lived Through the Roaring Twenties and the Great Depression* by David E. Kyvig. Rereading, too: Kathleen Norris, *Dakota: A Spiritual Geography.*

## OCTOBER 14

Rain, rain, rain!

*Until I moved to western South Dakota, I did not know about rain, that it could come too hard, too soft, too hot, too cold, too early, too late. . . . I had not realized that a long soaking rain in spring or fall, a straight-down-falling rain, a gentle splashing rain is more than a blessing. It's a miracle.*

—KATHLEEN NORRIS

Moisture blowing up from the Gulf and a cold front—the first serious cold front of the season—blowing down from the north. The two met over our county, producing what the local weather gurus call a "weather event." A minor event, as it turns out, only an inch, which isn't nearly enough when we're some fifteen inches behind our twelve-month thirty-inch average. But it came with a minimum of thunder and lightning and was so lovely that it was easy to ignore the mud tracked into the kitchen on muddy puppy paws and forgetful feet. Who can be even a little annoyed about mud when the grass and the garden are so grateful?

It was probably the advancing cold front that whisked the monarchs into our woods and swept them away again, carrying them on to the south. There are still quite a few queens, though, monarch lookalikes but smaller, who love to feast on the velvety blue mistflowers that thrive in the autumn sun on the south side of the house. Comely creatures, they sleep on the blossoms at night; as the sun rises and warms their bodies, they wake like slowly opening blossoms, fanning their wings to dry the dew. When I take my coffee onto the porch, the queens, startled, rise in swirling, bronzy clouds, turning, floating, at last settling back onto their mistflower cushions. Nothing more beautiful than a cloud of queens in the morning—unless it's a tree full of sleeping monarchs at dusk.

Back to the book today. Started on the second chapter, which I planned to tell from China's point of view. But McQuaid felt strongly that since he's a narrator in this book, the reader ought to hear from him early on. So he gets Chapter Two. Go for it, guy. It's all yours.

NEWS SUMMARY: *In their final and most contentious debate (moderated by Bob Schieffer), McCain and Obama argued domestic issues: the economy, health care, the environment, Joe the Plumber figuring largely in McCain's remarks. CNN's post-debate poll found that 58 percent of viewers thought Obama had won, 31 percent McCain. In CBS's poll, 53 percent felt Obama won, 22 percent McCain.*

OCTOBER 15

*Why?* Joe the Plumber is not a licensed plumber, owes back taxes, and didn't vote until this year. Not exactly the poster boy for middle-class Americans that McCain and Palin thought they were getting. So why in the world would either of them even mention his name? The answer: To appeal to other Joes and Jills of a similar persuasion.

Today, in my solar oven, I baked the spaghetti squash that I rescued from the carnage of the worm invasion. Tasty, with butter and fresh minced parsley, basil, chives. Last night, a stir-fry made with snow peas, young green beans, thin-sliced carrots from the garden. I also cooked the rice (probably grown somewhere on the other side of the globe—so much for eating locally) in the solar oven.

Finished Chapter Two, up to eighty-six hundred words. Feels pretty good, although I'm trying to suspend judgment and let the story find itself. Ran across this, in Sophy Burnham's *For Writers Only*: "Frank O'Connor, the Irish short story writer and novelist, likewise withheld all initial critical judgment. 'I don't care what the writing's like [at this stage],' he said. 'Any sort of rubbish. It's the design of the story which is the most important.'"

Yes. Story structure first. Style later.

*I think most of us start from where we are. I'm starting here. . . . [O]ur future is not one of the environmentally pure living perfect lives, but of ordinary people going forward from where they are.*

—SHARON ASTYK

OCTOBER 17

The financial news isn't bad just in this country, it's bad around the world. Iceland is bankrupt—literally down to its last krona—and is trying to borrow from Russia. But the ruble is down, and the yen down even further, so Iceland can't borrow from Japan, either. Oil is off its midsummer high by some sixty dollars a barrel, throwing oil producers into confusion. The American consumer can't afford to buy imported goods, and consumers in other countries can't afford to buy ours. And therein, as Thomas Friedman said in a recent *New York Times* column, lies the uncomfortable truth—the unintended consequence—of globalization: "We're all connected and nobody is in charge."

In defiance of all this grim, gloomy news, October here is simply beautiful this year—cool, even. We've had Octobers when the temperature hit the 100-degree mark for a straight week. This morning, I wear a jacket when Toro takes me for his walk.

Then head for the computer. When I stop to fix dinner this evening (red beans, rice, and sausage, with coleslaw and applesauce), the word count is a little more than eleven thousand, and the story is taking shape.

*I start with a tingle, a kind of feeling of the story I will write. Then come the characters, and they take over, they make the story.*

—ISAK DINESEN

*I know writers who write only when inspiration comes. How would Isaac Stern play if he played the violin only when he felt like it? He would be lousy.*

—MADELEINE L'ENGLE

NEWS SUMMARY: *Colin Powell endorsed Barack Obama, calling him a "transformational figure" who will change the way the world views the United States. Asked about Sarah Palin, Powell described her as a "distinguished woman" but said he doesn't believe she is "ready" to be president, "which is the job of the vice president."*

OCTOBER 19

Like everyone else, I have the feeling that this is an extraordinarily important presidential election, maybe the most important of my life. I'm still almost incredulous about Obama's candidacy and grateful for the issues it raises—issues that would never be discussed with another candidate on the ticket. Obama's faith, for instance. This morning, on *Meet the Press*, Colin Powell brought up the rumor (circulated by fervent right-wing talk shows and bloggers) that Obama is a Muslim. "Well, the correct answer is, he is not a Muslim, he's a Christian," Powell said.

He's always been a Christian, Powell continues. But the really right

AN EXTRAORDINARY YEAR OF ORDINARY DAYS

answer is: What if he is? Is there something wrong with being a Muslim in this country? The answer's no, that's not America. Is there something wrong with some seven-year-old Muslim American kid believing that he or she could be president? . . . This is not the way we should be doing it in America.

Exactly.

## OCTOBER 21

In *On Writing*, Stephen King says that his books "tend to be based on situation rather than story." He goes on, "I want to put a group of characters (perhaps a pair; perhaps even just one) in some sort of predicament and then watch them try to work themselves free."

I like that description. In *Holly Blues*, McQuaid's ex-wife Sally puts McQuaid and China into a situation where they (both are usually suspicious of Sally's motives) do something they wouldn't do under normal circumstances: they take her in, loan her money and a car to drive, even come to her defense when it appears that she's being stalked. But a few inconvenient facts begin emerging out of the fog of Sally's contradictory stories, her lies—although what the real story is, I don't know yet. And that's okay. King adds:

> *I am, after all, not just the novel's creator but its first reader. And if I'm not able to guess with any accuracy how the damned thing is going to turn out, even with my inside knowledge of coming events, I can be pretty sure of keeping the reader in a state of page-turning anxiety.*

I don't know about "page-turning anxiety." That's King's schtick. I don't know about an "inside knowledge of coming events," either. Don't feel like an insider just yet. More like an outsider peering in, through a glass, darkly.

Word count: sixteen thousand.

## OCTOBER 22

Bill's splitting firewood—cedar, oak, hackberry. He harvests dead trees in the woodlot and piles the logs to dry for a couple of years. Splitting involves renting a gasoline-powered splitter and running the logs through the machine (wearing protective ear muffs, leather gloves). The end result: enough wood to keep the fireplace burning

*Every human being has hundreds of separate people living under his skin. The talent of the writer is his ability to give them their separate names, identities, personalities, and have them relate to other characters living with him.*

—MEL BROOKS

from October through March. In cold weather, we turn on the furnace for a half-hour to take the morning chill off, wear sweaters during the day, and build a fire in the evenings. This, together with our other ef-forts to save household energy (the new roof, the insulation blanket around the hot water heater, drying clothes on the clothesline) is add-ing up. We're using about twenty-five gallons of propane a month; the national average, forty-five.

OCTOBER 24

Another awful day in the world markets, making it even clearer that whatever happens in the U.S. markets happens around the world. It's like some ugly, unstoppable pandemic—the dark side (one of the dark sides—there are many) of globalization.

On a cheerier note: making a pot of sausage soup for tonight's library supper. And it's a beautiful day, clear, bright, cool. Texas at its October best.

Sausage Soup

1 pound sausage
2–3 cloves garlic, minced
½ medium onion, chopped
2 (14-ounce) cans beef broth
1 (14.5-ounce) can diced tomatoes, undrained
1 cup carrots, sliced
2 small zucchinis, cubed
¾ cup small uncooked shell pasta
2 tablespoons fresh chopped basil
1 teaspoon oregano
¼ teaspoon black pepper
¼ teaspoon salt
2 cups fresh spinach leaves or other garden greens

In a stockpot or Dutch oven, brown sausage with garlic and onion. Stir in broth, tomatoes, and carrots, and season with salt and pepper. Reduce heat, cover, and simmer 15 minutes. Stir in zucchini, pasta, herbs. Cover and simmer another 15 minutes. Remove from heat and add spinach. Cover and allow the heat from the soup to cook the spin-ach. Soup is ready to serve after 5 minutes.

The library's Souper Supper was held in the cafeteria at the Bertram Grade School. I took my slow cooker filled with soup and added it to the lineup of some twenty slow cookers on the cafeteria counter, filled with everything from chicken and dumplings to broccoli and cheese soup. Plenty of soup for seconds; plenty of desserts, too. Apple pie for Bill, carrot cake for me.

But better than the food: the people. Everyone in this rural community knows everyone else, from church, from the schools they've attended together, from encounters at the local vet clinic or the bank or the beauty parlor. I didn't hear a word about politics. Everybody just handed over their six bucks, got in line with their bowls and spoons, and enjoyed a good meal with friends.

*If you have a garden and a library, you have everything you need.*

—CICERO

## OCTOBER 26

Backstory. In a long series, the previous books are all backstory to the current book, and there's always a question—in my mind, anyway—just how much to recap. If there's too much, delivered in big, bulky packages, the narrative bogs down. If there's not enough, there'll be gaps in the reader's knowledge. *Holly Blues* is the seventeenth book in the series. One of the central characters—Sally, McQuaid's ex-wife, Brian's mother—has been around since *Rosemary Remembered* (Book Four), popping in and out of China's life like a bad fairy. I've got to fill in enough of that background material so that the reader gets the general idea, without recapping every episode.

Sally's life has been going on "outside" the books as well, so I have to figure out how much of her personal history belongs in this book and where in the story it should come. I don't want to dump it into the narrative in large, indigestible chunks, of course—but where do I put it?

Figuring this out requires rewrites, moving things around, finding where the pieces fit. Discovering bits of Sally's past life that connect with the present, with her son Brian, with McQuaid, with China. Using her story (especially the parts she tries to hide) to illuminate the stories of the other characters. Using her history to create and define the mystery of her present.

*Thousands of people plan to be writers, but they never get around to it. The only way to find out if you can write is to set aside a certain period every day and try. . . . Work every day and the pages will pile up.*

—JUDITH KRANTZ

*Plot springs from character. . . . I've always sort of believed that these people inside me— these characters—know who they are and what they're about and what happens, and they need me to help get it down on paper because they don't type.*

—ANNE LAMOTT

*There are no garden-
ing mistakes, only
experiments.*

—JANET KILBURN
PHILLIPS

First frost last night. Early (not due for another week or ten days), but the garden was ready for it. Bill cut lengths of flexible plastic pipe and I fitted them over metal pegs along both sides of the raised beds. Over these hoops, I fastened lengths of row cover, turning the raised beds into hoop houses.

It worked. The temperature dipped into the upper twenties overnight, but when I took the row cover off this morning, the plants were perky. Except the potatoes. I didn't cover them, and they look . . . well, like frozen potato tops. Not necessarily a disaster since potatoes survive light freezes. We'll see.

In the meantime, the garden is still putting green beans, snow peas, and carrots on our table in lovely abundance. Today, I planted two rows of spinach, a row of beets, four rows of garlic, four rows of onions.

And planted more of Sally's backstory here and there in *Holly Blues*.

*The most noteworthy
thing about gardeners
is that they are always
optimistic, always enter-
prising, and never satis-
fied. They always look
forward to doing some-
thing better than they
have ever done before.*

—VITA SACKVILLE-WEST

NEWS SUMMARY: *A week before the election, the poll-of-polls gives the race to Obama, 50 percent to 43 percent. Individual polls range from a 1 percent difference (Gallup) to 14 percent (Pew).*

OCTOBER 28

Feeling more optimistic about the election, which (irrationally) makes me feel better about everything else.

A few years ago, our county commissioners relocated our polling place—not gerrymandering, in the strict sense of the word, but it had the same effect. Now, instead of voting conveniently in the nearby town of Bertram, we (and the Bertramites who live north of the railroad track) vote an inconvenient twelve miles away in the tiny community of Joppa. You have to be an extraordinarily determined voter to find this polling place—or even to find a *map* to the polling place. In fact, a few of our more contrarian neighbors said (right out loud) that the polling place was relocated to keep some folks from voting against one particular county commissioner. (Didn't work: he lost anyway.)

There's a lot less of Joppa now than there was a century ago, when the village boasted a cotton gin, grist mill, general store, blacksmith shop, school, church, post office—and a hat shop, where Mrs. Hattie Snow Smith turned yesterday's bonnet into tomorrow's trendy chapeau. Nothing left now but the old school building, which serves as a community center and polling place—for any voter who can locate it on election day.

I didn't wait to vote in Joppa. I voted early today at the Burnet County courthouse. Located smack in the middle of the square in Burnet, it's not hard to find. I can only trust that the electronic voting machine that recorded my vote did so accurately. Unfortunately, I will never know for sure because there were no paper tallies. When I asked the election clerk about the backup for these machines, she acted as if I'd asked her to tell me her sexual history. None of my business.

Still, I'm happy. No, more than happy: I am awed. This is an extraordinary presidential election in an extraordinary year, and as I pushed the buttons, I felt extraordinarily privileged to be taking part in it. Even though my vote doesn't count. This is a red state. All of Texas' electoral votes will go for McCain/Palin. If I were queen of the world, I'd get rid of the electoral college. Tomorrow, if not sooner.

*The people who cast the votes don't decide an election, the people who count the votes do.*

—JOSEPH STALIN

*It's a ridiculous setup, which thwarts the will of the majority, distorts presidential campaigning and has the potential to produce a true constitutional crisis. . . . The majority does not rule, and every vote is not equal—those are reasons enough for scrapping the system.*

—*NEW YORK TIMES,* EDITORIAL (AUGUST 29, 2004)

## OCTOBER 29

"Indian summer" cool, crisp days, cooler nights. The cedar elms and the pecans are turning gold, the cypress trees are russet, the Virginia creeper holds the hackberry trees in a scarlet embrace, and the flameleaf sumacs have set the meadow afire. Bill has finished the fall mowing, and the winter's firewood is stacked on the porch. Toro is ecstatic on these bright mornings, eager to chase the white-tailed deer that bed down every night in the east meadow. I watch them leap across the tall brown grasses and wonder how many of these beautiful animals won't be here this time next week. Deer season begins in a couple of days.

I have mixed feelings about this. Hunting helps to limit herd size to the carrying capacity of the land. But from this point of view, it would be smart of the hunters to harvest (they prefer "harvest" to "kill") the weaker, slower animals, wouldn't it? Let the fit survive to breed more and fitter animals?

This may happen on managed game-hunting ranches, where the guides approve the target ("The guide's decision in the field is final," warns one Web site) and the shots average a hundred yards to give the hunter a chance to test his shooting skills. But there's little of that

*A peculiar virtue in wildlife ethics is that the hunter ordinarily has no gallery to applaud or disapprove of his conduct. Whatever his acts, they are dictated by his own conscience, rather than by a mob of onlookers. It is difficult to exaggerate the importance of this fact.*

—ALDO LEOPOLD

around here. The hunters are after the biggest bucks and the largest does, the gene pool be damned. And the easier the shot, the better. Up close and personal.

Our neighbor, for example, who has set up his deer blind about twenty yards from the feeder. This intrepid hunter, a man of substantial girth, will not have to shoot far to test his aim or walk any distance to harvest his kill. He can't walk very far, anyway, without crossing one of our fences, or another neighbor's fence. Which he is not supposed to do.

OCTOBER 30

Baked a pecan pie in the solar oven today. It's just right for baking a slow, custardy pie, not so good for something like a pizza, which requires a hot, fast oven. The pie baked for about fifty minutes, and it was perfect. Using the sun to cook food deeply appeals to me, so I don't mind the inconvenience of going outside every half hour to adjust the oven in relation to the sun. In fact, in the days since I've begun doing this, I am much more aware of the sun's place in the sky, its movements, and the occasional clouds that reduce the cooking temperature, slow the process.

Another reminder that I'm a solar creature, doing a solar task.

A Proper Pecan Pie
This recipe comes from my friend Catherine Cogburn, who gave it to me fifteen years and many delicious pies ago.

10-inch unbaked pie shell
3 eggs
2/3 cup dark brown sugar
1 teaspoon vanilla
dash salt
1/2 cup melted butter
1 cup Karo syrup (light)
2 cups pecans, coarsely chopped

Beat eggs, add sugar, vanilla, and salt. Add melted butter, syrup, and pecans. Stir until blended and pour into pie shell. Bake at 350 degrees for about 40–45 minutes, just until center is set. (Pie will continue to "cook" as it cools.) Tip: if you microwave the butter in a heatproof measuring cup and use the same cup to measure the Karo, the syrup will come out of the cup without sticking.

Read today (on the Internet, of course) the extraordinary news that the *Christian Science Monitor* is scrapping its daily print edition and moving to Web-based publication. It's not the only one, either—newspapers everywhere are leaving print, moving to the Web. Out here in the Texas boonies, the delivery of a print newspaper has never been a reasonable option, so I'm happy to get my daily news fix on the Internet.

Still, this feels like the end of the era I grew up in. The paper/ink era. And the beginning of an era we are all growing into, like it or not.

*Every time a newspaper dies, even a bad one, the country moves a little closer to authoritarianism; when a great one goes, like the* New York Herald Tribune, *history itself is denied a devoted witness.*

—RICHARD KLUGER

## October Reading and Listening

*Daily Life in the United States, 1920–1940: How Americans Lived Through the Roaring Twenties and the Great Depression,* by David E. Kyvig

*Dakota: A Spiritual Geography,* by Kathleen Norris

*Depletion and Abundance: Life on the New Home Front,* by Sharon Astyk

*The Forgotten Man: A New History of the Great Depression,* by Amity Shlaes

*For Keeps: Women Tell the Truth About Their Bodies, Growing Older, and Acceptance,* edited by Victoria Zackheim

*The Sign of the Book,* by John Dunning

| JANUARY | FEBRUARY | MARCH | APRIL |
|---------|----------|-------|-------|
| MAY | JUNE | JULY | AUGUST |
| SEPTEMBER | OCTOBER | **NOVEMBER** | DECEMBER |

## NOVEMBER 1

Lovely November weather, clear, bright, cool. The monarchs have gone south, coasting on a fast-moving cold front, and the overhead flyway has been crowded with migrating geese and ducks. Yesterday, Bill called me to see a large flock of sandhill cranes, a couple of hundred birds, flying high overhead in a wobbly vee, celebrating themselves, the wide sky, the earth below, and the wind, in those wild, warbling, heart-seizing cries that call me to rise and fly with them.

But I have things to do here. In *Holly Blues*, the story is pulling me forward, and I'm thinking about Elmore Leonard. When somebody asked him about pacing, he said, "I just leave out the boring parts." Which means keeping the action moving swiftly, even when it's mostly dialogue. (Dialogue can be action, too.) Every scene needs to move the plot another step forward, has to reveal something not yet known about the characters' beliefs, thoughts, feelings. Some little something. Something new.

*To celebrate. Here. Now. To express gratitude. For life? For being alive.*

—JOYCE CAROL OATES

*Plot is no more than footprints left in the snow after your characters have run by on their way to incredible destinations.*

—RAY BRADBURY

## NOVEMBER 2

"Move the *plot* another step forward."

I wrote that yesterday, but it's not quite right. For me, it's *plots* with an *s*, plots, plural. Most scenes are connected with more than one plot.

Back in 1991, my first adult mystery went the rounds of the New York houses and came back home with a fistful of rejection slips. One of those slips—from the editor at Mysterious Press, I think—advised me to drop the red herrings in favor of another couple of plots.

The project sold (to Scribner, no less!), but that editor did me a huge, huge favor. I stopped thinking about *the* plot of the story (plot, singular) and started thinking about each character's plot, his or her story line—which is as much a matter of characterization as of action. In *Holly Blues*, for instance, there's Sally's story (she's trying to stay out of the clutches of the villain who's after her, which is *his* story); McQuaid's story (he's trying to find out what really happened ten years ago, when Sally's parents were killed); Ruby's story (she's trying to deal with her mother, suffering from Alzheimer's, who has her own sad story); and China's story (she's trying to keep Sally out of jail). The whole story is the sum of these individual stories and, like most sums, is greater than its parts. And yes, they are also plots. Plot = story. Story = plot.

What with all these intersecting, character-driven plots, something inevitable, unpredictable, or dreadful has always just happened to one of the characters, is about to happen, wants to happen, threatens to happen, doesn't happen (why not?). And with all this story material to work with, there's no room for fluff, no need to pad the action with extraneous dialogue or commit another murder or two just to keep the middle of the book from sagging.

The trick is to lace these multiple story lines together in interesting, non-confusing ways and tie them up at the end—although this sometimes feels like a tall order. One of my pet peeves with a couple of popular mystery authors (not naming names) is their habit of dropping a story line or two. I get to the end of the book with the feeling that I've missed something. "Whatever happened to—?" Without re-reading, I can't know whether it's my fault or the author's. I usually tend to blame the author.

NOVEMBER 3

Everything in the country seems to be on hold, all eyes, all thoughts focused on the election. On television, it's all politics, all the time.

But not for me. It's easier to track the polls online, and I'm bored with the endless, repetitive speculating of the talking heads on television. Evenings, we're watching *West Wing* on DVD (yes, all over again). I'm a fan of Aaron Sorkin's crisp, crackling dialogue—dialogue that makes me feel as if I'm eavesdropping on real people's real lives. If I could create dialogue like that, I would be the world's happiest writer.

Not on hold: the writing. *Holly* is at thirty thousand words. Reading, too: Margaret Atwood, *Payback: Debt and the Shadow Side of*

*Wealth* and *Crossing Open Ground* by Barry Lopez; *Writing in an Age of Silence* by Sara Paretsky, a strong, brave book.


## NOVEMBER 5

The election is over. Finished and definitive: no verdict required from the Supremes. I woke up this morning feeling unspeakably relieved. As Oprah Winfrey put it late last night in Chicago, "America did the right thing."

Fortified with pizza, snacks, and soft drinks, we watched the returns until McCain conceded (at the glitzy Biltmore Hotel in Phoenix) and Obama spoke at Grant Park to a hundred thousand exuberant citizens. A substantial win, a muscular mandate: Obama rounded up 338 electoral votes and 52 percent of the popular vote to McCain's 161 votes, 46 percent.

I think back over all the presidential elections that I can remember—beginning with Harry Truman's trouncing of Thomas E. Dewey in 1948, when I was eight (I remember radio broadcaster Gabriel "There's Good News Tonight!" Heatter relating the story)—and know, beyond any question, that Barack Obama's decisive victory holds the greatest symbolism and the greatest significance of all. And the very greatest *importance*, for we are facing stalemated, stagnated wars in Iraq and Afghanistan, resource depletion, a global climate crisis, a shredded global economy—the worst situation in our lifetime, economists say, and no good news on the horizon.

I had no confidence at all—zero, zip, zilch, nada—in the Bush administration. No confidence, either, in the McCain/Palin team, one of whom cannot even frame a coherent sentence to describe her disappointment at her electoral loss.

Whether confidence in Obama is justified is still an open question. But I can hope.

Today, I am buoyed by hope.

*If there is anyone out there who still doubts that America is a place where all things are possible, who still wonders if the dreams of our founders are alive in our time, who still questions the power of our democracy, tonight is your answer.*

—BARACK OBAMA
(NOVEMBER 4, 2008)

*Hope—hope in the face of difficulty. Hope in the face of uncertainty. The audacity of hope! In the end, that is God's greatest gift to us, the bedrock of this nation. A belief in things not seen. A belief that there are better days ahead.*

—BARACK OBAMA


## NOVEMBER 6

Still happy, hopeful, feeling able to look ahead. Looking ahead to a new agenda, a major change in direction, important policy shifts.

To match the mood, extraordinarily beautiful weather, but still extraordinarily dry. On the U.S. Drought Monitor Map, we're in an area of "extreme" drought. Bill has decided that the problem with our well is not a sticky gauge or fire ants in the switch. It's slow recharge, caused by the drought. This is not fixable, but he's come up with a workaround: he's coupled the system to our second well, two hundred yards away. We are now pumping out of both wells. But we're conserving water as much as possible. Shorter showers, less laundry, essential watering only.

Reading: Michael Pollan's *Second Nature: A Gardener's Education* and a collection of warm, wry essays, *In Deep* by poet Maxine Kumin. About her life on a small New Hampshire farm, where she and her husband grow their own vegetables and cut their own wood, she remarks, "it is a life not noted for slack to begin with."

I understand, smile, concur. No slack here, either.

## NOVEMBER 7

Obama held his first post-election press conference this afternoon. There's talk of a large government investment in infrastructure projects—the electrical grid, roads, and bridges—which will create jobs. Employment has to be at the top of the to-do list, for the latest report is dismal: another quarter million jobs gone in October, 1.2 million for the year. Worse, the number of long-term unemployed: 4.4 million, twice as many people as live in Houston. But these aren't just numbers. They're people with families and debts: mortgages and car payments and health care bills and credit card balances. And no jobs.

My job (for which I am unspeakably grateful), *Holly Blues*: at thirty-three thousand words on the twenty-second day of the project.

## NOVEMBER 8

Saw a handsome eight-point buck in the south meadow at dusk last night, silhouetted against the pale grasses. I hope he survives the season and lives to improve the gene pool, instead of being shot and his proud antlers hung on somebody's trophy wall. Happily, there's been no sign of our intrepid short-range hunter-neighbor. The deer blind is still there, but maybe our letter discouraged him.

Harvesting, still—snap beans, snow peas, carrots, cabbage—with amazement and infinite gratitude for the bounties produced by the smallest seeds dropped into the hospitable earth, transformed into an abundant harvest by the genial sun. "Entropy undone," as Michael Pollan puts it, a hopeful thought in this era of depletions.

## NOVEMBER 9

There's a new dog at our house.

Since the Labs left us, we've talked intermittently about getting another dog to keep Toro company. As Dave Barry once said, it's always good to have an emergency backup dog, in case something happens to your main dog (Toro being the Emergency Backup who was promoted to Main Dog upon the deaths of his compatriots). But only once have we deliberately set out to acquire a dog: that was when we phoned Lab Rescue to ask about available Labs and ended up (to our enormous satisfaction) with Zach. All our other dogs have been unsolicited gifts from a beneficent universe.

Yesterday the universe stepped in once more and took control of our lack-of-dog situation. Dolly (the rancher friend from whom we got our cows) called to say that she needs to find a new home for a blue heeler, Molly Maguire, who kills chickens. We don't have any chickens (at the moment), and we're down to one Main Dog. So, at our invitation, Molly Maguire came to visit, to see if she, we, Toro, and the cat are compatible. Looks like she'll stay, likely. She's agreeable, biddable, playful, and affectionate—what more would we want in a dog?

Molly comes with verbal assurances that she's had her shots and is spayed, but the tags on her oversize collar are not hers, suggesting that the vaccinations, and maybe the spaying, are somebody's wishful thinking. She also has an unmistakable case of worms and an eye infection. We'll drop her off at the clinic and ask the vet to give her a good looking-over. He'll be pleased. We haven't visited very often since Zach and Lady left us, which has no doubt had a negative effect on the clinic's bottom line. Adopting Molly might be good for the local economy.

> *The animals are my confederates. They arrive, sometimes with speaking parts, in my dreams. They are rudimentary and untiring and changeless, where we are sophisticated, weary, fickle. They make me better than I am. . . . Guileless, predictable, they help define who I am.*
>
> —MAXINE KUMIN

## NOVEMBER 10

Reading Circle today, discussing *Circling My Mother* by Mary Gordon, who also wrote a memoir about her father, *Shadow Man*, and *Seeing Through Places*, about the houses in which she grew up. The consensus of our discussion: *Circling* is a splendidly complex book, lyrical, beautiful, rich. We talked nonstop for an hour and could easily have talked for another hour. I need to go back and reread the other two books before I read *Circling* again. A quite remarkable trilogy.

> *Of course, with autobiographical writing, in a way, one is always in bad faith, because you're still only telling what you want to tell. And who knows what's being hidden? Who knows what, in fact, might be the true, dark, unsayable, unbearable story?*
>
> —MARY GORDON

Molly Maguire is now officially our dog. We've forked over $185 for an examination, shots and tags, ear medicine, worm medicine, and eye medicine (she has a UFO—an unidentified foreign object—lodged in one eye and an infection in both eyes). The good news: the UFO will probably pose no problems, and yes, she's spayed. She is about twenty-four months old, and she is giving Toro lessons in how to play. He's forgotten, having lived with couch potato Labs for the past four years. Molly is remarkably good about letting us treat her eyes and ears, open her mouth and look at her teeth, and handle her paws—intrusions that you want your dog to tolerate, if you are going to have a long and happy life together. She's not so good at leaving Toro alone when he wants to eat his dinner (he's slower than she is, and she'd like to steal his food) or have a nap. And her outdoor play habits resemble nothing so much as a hard, no-holds-barred scrum.

Back at work. It's always a challenge to pick up the book again after a time away, but I made good progress on *Holly* today. The story remains disconnected, in bits and pieces—I'm still moving this part here, that there—but there's enough conflict and tension to pull the whole together, eventually.

*For 99 percent of all novels, conflict is the core of the plot. Without it there is no tension and there's no reason to turn the page. Essays are the place for gentle reflection. Novels are not.*

—RITA MAE BROWN

## NOVEMBER 12

Rain! Not much, only a half inch, but most of the county didn't get any at all, so we're feeling lucky. A small thunderstorm parked itself over our thirty-one acres and rained on us for a whole half-hour.

Dolly came to pick up Molly's crate today and brought two bags of fresh chile peppers—poblanos for me, habaneros for Bill. I can't handle habaneros, literally. They set my hands afire, and Bill will have to deal with them. But I halved and seeded the poblanos, dried them in the dehydrator, and put them through the blender, then the coffee grinder, to make chile powder. A pound and a half of fresh peppers became three ounces of chile powder in less than twenty-four hours. I call it hot. Bill calls it sweet and fruity.

## NOVEMBER 13

The first hearth fire of the winter season. Bill brought in an armload load of seasoned cedar, ash, and oak and laid the fire. Bright and love-ly, flames dancing in the dusky room, dogs warming themselves on the hearth. Carrot-and-potato soup and fresh-baked bread for supper, good conversation, the fire. A perfect evening.

## NOVEMBER 14

A hard freeze—29 degrees when I got up this morning. I spent a half hour last night, just before sundown, putting on the row covers. This morning, the snow peas were still pert and perky, the lettuce limp but carrying on bravely, the broccoli and cabbage none the worse for the freeze.

Writing all day, every day.

## NOVEMBER 15

Our Mitsubishi truck is twenty-five years old and still running, with nearly two hundred thousand miles on the odometer. A truck doesn't get to be twenty-five without showing signs of age and hard wear, so it's not pretty. We use it only as a ranch truck, but it's a long-bed model and we do use it, often, to haul brush, dogs, tools, fencing, firewood, and similarly bulky items. If you don't count the perennial problem of flat tires (the inevitable, incontestable mesquite thorns picked up by driving across the pastures), the truck has been remarkably reliable.

Until the water pump went out. Bill is a DIY kind of guy, so he attempted the repair—until he figured out that you can't get to the water pump unless you're prepared to pull the engine. Wisely, he refrained. He decided to tow the truck to the auto shop, fifty-some miles away in north Austin.

Now, most normal men would have called a tow truck. But not Bill. He bought and installed a tow bar on the Element, hooked up the truck, and we set off for Austin, sixty miles away, Bill driving the Element with the Mitsubishi in tow, I following in the Civic (backup, in case of an emergency), muttering prayers for safe passage. Towing makes me nervous.

Halfway to Austin, I noticed that the license plates on the Mitsubishi (staring me in the face since I was following close behind) were not current and that the inspection sticker was two years out of date. Logical, since the truck doesn't normally go out on the road, in public. But this meant that when the repair was finished a couple of days later, Bill had to drive the truck back home under cover of darkness, with me following in the Civic, again muttering prayers. This time,

*It is no accident that the word* heart *is central to the word* hearth. *If we reflect for a moment about the heart of our home, we will have a sense of it straight away—whether it is lit with wood and matches or not, it is still the hearth place.*

—GUNILLA NORRIS

*I thought I started rebuilding this truck because I needed a truck. Then I thought I was doing it to thumb my nose at the excesses of the modern motor vehicle. And then I thought—notice how the rationales become gaudier as I get further from an old truck sitting in the driveway and deeper into a barn full of junk parts—that my truck-building was a political act in revolt against the technocracy.*

—JOHN JEROME

I was praying for passage home without being apprehended by the DPS.

And all's well that ends without a train wreck, as my father used to say. I'm back at the desk, happily at work on the writing, and the truck is back in business—except that this morning, it had a flat tire.

NEWS SUMMARY: *A recession rages, but tell that to the e-book business. In the United States, wholesale revenue zoomed from $8 million in the third quarter of 2007 to $14 million for the same quarter of '08.*

### NOVEMBER 16

Unsettling news today, if you're a print book publisher. Book sales are down "substantially" for September: adult hardcovers off by nearly 30 percent, paperbacks 9 percent, audiobooks 12 percent. The only category to post an increase: e-books, up 78 percent for September, 75 percent for the third quarter.

Considering this, I have to be glad that all of my books, as well as the books Bill and I wrote together, are available as e-books. But the fall-off in print sales is ominous. We won't know the impact until the next round of royalty statements, next March.

Pressing on, nevertheless: *Holly* at the halfway point.

### NOVEMBER 17

Author Studs Terkel died last month. At his bedside, a copy of his latest book, *P.S.: Further Thoughts from a Lifetime of Listening*, due out in a few weeks. He was ninety-six. Ninety-six, still listening, thinking, writing. I can't imagine a richer life.

### NOVEMBER 19

Cool and drizzly this morning, to the dogs' great delight. Tail nubbins wagging furiously, noses to the ground, Toro and Molly are off to pick up the messages left behind by the nocturnal traffic.

A couple of yards off the path, deer have built a bedroom, trampling and matting the grass where they bed down for a few hours every night. Nearby, a small sumac sports a bright new buck rub—

*Whenever I have endured or accomplished some difficult task—such as watching television, going out socially or sleeping—I always look forward to rewarding myself with the small pleasure of getting back to my typewriter and writing something. This enables me to store up enough strength to endure the next interruption.*

—ISAAC ASIMOV

*I never ask about sales. It's better not to know. I feel like I write a book. I give it to my editor, then I go back and write another one. That's what I do.*

—ALICE HOFFMAN

*We are the most powerful nation in the world, but we're not the only nation in the world. We are not the only people in the world. We are an important people, the wealthiest, the most powerful and, to a great extent, generous. But we are part of the world.*

—STUDS TERKEL

a two-foot strip where a white-tailed buck has scrubbed his antlers against the tree, stripping off the bark. They rub at this time of year, I'm told, not just to remove velvet, but to leave their scent, to advertise: "Hey, buckos, it's me. I'm here, Boss Buck, and don't you forget it."

I don't know whether Toro and Molly get the message, but they find the rub extremely interesting—until their attention is distracted by fresh coyote scat, full of wads of fur (midnight mouse snack?), and then by raccoon droppings studded with sumac seeds. A little farther along, we are startled when a deer, sleeping late, darts out from under a mesquite and the dogs are off, returning with tongues lolling, bragging about the chase, which was fruitless (of course—they don't have a prayer of catching that deer) but fun.

A good morning to be a dog at Meadow Knoll. A good morning to be a human here, too.

NOVEMBER 20

Got an e-mail today from Peggy Turchette, the artist who does the covers for the Cottage Tales. She's getting started on *The Tale of Applebeck Orchard* and wanted suggestions for the drawing. Authors usually don't have any say in their covers, but Peggy and I have worked together on other projects. Our collaboration on this one is a bit sub rosa. I'm glad to send her a couple of ideas and to know that the book (which I turned in at the end of August) is on track for publication next year.

Another e-mail, this one from my editor, letting me know that the copyedited manuscript of *Wormwood* will be here in a few days. Both of these snippets of production news are welcome. With all the economic uncertainty, hearing that the books are on schedule makes me feel a little more secure.

NOVEMBER 21

We're planning a winter trip to New Mexico, a bit more happily now that gasoline prices are nearing two dollars a gallon. From a conservationist's point of view, of course, lower prices are *not* good: cheaper gas means that people will go back to driving their gas-guzzlers and we'll run out of oil that much faster.

But I'm putting those thoughts aside and packing books (William R. Catton's *Overshoot*, for rereading, deeper consideration; *Portrait*

*Dogs need to sniff the ground; it's how they keep abreast of current events. The ground is a giant dog newspaper, containing all kinds of late-breaking dog news items, which, if they are especially urgent, are often continued into the next yard.*

—DAVE BARRY

*Clearly, the impulse for poems is here for me, in the vivid turn of the seasons, in the dailiness of growing things, . . . Without religious faith and without the sense of primal certitude that faith brings, I must take my only comfort from the natural order of things.*

—MAXINE KUMIN

*Bringing out our little books was hard work. The great puzzle lay in the difficulty of getting answers of any kind from the publishers to whom we applied.*

—CHARLOTTE BRONTË

of an Artist: A Biography of Georgia O'Keeffe by Laurie Lisle; *Raven's Exile: A Season on the Green River* by Ellen Meloy; *Winter: Notes from Montana* by Rick Bass; and *Wintering* by Diana Kappel-Smith. Also yarn and needles for knitting, carded fleece and spindles for hand-spinning, and the episodes of *West Wing* I haven't yet seen. We're leaving at the end of next week, right after Thanksgiving. My brother John and his wife Jean will be visiting for a few days in early December. Bill will stay for another week or so, then drive back to Texas, giving us each a few weeks of much-anticipated and separate solitude.

It's not that we don't want to be together. It's just that we look forward to being alone.

## NOVEMBER 22

The copyedited manuscript of *Wormwood* arrived as promised. Bill is spending the weekend with his mother and brother in Houston, so I settled in for a comfortable all-day-Saturday read in the living room, with a fire, a pot of hot tea, and the manuscript. The editor did a good job, the manuscript was fairly clean, and I enjoyed it.

*Wormwood* is going to surprise some readers. It's set in a Shaker village in Kentucky (not in the usual Pecan Springs) and part of the narrative is told through 1912 Shaker journals and newspaper clippings. Readers will have to work harder than usual to pull it all together. Some will probably think I should have made it a little easier.

The book's ending involves a bit of deus ex machina. The villain certainly deserves to get what's coming to him, but my detective (China Bayles) is in a situation where she can't shoot, whack, ambush, or otherwise interfere with his escape. I'm happy with the ending. Definitive, final, and realistic—a bolt from the blue.

## NOVEMBER 23

Bill's back from Houston and we're celebrating his birthday. Chocolate cake, chocolate frosting. Not enough candles (sixty-three), so he settled for a single fat one.

Bill and his family (dad, mom, brothers David and John) moved from New York to Houston in 1952, when he was six. A couple of years later, they settled in Bellaire, then a new outlying suburb, now walled in by the sprawling megalopolis. The brothers rode their bikes for miles in all directions, exploring cow pastures, open coastal prairie, rice fields, and Brays Bayou, which flows out of Fort Bend County to the Gulf. When they were teens, that's where they discovered a number of Pleistocene mammal fossils—mammoth tusks, bison molars, horses' teeth—and Paleo-Indian artifacts, the beginning, for Bill, of a lifelong love of field science.

After high school, he went to the University of Texas at Austin, where he majored in many subjects, including pre-med, psychology, geology, mechanical engineering, statistics, and finally, industrial management. After being ordered to Vietnam, he was reassigned to an Army unit whose tactical mission was to defend the White House. This was during the antiwar years when the crowds were large, the protesters were determined, and the situation was dicey. But not as dicey as Vietnam.

His war finished, Bill went to work as a statistician for the Texas governor's office, where he discovered that computers were better at sorting data than humans with index cards. (He still has a huge collection of index cards. Unsorted.) When we met, he was managing the computers that store birth records in the state Health Department's Bureau of Vital Statistics.

Thanks to his on-the-job training in PCs, our computers are never down. Not for long, anyway.

Happy birthday, Bill. And thank you for all the wonderful, amazing years.

*Once the realization is accepted that even between the closest human beings infinite distances continue, a wonderful living side by side can grow, if they succeed in loving the distance between them which makes it possible for each to see the other whole against the sky.*

—RAINER MARIA RILKE

NEWS SUMMARY: *On November 19, the Dow Jones fell 427 points, to 7,997, the lowest since 2003. The next day, lawmakers rejected a plea for $25 billion in government loans from automakers Ford, GM, and Chrysler. Two days later, the U.S Treasury and the FDIC agreed to back up to $306 billion in financial sector losses and put another $20 billion in cash into Citigroup. The market continues to slide.*

NOVEMBER 24

Big chunks of sky still crashing. The Big Three automakers had to get on their corporate planes and fly home without a bailout last week. And frugality seems to be the new buzzword. From Thomas Friedman's *New York Times* column:

*I go into restaurants these days, look around at the tables often still crowded with young people, and I have this urge to go from table to table and say: "You don't know me, but I have to tell you that you shouldn't be here. You should be saving your money. You should be home eating tuna fish.*

This financial crisis is so far from over. We are just at the end of the beginning. Please, wrap up that steak in a doggy bag and go home."

I have the same feeling when I go into a store and see people loading their carts with stuff. I want to shout, "Save your money. Don't put junk on your credit card!" (Of course, if they are buying books, mum's the word.)

On the other hand, if everybody got serious about practicing thrift, the economy would sink faster than the *Titanic*. Reminds me of St. Augustine's famously ambivalent prayer: "Lord make me chaste, but not yet."

Maybe if everybody bought *lots* of tuna fish, the country would stay afloat.

But everybody buying lots of tuna fish would mean that the tuna fish would disappear, wouldn't it? And then the killer whales and pilot whales and sharks would have to find something else to eat, and the tuna fishermen would have to find other jobs.

The law of unintended consequences.

## NOVEMBER 25

Watching my 401k fade slowly, like an old Polaroid photo, gradually getting fainter and fainter. Deeply distressing, since the IRS says I have to start taking money out of it soon, assuming there's any left. And a great many seniors are crowded into the same boat. The same *Titanic*. No lifeboats.

Back to *Holly*, slow forward progress. Too many interruptions, distractions. This time of year, the holidays looming, life gets in the way of work. Which is okay. *Holly* can wait. Christmas can't.

## NOVEMBER 26

Wrapped and mailed the gifts I've been working on during the year: socks, mittens, scarves, hats. I suspect that these knits are nicer for me—making them, that is, enjoying the yarn, the colors, the needles in my fingers—than they are for the people who get them.

NEWS SUMMARY: *Terrorist attacks in Mumbai, India, at least eighty dead, more than two hundred injured.*

## NOVEMBER 27

Thanksgiving, a gray, chilly day, just the two of us. A simple, no-fuss Thanksgiving dinner in front of the fire—ham and gravy, sweet potatoes, broccoli, cranberry sauce, pecan pie. Son Bob called, and there were e-mails from Michael and Robin. I'm sorry we can't all be together, but the quiet day has its own special loveliness—except for the television news. Another day when I wish I could simply ignore it. But I can't. Feeling gratitude for our small enclave of peace and, yes, privilege. Sadness for the violence elsewhere.

*If the only prayer you said in your whole life was "thank you," that would suffice.*

—MEISTER ECKHART

## NOVEMBER 28

Chilly, drizzly morning. Bill has left for New Mexico, after much hurry-scurry, last-minute loading and other activity. I leave tomorrow, early. Packing right now. Molly Maguire hasn't been with us long enough to know what's afoot, but Toro knows and is beside himself with happiness at the thought of an all-day ride in the car. Dogs are easy to please.

## November Reading

*Circling My Mother: A Memoir*, by Mary Gordon
*Crossing Open Ground*, by Barry Lopez
*The Gift of Years: Growing Older Gracefully*, by Joan Chittister
*In Deep: Country Essays*, by Maxine Kumin
*Overshoot: The Ecological Basis of Revolutionary Change*, by William R. Catton
*Payback: Debt and the Shadow Side of Wealth*, by Margaret Atwood
*Second Nature: A Gardener's Education*, by Michael Pollan
*Seeing Through Places: Reflections on Geography and Identity*, by Mary Gordon
*Shadow Man*, by Mary Gordon
*Writing in an Age of Silence*, by Sara Paretsky

| JANUARY | FEBRUARY | MARCH | APRIL |
|---------|----------|-------|-------|
| MAY | JUNE | JULY | AUGUST |
| SEPTEMBER | OCTOBER | NOVEMBER | **DECEMBER** |

## DECEMBER 1, COYOTE LODGE, NEW MEXICO

Arrived yesterday evening after eleven hours on the road. The mountains are covered in snow; snow drifts across the valley and blankets the roads—entirely, indescribably beautiful. Walking this morning, the dogs are ecstatic. Gophers and voles and the secret creatures that winter under the snow—new experiences for Molly Maguire, and she's incredulous, all tail-wagging joy. Butt-wagging, for she has no tail. Toro is glad to be here again, and especially glad to see Bill. I'm glad, too. Hoping to be here through mid-January, with the dogs, if all goes as planned.

Today: unpacking, making a grocery list, organizing the sleeping arrangements for my brother John and his wife Jean, arriving tomorrow for several days. I brought my desktop computer from home (easier than transferring files and e-mails to the laptop) and am ready to go back to work on *Holly Blues*, at the end of the week, looks like.

*Some of the users of snow are nearly invisible. In the high dry meadow by the house, short-tailed shrews spend their winters foraging for seeds, insects, worms, buds; they are busy tiny animals like velvety torpedoes. . . . [T]hey couldn't survive long cold winters if they didn't live under the snow, which insulates their warrens and protects them from shifts of weather and the view of owls.*

—DIANA KAPPEL-SMITH

## DECEMBER 4

John and Jean left this morning, after a pleasant two-day visit. Hours of good conversation, catching up on kids, mutual friends, projects, lives. After a career in corporate communications, John now writes article-length nonfiction, mostly for automotive magazines. He showed me a couple of pieces just published in *Classic Motorsports*, where he's on the masthead as contributing editor. A strong, descriptive style, brassy, brash, exactly the voice to keep his audience reading.

While they were here, we took a couple of day trips. Yesterday, over to Mora, to the Tapetes de Lana Weaving Center. A large open space, with a half-dozen large looms, handwoven rugs on the walls, shelves of spun wool, racks of hand-knitted items, a stove with a roaring fire. I spoke with Carla Gomez, the founder of this community weaving enterprise, for a few minutes. Found out that the Center rents weaving time on the looms, so maybe I can do some serious weaving next summer when I have some uncommitted time. (Really? Ever?) I bought a bag of Karakul roving, a lustrous, silver-gray, long-stapled wool, primarily used for weaving rugs. Stopped at the Victory Alpaca Ranch before adjourning to lunch (huge, tasty burritos) at Crystal's Café in Mora. Then back home to a quiet afternoon.

Bob Goodfellow joined us for dinner last night. Comfort food: lasagna, broccoli, salad, and Bob's favorite key lime pie (purchased, no time to bake). Afterward, Bob went home up the mountain and the four of us sat down to a quietly companionable evening of reading, not a word said. I wonder: in how many American households might you find four people sitting together for two after-dinner hours, each with a book?

DECEMBER 5

November 18, 1928. It is lucky I bought the typewriter. The rest of my money is gone. The bank failed last Friday, so the whole community is pretty blue. Since the July 1 hailstorm farmers have drawn out more than $50,000 and had nothing to put in. Now the money, some of it borrowed, they counted on for living expenses this winter and for seed grain in the spring is gone. Our student association lost the $124.00 we had made to pay for basketball suits. The teachers lost any money they had. Miss Lundeen is left with 15¢ and in debt for clothes she charged in Minneapolis.

—ANN MARIE LOW

Reading *Dust Bowl Diary*, which I left here on the shelf and rediscovered yesterday. It was written by a young woman (Ann Marie Low), trying, with her family, to make a go of a North Dakota farm during the droughts and Depression of the 1930s. Hard times, extraordinarily hard work, an almost unimaginably hard life—how they got through, Lord knows. Some didn't. Some died, all were marked by their trials.

Reading this poignant story, thinking about the massive job losses this year (another half-million-plus jobs gone in November, with unemployment running nearly 7 percent), I wonder whether Americans have the strength and stamina to get through whatever lies ahead. In the thirties, people still knew how to *do* things: grow a garden, cook economically, make clothes, do repairs. They lived within walking distance of work and school. Now, we drive everywhere, few people grow their own food, almost nobody makes any of the products they consume. We don't have the knowledge or the resources our Depression-era grandparents had, when it comes to getting by, making do.

Which has given me the idea for a new writing project. Mysteries, a series, set in the early thirties, in the Depression. Small Southern town, Alabama, Georgia. Women, strong women, garden club members dedicated to keeping their families fed, kids clothed and shod, everyone as cheerful as possible. Character-driven, realistic, hopeful.

## DECEMBER 6

I put out the bird feeders this morning to the instant delight of the juncos and nuthatches. The ravens flew down to sit in a circle underneath the feeders, discussing the situation and waiting for seeds to be dropped by the smaller birds.

Back at work on *Holly Blues*. Spent the morning writing out the backstory in detail, thinking through and being explicit about story elements that I'd only roughed out (very roughly) earlier. The ending still isn't clear—that is, the mechanism by which good triumphs and the villain gets his just desserts—but I have faith (borne out of the writing of seventeen previous novels in this series) that justice will be done when the time comes. The three hours invested in the backstory were well worth it. I settled down to a productive afternoon, working from the beginning, revising. Reached page 25 before the dogs came upstairs to my writing loft to tell me (urgently) that it was time to turn off the computer and let them take me for my walk.

> *I don't wait for moods. You accomplish nothing if you do that. Your mind must know it has got to get down to work.*
>
> —PEARL S. BUCK

## DECEMBER 7

Beautiful day, bluest blue sky, windy, magpies chattering in the pine trees beside the deck, dogs and cat comfortably napping in the sunshine, out of the wind.

Working on *Holly Blues* today, editing, cutting, smoothing, sharpening. In these books, the story unfolds in a leisurely way, unlike police procedurals and P.I. novels, which start with a loud bang, with the dead body sprawled across the first page. I like to open with a situation that seems normal—a little chaotic, maybe, a few tensions and conflicts, but nothing out of the ordinary. Then the balance begins to shift, difficulties emerge, there's a growing sense of uneasiness, of misalignment. The murder (most of these books involve at least one death) is the climax of this part of the story, which often takes a hundred pages. I always have to hope that the reader is still with me. Some people like their murders served up a little sooner: the main course first, forget the appetizers.

Thinking about the Southern series. Thought of a series title: The Darling Dahlias. The town's name is Darling, the garden club calls

> *I want to be near that blue sky again. Just like a raven or a magpie. I want to soar with that land.*
>
> —NATALIE GOLDBERG

itself the Dahlias. Plants in the titles, probably. A possible first book title: *The Darling Dahlias and the Cucumber Tree*. Cucumber tree, magnolia.

Reading a wonderful old (1948) book: *Northern Farm: A Chronicle of Maine* by Henry Beston. Lovely, lovely descriptions of winter. It's snowing outside my New Mexico window; inside, I'm with Beston, in Maine.

NEWS SUMMARY: *The* Chicago Tribune *has filed for bankruptcy. In Detroit, the* Free Press *and the* Detroit News *will be delivered only three days a week. The* Albuquerque Journal *is stopping home and rack deliveries in thirty communities around New Mexico.*

## DECEMBER 8

More signs of the times, dreadful: newspapers cutting back, going under. There are a great many subscribers to the *Journal* in this area—I can see the orange tubular delivery boxes all along the road. Many people in this rural corner of New Mexico are older, don't have computers, Internet access. They'll miss the local news. And without a newspaper to record and preserve local history, will there be any community memory of local events, of the local past?

It's colder these mornings, high teens, low twenties, still and clear, air very dry. I stand outside, just looking, looking, almost not believing all that I see. The mountainside is quiet here, the few trucks venturing down our road are rude and loud in the silence. Molly loves the snow. She finds a chunk, picks it up in her mouth and carries it for a distance, until her tongue gets cold, I suppose, then spits it out. She and Toro are learning to live together, with only a few snappish disagreements over property rights to toys, food, personal space. Rather like Bill and me, in the beginning. Property rights. Took a while to learn to be together without rubbing each other raw.

Hit a rough patch in *Holly Blues* that required considerable revision, based on the backstory sketch I made a couple of days ago. The rewrite took a while. But I combed out the worst of the snarls and am in the process of reweaving the pieces. Easy enough with the computer; but just imagine the challenge of this fairly substantial reworking in the days before word processing.

## DECEMBER 9

The publishing industry has shifted into panic mode. Houghton Mifflin Harcourt is reducing staff, "streamlining" its educational program, and "taking a serious look" at acquisitions. Translation: taking fewer manuscripts. Random House is consolidating departments. Simon & Schuster cut thirty-five positions. Thomas Nelson fired fifty-four people. Closer to home, my publisher's parent company (Penguin Group) announced a wage freeze and refused to rule out possible cuts in staff jobs.

The Internet is filled with rumors of authors' contract cancellations and reductions in advances. I've been expecting to hear sad news from author friends, but there's been nothing more specific than the usual laments over the axing of mid-list authors (writers who consistently produce acceptable but not best-selling titles) and protests over the six- and seven-figure advances for celebrity books of no literary merit. Bleak days. Authors are expecting the worse.

## DECEMBER 10

Cold mornings (in the teens), chilly afternoons (in the twenties). The weather keeps me inside, exactly where I want to be, reading, writing, thinking. The landscape is snowy, surrealistically serene, especially as we hear the news from the world beyond this high mountain valley. More layoffs, job losses, bailouts, bankruptcies, home foreclosures.

Hearing all this, I'm thinking about limitations, feeling that the last couple of decades we've been practicing sky's-the-limit thought, where the horizon recedes beyond our imagination. But all these seemingly limitless possibilities, these dreams of affluence, all are funded by debt: personal, corporate, national, international. Everybody owes everybody else, and many—maybe most—debtors will never be able to repay everything they owe. No easy forgiveness, anywhere. Add to this my own growing awareness of looming resource limitations (oil, natural gas, water, minerals) and climate change, and it seems to me that the universe of possibilities has dramatically shrunk within the past year. It is much smaller than I thought just twelve months ago.

Has this universe really shrunk? If that's true, is it because I'm a year older, about to move from my sixty-ninth year into my seventieth

*The unlicensed pipe fitter known as Joe the Plumber is out with a book this month, just as the last seconds of his 15 minutes are slipping away. I have a question for Joe: Do you want me to fix your leaky toilet? I didn't think so. And I don't want you writing books. Not when too many good novelists remain unpublished. Not when too many extraordinary histories remain unread. Not when too many riveting memoirs are kicked back at authors after 10 years of toil. Not when voices in Iran, North Korea or China struggle to get past a censor's gate.*

—TIMOTHY EGAN

*It is so dark inside the wolf.*

—BROTHERS GRIMM

and hence more conscious of my own limitations of time, energy, physical activity?

Or is it, as Robert J. Samuelson says in *The Great Inflation and Its Aftermath* (a book I downloaded on my Kindle and am reading now), a product of an increasingly gloomy national sense of "affluent deprivation," a clumsy but interesting term that Samuelson defines as a "period of slower economic growth that doesn't satisfy what people regard as reasonable private wants and public needs." Too little pie, divided into too few pieces.

And yet there is something profoundly, surprisingly liberating about this new realism. Americans will have to adapt to something that those in other countries understand all too well: less prosperity, fewer consumer goods, a lower level of financial security. We'll have to develop more realistic expectations, a more pragmatic view of our challenges, a more sustainable sense of what we can actually achieve, given our resources, personal and national.

But there *is* abundance here. I step into it when I step outside my door, into the falling snow, the brittle air, the silence, the awareness of what is, still, abundantly available. No, the universe isn't infinite. But there is an infinity within it, yet to be discovered, experienced.

Which is not to say that we humans have the ability to discover or experience it.

DECEMBER 11

The neighbors for drinks last night. The usual flurry of late afternoon preparation, vacuuming the area rugs and sweeping the floors, removing the dog hair from our "guest" chairs, dusting, making hors d'oeuvres. Tonight, "shrimp cups" in miniature muffin tins (actually, mini-quiches). Also bean dip (simple: a can of ranch beans, mashed, with half a can of Bill's homemade chipotle sauce, onions, cheese), baked for twenty minutes and served with a basket of tortilla chips. The bean dip was a special hit, although it was so spicy-hot that one taste was enough to set my hair afire.

A long and interesting conversation, gloomy at points, since it soon emerges that we all genuinely believe that no matter what the Obama administration does, there's not much hope of halting the slide into economic depression. And that Congress doesn't have the political will to do anything meaningful about climate change.

But paradoxically, it feels good to be openly realistic about the elephant in the room.

*Anything I'm guilty of is forgiven when the snow falls. I feel powerful . . . not in control of my emotions, my happiness and furies, but in charge of loving the snow, standing with my arms spread out, as if calling it down, the way it shifts and sweeps past in slants and furies of its own, the way it erases things until it is neither day nor night—that kind of light all through the day—dusk, several hours early, and lingering, lingering forever.*

—RICK BASS

DECEMBER 12

Working on *Holly*. Rewrote an entire chapter to extend the character-ization and insert a new plot element—giving one of the characters a new challenge, a worrisome problem to solve, one that will force her to grow, or to fail. This slows me down when I'd rather be push-ing ahead, but it needs to be done. She wanted to be larger and more significant than the story I gave her allowed her to be. Anyway, there's time—the book isn't due until the end of March.

But comes another interruption: an e-mail from my editor, say-ing that the typeset first-pass pages of *Wormwood* will be sent out next week, which means three days away from *Holly* to work on that project. *Holly* isn't benefitting from these disruptions. The plot is complex and it's hard to keep track of the changes I'm making. The back-and-forth doesn't help. Wishing for some focused time.

*You are going to love some of your characters, because they are you or some facet of you, and you are going to hate some of your characters for the same reason. But no matter what, you are probably going to have to let bad things happen to some of the characters you love or you won't have much of a story.*

—ANNE LAMOTT

DECEMBER 14

Last night, the monthly village potluck in the community center, dec-orated for the holidays with a glittering tree and table greenery. The weather was threatening: high wind, cold, a predicted three to five inches of snow. But the people who live here are used to winter, and by the time grace was said, there were nearly fifty of us. Some stand-out dishes: a traditional posole, rich with chunks of chicken; a warm and vinegary German potato salad; a native squash casserole; turkey and ham, with cranberry and raisin-rum sauce. On the dessert table, cakes, cookies, and pies (including my pumpkin pie). We feasted heartily, merrily on this shared abundance. An even more nutritious feast: shared friendship and community.

*It isn't the landscape that matters so much as the way you live in it. . . . You have to make it your life. You just have to go and live in a place and let it tell you how to live.*

—GRETEL EHRLICH

DECEMBER 15

Countering this momentary reassurance of abundance, I'm rereading Michael Klare's *Rising Powers, Shrinking Planet*. Klare, an expert in re-source geopolitics, argues that the strategic materials needed by mod-ern industrial societies—not just oil and natural gas but uranium, coal, and copper—are being depleted at an accelerating rate and that without careful, collaborative efforts to develop new, climate-friendly sources of energy, global conflicts are inevitable. Understanding it better, second time around.

And rereading, at the same time, *Temporary Homelands* by Alison Hawthorne Deming. In her introduction, she writes:

*We live in a time of radical loss—loss of space, places, tribes, and species. Loss of a sense of belonging in and to a place. Loss of continuity and co- herence. We live with a painful sense that the human species is the most destructive force on the planet. Even so, the fact ironically remains that we are embedded in nature. Every second of every day we are in relationship with that force—it is what we are.*

Deming's is a more lyric representation of Klare's thesis, but the two—the poet, the professor of energy geopolitics—are asking the same question: How do we come to terms with what we've used, abused, lost? How do we face a future when there's less of everything, and it's our doing?

"We have less time than we knew," Annie Dillard says, "and that time buoyant, and cloven, lucent, and missile, and wild."

Yes. Wild.

NEWS SUMMARY: *An ice storm brought down the electrical grid and nearly four hundred thousand households in Maine, Massachu- setts, New Hampshire, and New York will be without power through the week. Hard hit: local retailers who were counting on pre-holiday sales.*

DECEMBER 16

More snow here, blowing hard, a white-out, mountains invisible, pine trees heavy with snow. The cows are huddled together in the valley, backs to the icy, snow-laden wind whipping down the mountain. The power was out briefly, but came back on again while I was getting the kerosene lamps from the cupboard. I've left them out, just in case. Longest outage here, according to neighbors: five days.

DECEMBER 18

Better weather. Bill and the cat drove back to Texas today—he just called to say that they arrived safely, no problems. The cat had no comment.

Watched *The Cutting Edge*, a film about film editing, editors. Thinking that film editing and cutting are like the revision process, which is where I am in *Holly Blues* right now. Cutting, mostly. Taking out the slow parts. Straightening out the plot kinks.

Just before bedtime, I put on coat, hat, boots, mittens and take the dogs out into a luminescent landscape. The mountains in moonlight, white shoulders bright against the black night sky, curtains of clouds like pale smoke blowing across the moon, painting moving shadows, blue, across the white snow. Cold and utter, utter stillness.

## DECEMBER 19

Nine degrees outside this morning, chilly in my writing loft. I've wrapped myself in a wooly shawl, turned on the heating pad to toast my feet, and am wearing a pair of fingerless mitts—knitted of yarn I've hand-spun, so I know it well, know the feel of it, the elastic strength of it. Through the window, up the mountain, more snow blowing horizontally. Ravens at the feeder, black, black against white, white.

## DECEMBER 20

A dozen wild turkeys under the bird feeders. The dogs, out on the deck for some fresh air, set up a flurry of barking, anxious to go out and corral these large birds—not as large as the Thanksgiving bird, but large enough. The turkeys are unfazed by all this noisy attention, stoic in the snow, picking their way with their peculiar graceful gracelessness through the white drifts, leaving their hieroglyphic markings, writing their passage across the face of the earth, the face of time.

## DECEMBER 21

I've put up a few holiday decorations, brought in a few pine boughs in lieu of a tree, put up some lights—the house wears a modestly festive air. Bob is coming for supper tonight: a pot of chili, cornbread, a pecan pie. He recently lost his second greyhound, so he's glad to get his "dog fix" from Toro and Molly, who are glad to see him, as well. As we sit down to eat, they settle companionably at our feet, while Bob and I talk about books and films, the economy, politics, the weather. And dogs.

*Editing is why people like movies, because in the end, wouldn't we like to edit our own lives? I think we would. I think everyone would like to take out the bad parts, take out the slow parts, and look deeper into the good parts.*

—ROB COHEN, FILM EDITOR

After he leaves, I go back to my book: Gretel Ehrlich's *The Future of Ice: A Journey into Cold*. A chronicle of winter, pondering, as she says, the story of a planet where ice is the canary, the crystal element that tells us how healthy our earth is, whether we are on the brink of a warming that will change everything.

### DECEMBER 22

The winter solstice, the sun's year closing, the sun's year beginning. At twilight, I leave the dogs at home and walk up the mountain and into the edge of the forest. The translucent snow seems to hold its own light, blue, purple, pale green. The pines are sweet, fragrant, the air is very cold, very still. It's as if the world has stopped turning for the briefest moment, as if the mountain is holding its breath, betwixt and between. As I am, my old year closing, shutting its window on the past, another year about to open.

### DECEMBER 23

A bright day, blue and clear. The dogs and I drove down to Las Vegas this morning for groceries and dog food. There's no cell phone reception here at the house, so I took my e-book reader and downloaded a book in the grocery store parking lot: *Down River* by John Hart. Looking for a book I can read without being perplexed, undone. A book about problems that seem real and important enough at the moment of reading, but stay inside the book when I close its cover.

### DECEMBER 24

Snow this evening, carols on the radio (a strong signal tonight from Albuquerque makes listening enjoyable), hot chocolate, socks on the knitting needles, a good book on my lap. I gobble *Down River* in a few hours: a strong story well told, although seasoned readers will probably guess the crux of the mystery, if not the outcome. I'll look for more of Hart's work.

Thinking back over the year's reading, though, I realize that—while reading was more important to me this year than in most years—I probably read fewer novels than in any other year of my adult life. A permanent change in reading preferences, or a temporary lull while I've been pursuing other, more urgent reading interests?

I also notice that one book leads to another in a fairly focused way, which comes from reading bibliographies and shopping online, rather than hanging out at bookstores or libraries, browsing the shelves. Makes it easy to get what I'm looking for, but eliminates that wonderful accidental find, when the book you absolutely need (but didn't know it) falls off the shelf and into your hand.

Out with the dogs at midnight, into fresh snow, a clear sky littered with stars, a magical sliver of moon, the powerful silence of mountains.

*Books can be dangerous. The best ones should be labeled, "This could change your life."*

—HELEN EXLEY

## DECEMBER 25

Woke up to more snow and a phone call from Bill, who is spending Christmas day with his mother in Houston. This is the first holiday we've been apart since our marriage. I miss him.

Otherwise, the day was leisurely, restful, celebratory. A quiet morning reading, a wonderful Christmas dinner with Editha Bartley, who lives on her family ranch up the mountain in a narrow valley above Upper Rociada. In 1905, Editha's physician father founded Valmora, a tuberculosis sanitarium on the Mora River, about twenty-five miles east of here. Later, he bought the ranch up the mountain and built guest cabins, often hosting celebrities and dignitaries from back East. Editha—a writer, columnist for the *Las Vegas Optic*—lives in the old ranch house. Today, she invited a houseful of family and friends for a holiday dinner. The potluck was sumptuous: fine food, finer company, as the snow fell outside the windows.

Drove down the mountain through the late afternoon twilight, coming home to the discovery that Molly (still a puppy, really, still in the Terrible Twos) had chewed up her bed and my favorite necklace of carved wooden beads. Shreds of foam rubber, chewed beads scattered over the floor. Girls will be girls.

*Here where the wind comes straight from the mountains [the] fine powder snow comes in hung on the bias, its warp driven at a slant. At the ground it is whirled up and is snatched and carried in great clouds like smoke, hissing and drifting to a stop in the backwaters of the air; behind fenceposts, the screen of orchard trees, the stone shoulder of the ledge jutting here, the house walls, brush, a stone, a broomlike tuft of grass.*

—DIANA KAPPEL-SMITH

NEWS SUMMARY: *Israel attacks Hamas in Gaza in retaliation for rockets fired across the border into Southern Israel. More than three hundred dead in the first two days, many wounded. Each side accuses the other of violating the cease-fire.*

## DECEMBER 28

This holiday, no peace on earth, no good will to man. It's being said that the Israelis are moving on Hamas in the last days of the Bush administration, wanting to do whatever they mean to do and have done with it before Obama takes office on January 20. A sad affair—difficult for me to square the politics of this with what I know of the Jewish faith.

Wrapping up *Holly Blues*, at least to the point where I can let the book sit for a while. I'll see it more clearly when I go through it once more, in February or March, before I turn it in.

Outdoors, it's ice, ice, all ice. Snow crusted with ice, pines glittering with ice, ice glinting in the sharp air, glassing the window panes, glazing the road. Ice is frozen around the bird feeders, and the seeds—especially the thistle seeds, the most popular among this flock—are all clumped together. I bring in the feeders to thaw them out before I refill and rehang them. Shovel the deck and the back steps, treacherous with ice. The dogs are adventurous, rowdy and reckless, racing, slipping, sliding across the icy crust. I'm loving the solitude here, the monastic quiet, but the dogs are a blessing. The three of us are our own society.

*The only certainty about writing and trying to be a writer is that it has to be done, not dreamed of or planned and never written, or talked about (the ego eventually falls apart like a soaked sponge), but simply written; it's a dreadful, awful fact that writing is like any other work.*

—JANET FRAME

## DECEMBER 31

There's other society, too. The Daigles, Rosi and Mike (up the road from Bob), are having their annual New Year's Eve party tonight and expecting a large turnout. The Daigles moved here from Louisiana, after Katrina, aiming for higher, drier land. Both are accomplished Creole cooks, so there'll be plenty of fine Louisiana food, maybe even a barbequed turkey. Some of the women will be dressed in party finery and makeup; others, like me, will be in jeans and sweaters, wearing our everyday faces. Either way, entirely comfortable. It'll be nice to have someone else to talk to besides the dogs.

The party is a potluck, as are most of our village get-togethers: I'm taking stuffed mushrooms—simple, easy to carry up the mountain.

Stuffed Mushrooms

12 whole fresh mushrooms
1 tablespoon butter
1 tablespoon minced garlic
1 (8-ounce) package cream cheese, softened

¼ cup grated Parmesan cheese
¼ teaspoon dried thyme
¼ teaspoon dried sage
¼ teaspoon ground black pepper
¼ teaspoon onion powder
¼ teaspoon ground cayenne pepper
paprika

Preheat oven to 350 degrees. Spray a baking sheet with cooking spray. Clean mushrooms with a damp paper towel. Break off stems and chop fine. Heat oil in a skillet over medium heat. Add garlic and chopped mushroom stems to the skillet and sauté. Cool. Stir in cream cheese, Parmesan, thyme, sage, black pepper, onion powder, and cayenne pepper. Fill each mushroom cap and arrange on prepared cookie sheet. Sprinkle caps with paprika. Bake for 20 minutes.

## JANUARY 1

The party went on just long enough. We wrapped it up when the ball came down in Times Square, 10 p.m. here in the mountains. We drank our champagne toasts, exchanged wishes for a happy new year—some of us wishing for a happier new year than 2008—and said our goodbyes. For me, goodbye until next August, since I won't be seeing anyone again before I leave. I walked home down the hill through a fresh-falling snow, in the sharp cold, the absolute silence of a deep winter night.

Today is the first day of the new year for most, the last day of the old year for me: my birthday is tomorrow. Another ending, another beginning, the beginning of my eighth decade, my seventieth year.

Another year of listening to the land, of loving life, of learning to recognize and describe the behaviors that change our world. A year of writing, of reading, of loving tenderly, of living in the embrace of garden, grass, woods.

Another extraordinary year of ordinary days. But nothing as extraordinary, I hope, as this one.

## December Reading

*Down River*, by John Hart
*Dust Bowl Diary*, by Ann Marie Low
*The Future of Ice: A Journey into Cold*, by Gretel Ehrlich
*The Great Inflation and Its Aftermath: The Past and Future of American Afflu-
ence*, by Robert J. Samuelson
*Northern Farm: A Chronicle of Maine*, by Henry Beston
*Portrait of an Artist: A Biography of Georgia O'Keeffe*, by Laurie Lisle
*Raven's Exile: A Season on the Green River*, by Ellen Meloy
*Temporary Homelands*, by Alison Hawthorne Deming
*Winter: Notes from Montana*, by Rick Bass
*Wintering*, by Diana Kappel-Smith

# A POSTSCRIPT TO THE READER

JULY 21, 2009

I've just gotten official word from the Press that this journal will be a book. So as I finish doing what needs to be done before I print the manuscript, I'll tidy up some loose ends that the journal left hanging.

The Press always "juries" its submissions. One of the two "jurors" of this manuscript asked what happened with our neighbors: the intrepid hunter who planned to shoot onto our property, and the neighbor who claims more land than she owns. The answer, in case you're wondering, too: nothing happened. The deer blind is still there, although the hunter didn't show up for deer season, and we didn't have to call the cops. And the fence is still there on the road right-of-way, with warning signs posted along its length. Which reminds me to tell you that life isn't a novel with a beginning, a middle, and an end. Life just keeps on keeping on, smuggling in new beginnings, muddling the middles, and offering counterfeit conclusions that don't resolve much of anything.

Like the election, which ended the campaign but hasn't yet brought about all the changes the candidate promised, although this has not yet diminished the broadly felt affection for him and his family. (Whatever people think of her husband, Michelle Obama is turning out to be a national treasure.)

The Texas drought, now entering its twenty-fourth month, hasn't ended, either. Called "exceptional" (the worst category) by the Weather Service, the drought has been amplified by a truly horrifying heat wave, with record strings of 100-degree days. In Austin, last month was the hottest June since people started writing down the temperatures, and July is well on the way to its own record.

*When we look back, 2008 will be a momentous year in human history. Our children and grandchildren will ask us "What was it like? What were you doing when it started to fall apart? Could you see it? What did you think? What did you do?"*

—PAUL GILDING

I'm not going back to Pendaries and Coyote Lodge next month, as I planned. The water level in the Trinity aquifer that feeds our wells is dropping, and although we still have water (if we're careful when we pump), wells to the south of us are drying up. The hills around Meadow Knoll are like tinder; there are new wildfires every day. Bill's pecans are so stressed that they've dropped all their immature nuts; he's hoping that the trees survive. And the spring-green needles on our cypress trees, the glory of Pecan Creek, have turned a deep, dire russet. Someone needs to stay home to look after the place, water as much as possible, and make sure that the cows and sheep have plenty to drink. Bill is still working on Coyote Lodge, so I've elected to stay. I'll go in November and December, when I can enjoy the snow.

The garden did well in the spring, yielding potatoes, green beans, broccoli, carrots, cabbage, and buckets of snow peas. Even the tomatoes produced well, until June's high temperatures sent them into a prolonged sulk. I don't blame them. However, I am undeterred. This week, Miles and I are at work on an expansion of the garden that will double it in size. The fall forecast includes a strong El Niño "event" in the Pacific Ocean, which may mean rain for us. I can only hope—and reflect on the irony that ocean surface heating in the Pacific has a beneficial effect on rainfall in arid southwestern North America.

On the writing front, I turned in *Holly Blues* at the end of March, then went with Bill on a cross-country driving tour to promote *Wormwood*—the last one, I've decided. The tours cost too much in terms of time and resources, including gasoline. I'm replacing live touring with Internet promotion. I've just finished *The Tale of Oat Cake Crag*, the seventh of the Cottage Tales. *Together, Alone* is coming out next month, about the same time as *The Tale of Applebeck Orchard*. This journal is becoming a book that the University of Texas Press will publish in September 2010. Oh, and my Berkley editor, Natalee Rosenstein, accepted my proposal for the Darling Dahlias series. I'll be starting the first book in another couple of weeks. It will be published in July 2010.

The election changed some things. After months of litigation, the Democrats now control (more or less) sixty votes in the Senate. But it's still politics as usual in Washington. Obama's administration is slogging it out with Republicans and blue-dog Democrats over health care reform, energy policy, and financial sector regulation. It looks as if he'll get his first Supreme Court Justice appointment, though: Sonia Sotomayor, a Hispanic woman from the federal bench. Not without a fight, of course. The white male Republicans were particularly offended by her "wise Latina" remark.

The Bush wars drag on and the sins of that administration are on everyone's mind this summer. It has been revealed that Cheney lied to Congress about a secret CIA assassination program, that Bush tried to coerce his hospitalized attorney general to sign off on a warrantless wiretap program, and that administration lawyers thought it was fine to ignore the Constitution. Doubtful that anything will come of any of this: there is no political will to prosecute the two men at the top and prosecuting the men underneath the men at the top seems to most people to be a waste of time. Frustrating for those who care about accountability. But since this is life, not a novel, just desserts are not likely to be served.

The saga of the recession continues, in spite of a sizable stimulus plan approved immediately after Obama took office—as large a package as he thought he could get out of the Congress, but not large enough, according to Nobel laureate economist Paul Krugman, to turn the tide of decline. Job losses continue to grow, foreclosures to mount, business assets to fall, banks to fail. While the slump may have slowed, there's no end in sight—and when the upturn comes, it's likely to be accompanied by rising gasoline prices, which will create another downturn. (On the other hand, surviving banks are making colossal profits and paying huge bonuses. Go figure.)

And there is no conclusion, of course, to the major concerns of my year of reading and learning: resource depletion, climate change, and the impacts of both on our industrialized food system. My journal for 2009 is full of these personal worries, which continue to broaden and deepen as I read and learn. And to my list of topics-that-require-awareness, I'm adding the H1N1 "swine" flu.

The media, too, are beginning to pay more attention to some of these issues, with TV specials and topical features focusing on diminished resources (especially oil) and climate change. Even "peak oil" is getting some serious commentary. More encouraging, the notion that we have to learn to live with less is spreading—among thinking people, anyway, people who understand that uncontrolled exploitation of the planet's resources is the surest way to planetary catastrophe. But catastrophe is difficult for many to see and to imagine. We are still living beyond our means. We continue to live the story that our national narrative of unlimited resources has urged us to live, while the life that scarcity will teach us is still beyond our horizons.

If you've read this far, you must be interested in these issues, too.

*I would hope that a wise Latina woman with the richness of her experiences would more often than not reach a better conclusion than a white male who hasn't lived that life.*

—SONIA SOTOMAYOR

*In the foreseeable future we shall feel more and more thwarted and subject to capricious manipulation by forces we cannot control, not necessarily because there will be more tyrants or unscrupulous profiteers, but principally because there will be more people, more resource-hungry technology, and more man-made substances crowding a world of fixed size.*

—WILLIAM R. CATTON

*Life seems sometimes like nothing more than a series of losses, from the beginning to end. That's the given. How you respond to those losses, what you make of what's left, that's the part you have to make up as you go.*

—KATHERINE WEBER

With that in mind, I have added a list of books with the hope that you will feel compelled to do some more reading—and to take whatever actions are appropriate and effective in the contexts in which you live and work.

The world we have made for ourselves offers no conclusions and no resolutions, and guarantees no happy endings. All we can do is be attentive and present to today, with all its rewards and challenges, and do the best we can to be ready for whatever comes tomorrow.

# RESOURCES

These are some of the books that may help you think in new ways about the world around you and the life you are creating for yourself and your family. The list includes many of the books I read during 2008, books I'm reading in 2009, and books on my to-be-read stack. You'll find other suggestions in my end-of-the-month reading lists in this book, and still others in an updated list on my Web site, www.susanalbert.com.

## THE CLIMATE WE'VE CREATED

Flannery, Tim. *The Weather Makers: How Man Is Changing the Climate and What It Means for Life on Earth.* Grove Press, 2001.

Kolbert, Elizabeth. *Field Notes from a Catastrophe: Man, Nature, and Climate Change.* Bloomsbury, 2006.

Lovelock, James. *The Revenge of Gaia: Earth's Climate Crisis and the Fate of Humanity.* Basic Books, 2007.

Pearce, Fred. *With Speed and Violence: Why Scientists Fear Tipping Points in Climate Change.* Beacon Press, 2008.

## LIVING WITH LESS OF WHAT WE'VE TAKEN FOR GRANTED

Darley, Julian. *High Noon for Natural Gas: The New Energy Crisis.* Chelsea Green, 2004.

Ehrlich, Paul R., and Anne H. Ehrlich. *One With Nineveh: Politics, Consumption, and the Human Future.* Island Press, 2004.

Greer, John Michael. *The Long Descent: A User's Guide to the End of the Industrial Age.* New Society Publishers, 2008.

Heinberg, Richard. *Peak Everything: Waking Up to the Century of Declines.* New Society Publishers, 2007.

Klare, Michael T. *Rising Powers, Shrinking Planet: The New Geopolitics of Energy.* Metropolitan Books, Henry Holt, 2008.

Kunstler, James Howard. *The Long Emergency: Surviving the Converging Catastrophes of the Twenty-First Century.* Atlantic Monthly Press, 2005.

Makansi, Jason. *Lights Out: The Electricity Crisis, the Global Economy, and What it Means to You.* Wiley, 2007.

Pearce, Fred. *When the Rivers Run Dry: Water—The Defining Crisis of the Twenty-First Century.* Beacon Press, 2007.

Reisner, Marc. *Cadillac Desert: The American West and Its Disappearing Water.* Penguin, 1993.

## UNDERSTANDING LIMITS

Bacevich, Andrew. *The Limits of Power: The End of American Exceptionalism*. Henry Holt, 2008.

Catton, William R. *Overshoot: The Ecological Basis of Revolutionary Change*. University of Illinois Press, 1982.

Diamond, Jared. *Collapse: How Societies Choose to Fail or Succeed*. Viking, 2005.

Johnson, Chalmers. *Nemesis: The Last Days of the American Republic*. Henry Holt, 2006.

McKibben, Bill. *Deep Economy: The Wealth of Communities and the Durable Future*. Times Books, 2007.

Orlov, Dmitry. *Reinventing Collapse: The Soviet Example and American Prospects*. New Society Publishers, 2008.

Schumacher, E. F. *Small Is Beautiful: Economics as if People Mattered*. Frederick Muller Ltd., 1973.

Speth, James Gustave. *The Bridge at the Edge of the World: Capitalism, the Environment, and Crossing from Crisis to Sustainability*. Yale University Press, 2009.


## HOW WE EAT, WHAT WE EAT, AND WHY

Cummings, Claire Hope. *Uncertain Peril: Genetic Engineering and the Future of Seeds*. Beacon Press, 2008.

Kingsolver, Barbara. *Animal, Vegetable, Miracle: A Year of Food Life*. HarperCollins, 2007.

Nestle, Marion. *Food Politics: How the Food Industry Influences Nutrition and Health*. University of California Press, 2002.

Pfeiffer, Dale Allen. *Eating Fossil Fuels: Oil, Food and the Coming Crisis in Agriculture*. New Society Publishers, 2006.

Pollan, Michael. *The Omnivore's Dilemma: A Natural History of Four Meals*. Penguin Press, 2006.

Roberts, Paul. *The End of Food*. Houghton Mifflin Harcourt, 2008.

Schlosser, Eric. *Fast Food Nation: The Dark Side of the All-American Meal*. Houghton Mifflin, 2001.

Shiva, Vandana. *Stolen Harvest: The Hijacking of the Global Food Supply*. South End Press, 2000.

Singer, Peter, and Jim Mason. *The Way We Eat: Why Our Food Choices Matter*. Rodale Press, 2006.


## LIVING SUSTAINABLY: PRINCIPLES AND PRACTICES

Ashworth, Suzanne. *Seed to Seed: Seed Saving and Growing Techniques for Vegetable Gardeners*. Seed Savers Exchange, 2002.

Astyk, Sharon. *Depletion and Abundance: Life on the New Home Front*. New Society Publishers, 2008.

Berry, Wendell. *The Gift of Good Land: Further Essays Cultural and Agricultural*. North Point Press, 1981.

Jeavons, John. *How to Grow More Vegetables (and Fruits, Nuts, Berries, Grains, and Other Crops) Than You Ever Thought Possible on Less Land Than You Can Imagine*. Ten Speed Press, 2002.

Seymour, John. *The Self-Sufficient Life and How to Live It: The Complete Back-to-Basics Guide*. D. K. Publishing, 2009.

# INDEX

Barnum, P. T., 40
Barrie, J. M., 40, 59
Barry, Dave, 36, 183, 187
Bartley, Editha, 203
Bass, Rick, 188, 198
Batterson, Anne, 152, 167
Battista, O. A., 17
Bear Stearns, 51, 67
Beath, Mary, 90
Bender, Sue, 82, 84
Berkley Books/Prime Crime (Penguin imprint), 14, 20, 41, 87, 208
Berkman's Books, 62
Bernanke, Ben, 156
Berry, Wendell, 16, 47, 67, 99, 155, 156, 160
Beston, Henry, 15, 48, 196
Bettler, Lucia, 74
Biden, Joseph, 3, 139–140, 165. See also presidential election of 2008
Blew, Mary Clearman, 25
blogging, 23, 25, 31, 41–42, 55, 65, 91, 142, 170
Bombeck, Erma, 69
book promotion, 23, 40, 52, 56–57, 62, 65, 66–69, 72–75, 83–84, 164, 208
book publishing, 41, 57, 64, 197. See also e-books
book reviews, 167
bookstores/book selling, ix, 6, 22, 40, 57, 62, 63, 64, 66, 68, 74, 92, 134–135, 160, 186, 203
Borges, Jorge Luis, 64
Boulding, Kenneth E., 78
Bowers, Janie Emily, 99, 107
Bradbury, Ray, 47, 179
Brokaw, Tom, 165
Brontë, Charlotte, 187
Brooks, Mel, 171
Brothers, Joyce, 68
Brothers Grimm, 197
Brown, Margaret Wise, 56
Brown, Rita Mae, 184
Browning, Elizabeth Barrett, 32
Bruère, Martha, 124
Buck, Pearl S., 195
Bullock, Alice, 7
Burnham, Sophy, 50, 166, 169
Burroughs, William S., 14

Bush, George W., 42, 54, 79, 98, 99, 100, 106, 164; administration of, viii, 3, 18, 51, 71, 78, 86, 99–100, 107, 116, 152, 157, 181, 204, 209
Butela, Sharon, 94
Buyer, Laurie Wagner, 65

Cabeza de Vaca, Álvar Núñez, 53, 94
Campbell, Joseph, 74
Caras, Roger, 27
carbon emissions, 31–32, 35, 39, 154. See also climate change
Cariou, Heather, 34
Carleton, Will, 38
Carlyle, Thomas, 22
Carson, Rachel, 32, 70
Carter, Jimmy, 19
Carver, Raymond, 166
Catton, William R., 110, 125–126, 187, 209
Cerro Pelón, 1, 5, 137
Chandler, Raymond, 41
Cheney, Dick, 71, 99, 100, 209
China, 61, 85, 96
China Bayles' Book of Days, 28
China Bayles series, 1, 13, 40, 46–47, 52, 64, 74, 89, 148. See also under individual titles
Churchill, Winston, 79
Cicero, 173
Citigroup, 72, 189
climate change, 72, 78, 120, 131, 147, 155, 181, 197; and carbon footprint, 31; Congress's political will to address, 198; discussion of, online, 41–42; ignored by the Bush administration, 86, 118–119; impact of, on agriculture, viii; intersection of, with energy depletion, 79; presidential candidates discuss, 45, 85, 157; reading about, 69, 132, 202, 209
Clinton, Bill, 36, 140
Clinton, Hillary, 3, 27, 45, 72, 88, 98, 139–140
Coe, Sophie D., 145
Cohen, Rob, 201
Coldiron, Mary Ann, 102
Colette, 129
Connelly, Dianne, 74, 141

AN EXTRAORDINARY YEAR OF ORDINARY DAYS

115, 125, 170–171, 175, 180, 207; and debates, 157–158, 165, 169; polling for, 174; primaries for, 27, 40, 45, 72, 88; sense of hope about, 88, 98, 181; and vice-presidential candidates, 139–140, 141–142
Price, Pam, 142
Prime Crime. *See* Berkley Books/ Prime Crime
publishing. *See* book publishing; e-books; newspapers
Pyle, Robert Michael, 4, 70

Quammen, David, 10, 12
Quindlen, Anna, 30

Raymo, Chet, 5
recession, 16, 26, 160, 186, 209. *See also* economic crisis/downturn
Reich, Robert, 28
Reichl, Ruth, 48, 118
Relph, Edward, 208
Republicans, 3, 88, 141, 180, 208, 209. *See also* George W. Bush: administration of; presidential election of 2008
resource depletion, 75, 110, 132, 160–161, 181, 197–198, 200, 209; and oil/energy, viii, 19, 25, 27, 39, 41–42, 45–46, 69, 78–79, 120, 131, 152, 154, 157
Rice, Condoleezza, 99, 137
Richardson, Bill, 48
Rilke, Rainer Maria, 33, 189
Roach, Margaret, 38
Robertson, Adele Crockett, 145–146
Robin Paige Victorian Mysteries series, 30, 64
Rociada (New Mexico), 7, 137, 203
Rogers, Ken E., 119
Rogoff, Kenneth, viii
Romney, Mitt, 3
Roosevelt, Eleanor, 34
Rose, Phyllis, 25
*Rosemary Remembered* (Albert), 40, 173
Rosenstein, Natalee, 20, 48, 49, 50, 208
Rubin, Lillian, 20–21

Rumsfeld, Donald, 37, 99, 100
Russia, 132–133, 164, 170

Saakashvili, Mikheil, 132
Sackville-West, Vita, 38, 174
Samuelson, Robert J., 198
Sanders, Scott Russell, 8, 63, 64, 72
Sangre de Cristo Mountains, 1, 4, 5, 6, 8, 9, 134, 136, 137
Sarton, May, 36
Sass, Herbert, 53
Saudi Arabia, 71, 99
Scalia, Antonin, 111, 165
Schieffer, Bob, 169
Schmidt, Eric, 28
Schumacher, E. F., 139, 152
Schwarzenegger, Arnold, 146
Schweiger, Larry, 86
Seale, Jan, 147
Seinfeld, Jerry, 63
Semple, Robert B., 12
Shaffer, Romelda, 180
Shapiro, Laurie, 124
Shlaes, Amity, 164
Sikorski, Radek, 137
Simmons, Matthew, 71, 78
Sisters in Crime, 20, 65
Skolnik, Linda, 145
Snyder, Gary, 73, 83, 93
Sorkin, Aaron, 90, 180
Sotomayor, Sonia, 208–209
South Padre Island (Texas), 69–71
*Spanish Dagger* (Albert), 148
species extinction, 86, 120
Stalin, Joseph, 175
Stegner, Wallace, 9
Stevens, John Paul, 165
Stevenson, Robert Louis, 132
stimulus package, 18–19, 210. *See also* economic crisis/downturn
stock market, 115, 152, 160, 189. *See also* economic crisis/downturn
Story Circle Network, ix, 6–7, 20, 25, 59, 66, 148, 166; and book review Web site, 34, 65, 90; and Reading Circle, 48, 82, 84, 101, 120, 145, 149, 168, 183; and *Story Circle Journal*, 124
Stratemeyer, Edward, 46

book" syndrome, 107; as "play," 92; and revision, 196; and story structure vs. style, 169; technology's effects on, 36; and unfolding of story, 195. *See also* book promotion; book publishing

*Writing from Life: Telling Your Soul's Story* (Albert), 7

Yost, Paula, 34, 65, 147

Zackheim, Victoria, 168
Zimmerman, Elizabeth, 190
Zoellick, Robert, 61